Threads Primer

A Guide to Multithreaded Programming

Bil Lewis
Daniel J. Berg

SunSoft Press
A Prentice Hall Title

The publisher offers discounts on this book when ordered in bulk quantities. For more information, contact: Corporate Sales Department, Prentice Hall PTR, One Lake Street, Upper Saddle River, NJ 07458. Phone: 800-382-3419 or 201-236-7156, Fax: 201-236-7141, email: corpsales@prenhall.com

Cover designer: *M & K Design, Palo Alto, California*
Manufacturing manager: *Alexis R. Heydt*
Acquisitions editor: *Gregory G. Doench*

10 9 8 7 6 5 4 3 2

ISBN 0-13-443698-9

SunSoft Press
A Prentice Hall Title

Dedication

To Elaine, my wife and best friend, for her encouragement and understanding during all the late nights and weekends when I should have been spending time with her. Thank You!

— Dan

A mes enfants, Caleb, Matthew, et Rebecca. "Tu deviens responsable pour toujours de ce que tu as apprivoisé"

— Bil

Contents

≡

Threads Primer

Figures

≡

Tables

Threads Primer

Code Examples

Acknowledgments

Thanks to Matt Delcambre for his support of the book and his assistance in the review process. Thanks also to John Bost and James Hollingshead for their support and funding of the trips to California. Thanks also go to Mary Himelfarb for putting up with all the paper and time I consumed on her printer.

Special thanks to Ty "Tyrone" McKercher, for all the time in the review process and for always taking the time to listen to my wild new ideas; also for his keen insight during the many late night and weekend programming sessions where many of the examples in the book were born.

Many thanks to Tim Hayes, Jim Thompson, and Richard Robison for providing their customer testimonials and for their early adoption of threading technology in their production applications. Thanks also go to all the people who make up the POSIX committee for all their work on the pthreads draft and the threads documentation team for all their work on the quality documentation.

We owe an enormous debt to Devang Shah and Dan Stein for their constant support, answering innumerable questions, debating issues of presentation and concept. In spite of numerous barriers, we always managed to come to a consensus on the major issues— something which speaks well for the true nature of science.

Many thanks to Richard Marejka, Eric Jaeger, Adrienne Jardetzky, Richard Schaefer, and Charles Fineman for their assistance in the review process and their numerous accurate and insightful comments and suggestions; to Ron Winacott for coming all the way to Sweden to introduce me to the subject; to Chris Crenshaw for his comments and discussion; to Karin Ellison for starting us on this book and for her enormous energy in dealing with all those little problems that always seem to crawl out of the woodwork at 2 a.m. Roses to Marianne Muller who made the Web work for us and was always there with reassurance and support when things got rough.

Thanks to Bill Lindeman, Mukul Goyal, Ben Catanzaro, Morgan Herrington, Paul Lorence, Brian Kinnard, Larry Gee, Shaun Peterson, and Leif Samuelson for their help, comments, and guidance in the numerous fine points of writing, formatting, and interpretation; to my peers in Developer Engineering and the Shaysa council;

≡
_____

to RMS who did more to shape my writing abilities than he realizes; to Manoj Goyal who was so pivotal in making the personal interactions at Sun work like they should.

A special thanks to two computer scientists whom I have always held in awe and whose writing abilities and finely tuned senses of humor I admire more than I can express, Peter van der Linden and the great Quux. How two individuals can have such depth of understanding and also be such amazing copyeditors, I don't know!

Tusan tack till alla på Sun Sverige, och kram till dej, Madelene.

Ja Tarvi, Kati, Lõvi, Tiia, Epp, Mari ja Kaur, kuna mõnikord vajab inimene sõpru rohkem kui midagi muud.

　　　　　　— *Dan Berg*　　　　　　— *Bil Lewis*

Preface

Today, there are three primary sets of multithreading (MT) libraries: the "standards-based" libraries (all of the UNIX® implementations, which will move to POSIX upon ratification), the OS/2® library, and the Windows NT™ library. (The NT and OS/2 libraries are fairly similar, which should not be too surprising. NT did start life as OS/2, version 2, after all.) Although the APIs and implementations differ significantly, the fundamental concepts are the same. The *ideas* in this book are valid for all three; the details of the APIs differ.

All the specific discussion in this book focuses on the Solaris™ 2 and POSIX multithreading models, with comparisons to OS/2 and NT throughout. We concentrate on the Solaris implementation in greatest detail. We do so because the Solaris threads library is currently the most advanced and robust implementation available, has the maximum exposure, the best thread-aware tool suite, and conforms most closely to the POSIX standard. (The fact that we both work for Sun has nothing to do with it[1].)

A frank note about our motivation is in order here. We have slaved away for countless hours on this book because we're propeller-heads who honestly believe that this technology is a superb thing and that the widespread use of it will make the world a better place for hackers like ourselves. Sun's motivation for assisting us in the project is to promote the usage of MT, because (a) this means you can write better, faster programs on Solaris, increasing sales of the operating system, and (b) Sun is far ahead of everybody else in both MT and multiprocessor (MP) machines, so it should leverage hardware sales, too.

Your motivations for writing MT programs? You can write your programs better and more easily, they'll run faster, and you'll get them to market more quickly, they'll have fewer bugs, you'll have happier programmers, customers, and higher sales. The only losers in this game are the competitors, who lag behind Sun in MP hardware and MT software and will lag behind you in application speed and quality.

---

1. The particularly gullible reader is encouraged to peruse some pre-owned bridges that we have for sale, cheap!

MT is here today. It will soon be ubiquitous. As a professional programmer, you have an obligation to understand this technology. It may or may not be appropriate for your current project, but you must be able to make that conclusion yourself. This book will give you what you need to make that decision.

Welcome to the world of the future!

Who Should Use This Book

This book aims to give the programmer or technical manager a solid, basic understanding of threads—what they are, how they work, why they are useful, and some of the programming issues surrounding their use. As an introductory text, it does not attempt a deep, detailed analysis. After reading this book you should have a solid understanding of the fundamentals, be able to write credible, modestly complex, threaded programs and have the understanding necessary to analyze your own programs and determine the viability of threading them.

This book is written with the experienced C/UNIX programmer in mind. A non-UNIX programmer will find a few of the details unfamiliar, but the concepts clear. A non-C programmer will find the code fragments and API descriptions mildly challenging, though possible to decipher, while the concepts should be clear. A technically minded nonprogrammer should be able to follow most of the concepts and understand the value of threads. A nontechnical person will not get much from this book.

How This Book Is Organized

Chapter 1, *Introduction* — In which we present the motivation for creating thread libraries, discuss the advent of shared memory multiprocessors, and the interactions between threads and SMP machines.

Chapter 2, *Concepts* — In which the reader is introduced to the basic concepts of multitasking operating systems and of multithreading as it compares to other programming paradigms. The reader is shown a set of reasons why multithreading is a valuable addition to programming paradigms, and a number of examples of successful deployment are presented.

Chapter 3, *Foundations* — In which the reader is introduced to the underlying structures upon which threads are built, the construction of the thread itself, and the operating system support that allows an efficient implementation.

Chapter 4, *Scheduling* — In which we explain the myriad details of the different scheduling models. After the reader is given a firm grounding in the fundamental concepts, we explain the various alternative choices that could have been made. Finally, the reader is treated to a comprehensive explanation of the intricacies in the life of a thread.

Chapter 5, *Synchronization* — In which the reader is led on a hunt for the intimidating synchronization variables and discovers that they are not actually as frightening as had been thought. After the hardware and software issues surrounding them are explained, the reader is shown the trade-offs involved in selecting the proper one to use. The chapter concludes with an explanation of thread-specific data.

Chapter 6, *Operating System Issues* — In which we explore a variety of operating systems issues that bear heavily upon the usability of the threads library in actual programs. We also examine a set of general operating system functions and their value.

Chapter 7, *POSIX Threads (pthreads)* — In which the details of the POSIX concepts are explained and contrasted to those of Solaris. A brief consideration of the issues of moving from Solaris threads to POSIX threads concludes the chapter.

Chapter 8, *Programming Tools* — In which we consider the kinds of new tools that a reader would want when writing an MT program. Details of the Solaris tool set are discussed in the context of working with actual programs.

Chapter 9, *Programming With Threads* — In which some pointers on programming with threads are given. Differences between single-threaded thinking and multithreaded thinking are emphasized.

Chapter 10, *Examples* — In which several example programs are presented, and their details and issues surrounding the way they use threads are discussed.

Recommended Reading

As of this writing, there are no other books specifically on the topic of multithreading concepts, although we know that several will be coming out within a year of this publication. Many of the operating system books and programming guides contain listings of the APIs but do not attempt to deal with the concepts of MT.

Related Books

Advanced Windows NT: The Developer's Guide to the Win32 Application Programming Interface. Jeffrey Richter. Microsoft Press, 1994. ISBN 1-55615-567-0. This book contains about 200 pages that cover the NT threads API and its usage. It covers the API well, contains a good amount of code, but very little theory.

Multithreaded Computer Architecture: A Summary of the State of the Art. Edited by Robert A. Iannucci. Kluwer Academic Publishers, 1994. ISBN 0-7923-9477-1. This book is a collection of papers dealing with hardware design considerations for building specialized machines that can support multithreaded programs.

Programming with Threads. Steve Kleiman, Devang Shah, Bart Smaalders. SunSoft Press/Prentice Hall PTR, Publication date late fall 1995. ISBN 0-13-172389-8. This book will be the definitive guide to developing multithreaded programs on UNIX, going into great depth on theory and practice.

Real-World Programming for OS/2 2.1. Derrel R. Blain, Kurt R. Delimon, Jeff English. Sams Publishing/Prentice Hall PTR, 1993. ISBN 0-672-30300-0. This book contains about 50 pages that cover the OS/2 threads API and its usage. It covers the API well, contains one nice example but very little theory.

Solaris Multithreaded Programming Guide. SunSoft Press/Prentice Hall PTR, 1995. ISBN 0-13-160896-7. This is the documentation that comes with Solaris and contains all the information about the API. It is also available as part of the Solaris AnswerBook® and via the threads page on the WWW (see Appendix C, *Threads on the Net*).

Using Multi-C: A Portable Multithreaded C Programming Library. Prentice Hall PTR, 1994. ISBN 0-13-606195-8. This book describes the API and use of the MIX Multi-C library, which is a proprietary library providing similar kinds of functionality to POSIX threads.

Related Papers

There are a number of papers from technical conferences that go into great detail of the different aspects of multithreading. You can find those that we felt were most interesting on the thread's home page. (See Appendix C, *Threads on the Net*.)

Introduction

In which we present the motivation for creating thread libraries, discuss the advent of shared memory multiprocessors, and the interactions between threads and SMP machines.

The basic concept of multithreaded programming (MT) has existed in R&D labs for several decades. Co-routine systems such as Concurrent Pascal & InterLisp's Spaghetti stacks were in use in the mid-70s and dealt with many of the same issues. Ada's tasks are a language-based construct that maps directly onto threads (so directly, in fact, that current Ada compilers implement tasks with threads). Other versions of co-routing have existed even longer.

The advent of this concept emerging into industry as an accepted, standardized programming paradigm is a phenomenon of the 90s. As with many other concepts, the research and the experimental use of threads has been widespread in universities and research institutes, and it is entering industry as a relatively well-formed whole on all fronts almost simultaneously. In 1991, no major commercial operating systems contained a robust user-level threads library. By 1996, every major player in the computer industry will have one.

Some of the motivation for this can be ascribed to general good sense and the recognition of a technology whose time has come. Some can be related to the unification efforts surrounding UNIX, SVR4, and now SPEC 1170 (*Single UNIX Specification*). Probably the greatest push, especially when viewed from the point of view of the ISV and the end user, is the emergence of shared memory symmetric multiprocessors (SMP). MT provides exactly the right programming paradigm to make maximal use of these new machines.

The threading models we describe in this book are strictly software models that can be implemented on any kind of general-purpose hardware. Much research is going into the problem of creating a better kind of hardware that would be uniquely suited for threaded programming. We do not address that aspect in this book.

To those of us who are concerned with the theoretical underpinnings of programming paradigms and language design, the true value of multithreading is significant and obvious. It obviously provides a far superior paradigm for constructing programs. For those others who are concerned with the practical details of getting real tasks done using computers, the value is also significant and obvious. Multithreading obviously makes it possible to obtain vastly greater performance than was ever before possible by taking advantage of multiprocessor machines.

In deference to those concerned with making a buck (or a bridge, or a Buick), we shall spend some time considering the value of MT to SMP machines.

At whatever price point, the purchasers of workstations want to get maximal performance from their machines. The demands of computationally intensive users are always growing, and they invariably exceed the provisions of their wallets. They might want a "personal Cray," but they can't afford one.

One of the solutions to this demand lies in the ever-increasing performance of CPUs. Along with the obvious technique of increasing the clock speed, a wide range of other methods are used to increase the performance of individual CPUs. The use of long instruction pipelines or superscalar techniques have allowed us to produce multiple-instruction machines that can do a lot more in a single clock tick. Finer compiler optimization techniques, out-of-order execution, predictive branching, VLIW, etc., allow us to obtain better and better performance from processors. However good these methods are, they still have their limits.

One of the major limiting factors is the problem of limited bus, memory, and peripheral speeds. We can build CPUs today that operate at 300 MHz, but we can't build communications buses that operate at the same speed. RAM speeds are also falling further and further behind the demands of the CPUs. It is expensive to build 150 MHz CPUs, but as there are only a few in a system, it's affordable. To build memory that can keep up with these speeds would be prohibitively expensive. A great many machines today implement two-level caches to deal with this problem (single-level caches weren't enough!). Multilevel caches work effectively with well-behaved programs, where sequential data and instructions references are likely to be physically adjacent in memory. But truly random-access programs wreak havoc on this scheme, and we can point to any number of programs that run faster on slower machines that lack that second-level cache.

None of the issues addressed above play favorites with any manufacturers. Sun, Intel, HP, IBM, DEC, etc., have come up with techniques for dealing with them. Some techniques have proven to be more effective than others, but none of them avoid the fundamental limitations of physics. Nature is a harsh mistress.

This is where SMP comes into play. It is one more weapon in our arsenal for performance. Just as the above techniques have allowed us to increase our single-CPU performance, SMP allows us to increase our overall system performance.

And that's what we really care about—overall system performance. As one customer put it "SMP, superscalar— buzzwords! I don't care if you have little green men inside the box! I want my program to run faster!"

We can build 64-processor machines today (e.g., the Cray CS6400) that will yield 64 times the performance of a single-processor machine[1]. The cost of that 64-CPU machine is a fraction of the cost of 64 single-processor machines. In a 64-way SMP machine, all 64 processors share the system costs: chassis, main memory, disks, software, etc. With 64 uniprocessors, each processor must have its own chassis, memory, etc. This fact makes SMP highly attractive for its price/performance ratio. An additional attraction to SMP is that it is also possible to purchase a machine with a small number of CPUs and add more CPUs as demands (and budgets) increase. In the chart below, these advantages of SMP are clear.

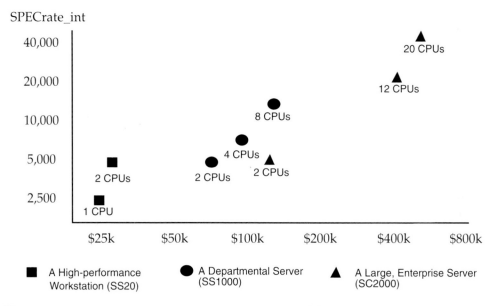

Figure 1-1   Cost vs. Performance for SMP Workstations and Servers

The economics of purchasing an SMP machine are pretty much the same as the economics of purchasing any machine. There are some extra unknowns ("I have 600 different applications that I run from time to time, how much faster will they all run? How much time will I save in a day?"), but if we focus on the primary

---

1. On some problems! Perfect, 100% scaling is unusual, but 60%–80% is common.

applications in use, we can get reasonable data upon which to make our decisions. The basic question is "If my applications run an average of N% faster and a dual-CPU machine costs M% more, is it worth it?"

Only you (or your customers) can answer this question, but we can give you some generalities. Here is a typical situation: The customer's major application is MARC Analysis' MARC Solver (for circuit simulation). The MARC Solver runs about 80% faster on a dual-processor SPARCstation™ 20 than it does on a single-processor SPARCstation 20. The single-processor machine costs $16,000, the dual-processor costs $18,000 (about 12% more). If the designers (who cost at least $100,000/year) are constantly waiting for the solver to complete its runs, is it worth it? Obviously, yes. You will save a lot of money on a minor investment. Indeed, MARC sells very well on SMP machines.

If you are a program developer (either in-house or an ISV), your question is going to be "Should I spend the time to write my program so that it will take advantage of SMP machines?" (This probably means threading, although there are other possibilities.) Your answer will be related to your anticipated sales. If your program runs 50% faster on a dual-processor machine, will your customers buy SMP machines and more of your software? Or, to pose the question differently, if you don't do it, will some competitor do it instead and steal your customers?

The answer depends upon your program. If you write a simple text editor that is never CPU-bound, the answer is a clear "no." If you write a database that is always CPU-bound, it's "yes." If you write a page-layout program that is sometimes CPU-bound, the answer is "maybe." In general, if users ever have to wait for your program, you should be looking at threading and SMP.

But there is more value to threading than just SMP performance. In many instances uniprocessors will also experience a significant performance improvement. And that bit about programming paradigms? It really does count. Being able to write simpler, more readable code helps you in almost all aspects of development. Your code can be less buggy, get out there faster, and be easier to maintain.

Multithreading is not a magic bullet for all your ills[2], and it does introduce a new set of programming issues which must be mastered, but it goes a long way toward making your work easier and your programs more efficient.

---

2. If you have ever spent days debugging complex signal handling code, you may disagree. For asynchronous code, it *is* a magic bullet!

Concepts

In which the reader is introduced to the basic concepts of multitasking operating systems and of multithreading as it compares to other programming paradigms. The reader is shown a set of reasons why multithreading is a valuable addition to programming paradigms, and a number of examples of successful deployment are presented.

Background: Traditional Operating Systems

Before we get into the details of threads, it will be useful for us to have some clear understanding of how operating systems without threads work. In the simplest operating system world of single-user, single-tasking operating systems such as DOS, everything is quite easy to understand and to use, though the functionality offered is minimal.

DOS divides the memory of a computer into two sections: the portion where the operating system itself resides (*kernel space*[1]) and the portion where the programs reside (*user space*). The division into these two spaces is done strictly by the implicit agreement of the programmers involved——meaning that nothing stops a user program from accessing data in kernel space. This lack of hardware enforcement is a good thing, because it is very simple and works very well when people write perfect programs. When a user program needs some function performed for it by kernel code (such as reading a file from a disk), the program can call the DOS function directly to read that file.

Each program has some code that it runs (which is just a series of instructions, where the *program counter* points to the current instruction), some data (global and local) that it uses, and a stack where local data and return addresses are stored (the *stack pointer* designates the current active location on the stack).

Figure 2-1 illustrates the traditional operating system memory layout.

---

1. "Kernel space" is UNIX-lingo for this concept, but the concept is valid for all operating systems.

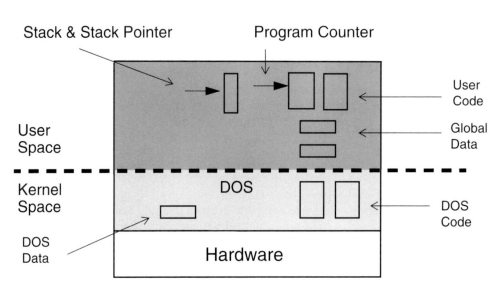

Figure 2-1   Memory Layout for DOS-style Operating Systems

Thus, the division between user space and kernel space, as shown in Figure 2-1, is a division by agreement of the programmers; there is no hardware enforcement of the policy at all. The drawbacks to this technique are significant, however. Not all programs are written flawlessly, and a programming mistake (or virus!) here can bring down the entire machine or, worse, destroy valued data. Neither can a machine run more than one program at a time, nor can more than one user log in to the machine at a time. Dealing with networks from DOS machines is somewhat awkward and limited. Configuring DOS machines cannot be discussed in polite company.

In a typical multitasking operating system such as VMS, UNIX, Windows NT, etc., this dividing line between the user space and the kernel space is solid (Figure 2-2); it's enforced by the hardware. There are actually two different modes of operation for the CPUs: *user mode*, which allows normal user programs to run, and *kernel mode*, which also allows some special instructions to run that only the kernel can execute. These kernel-mode instructions include such things as I/O instructions, processor interrupt instructions, instructions that control the state of the virtual memory subsystem, and, of course, the *change mode* instruction.

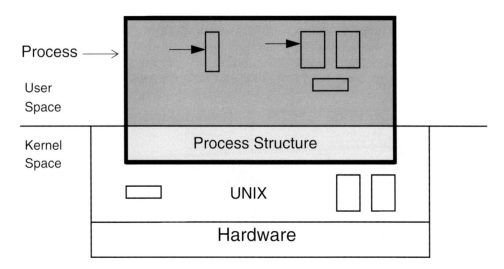

Figure 2-2   Memory Layout for Multitasking Systems

So, a user program can execute only user-mode instructions, and it can execute them only in user space. The data it can access and change directly is also limited to data in user space. When it needs something from the kernel (say, it wants to read a file or find out the current time), the user program must make a *system call*. This is a library function that sets up some arguments, then executes a special *trap* instruction. This instruction causes the hardware to trap into the kernel, which then takes control of the machine. The kernel figures out what the user wanted (based upon the data that the system call set up), and whether the user has permission to do it. Finally the kernel performs the desired task, returning any information to the user process.

Because the operating system has complete control over I/O, memory, processors, etc., it needs to maintain data for each process it's running. The data tells the operating system what the state of that process is—what files are open, which user is running it, etc. So, the concept of *process* in the multitasking world extends into the kernel (see Figure 2-2), where this information is maintained in a *process structure*. In addition, as this is a multitasking world, more than one process can be active at the same time, and for most of these operating systems (notably neither Windows NT nor OS/2), more than one user can log in to the machine independently and run programs simultaneously.

Processes

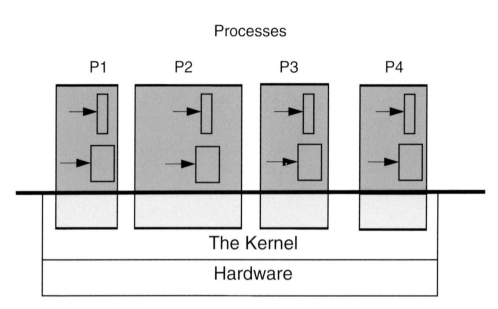

Figure 2-3   *Processes on a Multitasking System*

Thus, in Figure 2-3, Process P1 can be run by user Kim, while P2 and P3 are being run by user Dan, and P4 by user Bil. There is also no particular restriction on the amount of memory that a process can have. P2 might use twice as much memory as P1, for example. It is also true that no two processes can see or change each other's memory, unless they have set up a special *shared memory* segment.

For all the user programs in all the operating systems mentioned so far, each has one stack, one program counter, and one set of CPU registers per process. So, each of these programs can do only one thing at a time. They are *single threaded*.

What Is a Thread?

Just as multitasking operating systems can do more than one thing concurrently by running more than a single process, a process can do the same by running more than a single *thread*. Each thread is a different stream of control that can execute its instructions independently, allowing a multithreaded process to perform numerous tasks concurrently. One thread can run the GUI, while a second thread does some I/O, while a third one performs calculations.

A thread is an abstract concept that comprises everything a computer does in executing a traditional program. It is the program state that gets scheduled on a CPU, it is the "thing" that does the work. If a process comprises data, code, kernel state, and a set of CPU registers, then a thread is embodied in the contents of those registers—the program counter, the general registers, the stack pointer, etc., and the stack. A thread, viewed at an instant of time, is the state of the computation.

"Gee," you say, "That sounds like a process!" It should. They are conceptually related. But a process is a kernel-level entity and includes such things as a virtual memory map, file descriptors, user ID, etc., and each process has its own collection of these. The only way for your program to access data in the process structure, to query or change its state, is via a system call.

All parts of the process structure are in kernel space (Figure 2-4). A user program cannot touch any of that data directly. By contrast, all of the user code (functions, procedures, etc.) along with the data is in user space, and can be accessed directly.

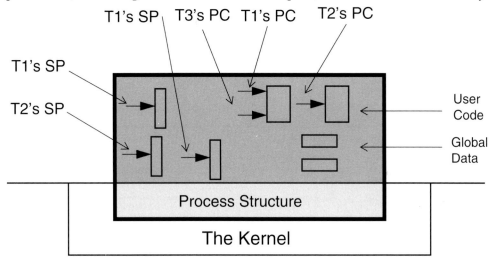

Figure 2-4   Relationship Between a Process and Threads

A thread is a user-level entity[2]. The *thread structure* is in user space and can be accessed directly with the thread library calls, which are just normal user-level functions. Note that the registers (stack pointer, program counter, etc.) are all part of a thread, and each thread has its own stack, but the code it is executing is not

---

2. This is not completely accurate. However we will persist in using this description for pedagogical purposes. Later, when you have sufficient background to grasp the details more easily, we'll be more accurate. (See *Threads Are Not Always User-level Entities* on page 44.)

Unrelated to this is the fact that some kernels are also built using threads. Obviously these "kernel threads" are kernel objects, but you will never interact with kernel threads directly unless you're doing kernel-level programming. Solaris kernel threads are not intended for external usage, and we will mention them only in passing.

part of the thread. The actual code (functions, routines, signal handlers, etc.) is global and can be executed on any thread. In Figure 2-4, we show three threads (T1, T2, T3), along with their stacks, stack pointers (SP), and programs counters (PC). T1 and T3 are executing the same function. This is a normal situation, just as two different people can read the same road sign at the same time.

All threads in a process share the state of that process (see Figure 2-5[3]). They reside in the exact same memory space, see the same functions, see the same data. When one thread alters a process variable (say, the working directory), all the others will see the change when they next access it. If one thread opens a file to read it, all the other threads can also read from it.

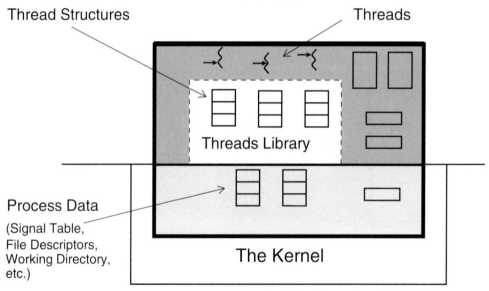

Figure 2-5   The Process Structure and the Thread Structures

Let's consider a human analogy: a bank. A bank with one person working in it (traditional process) has lots of "bank stuff" such as desks and chairs, a vault, and teller stations (process tables and variables). There are lots of services that a bank provides: checking accounts, loans, savings accounts, etc. (the functions). With one person to do all the work, that person would have to know how to do everything, and could do so, but it might take a bit of extra time to switch among the various tasks. With two or more people (threads), they would share all the

---

3. From here on, we will use the squiggle shown in the figure to represent the entire thread—stack, stack pointer, program counter, thread structure, etc.

same "bank stuff," but they could specialize on their different functions. And if they all came in and worked on the same day, lots of customers could get serviced quickly.

To change the number of banks in town would be a big effort (creating new processes), but to hire one new employee (creating a new thread) would be very simple. Everything that happened inside the bank, including interactions among the employees there, would be fairly simple (user space operations among threads), whereas anything that involved the bank down the road would be much more involved (kernel space operations between processes).

When you write a multithreaded program, 99% of your programming is identical to what it was before—you spend you efforts in getting the program to do its real work. The other 1% is spent in creating threads, arranging for different threads to coordinate their activities, dealing with thread-specific data, and signal masks. Perhaps 0.1% of your code consists of calls to thread functions.

So here's the essential point about threads: They are user-level entities. Virtually everything you do to a thread happens at user level with no system calls involved. Because no system calls are involved, it's fast. There are no kernel structures affected by the existence of threads in a program, so no kernel resources are consumed—threads are cheap. *The kernel doesn't even know that threads exist.* (This is important. We're going to repeat it about ten times.)

Kernel Interaction

We've now covered the basic concept of threads at the user level. As noted, the concepts and most of the implementational aspects are valid for all the thread models. What's missing is the definition of the relationship between threads and the operating systems. How do system calls work? How are signals handled? And how are threads scheduled on CPUs?

It is at this level that the various implementations differ significantly. The operating systems provide different systems calls, and even identical system calls can differ widely in efficiency and robustness. The kernels are constructed differently and provide different resources and services.

Keep in mind, as we go though this implementation aspect, that 99% of your threads programming will be done above this level, and the major distinctions will be in the area of efficiency. For UNIX machines, you will be writing strictly at the user level, so as soon as all the vendors implement the POSIX standard, your program can be completely portable, requiring no more than a single TSR (Theoretical Simple Recompile) in order to move to different platforms.

2

System Calls

A system call is basically a function that ends up trapping to routines in the kernel. These routines may do things as simple as looking up the user ID for the owner of the current process, or as complex as redefining the system's scheduling algorithm. For multithreaded programs, there is a very serious issue surrounding how many threads can make system calls concurrently. For some operating systems the answer is "one"; for some, it's "many." The most important point is that system calls run exactly as they did before, so all your old programs continue to run as they did before, with no degradation.

Signals

Signals[4] are one of the harder aspects of multithreaded programming to understand and to use effectively. Truth be known, they are not so simple in regular UNIX programming. The primary requirement, when designing the multithreaded signal model, was to ensure that the original UNIX semantics were retained. Single-threaded programs had to run exactly the same way as they did before, and on top of this, the multithreaded programs had to have some sort of "reasonable" semantics. The details we'll reserve until later, but the important point here is that for your old programs, nothing changes.

Synchronization

Synchronization ensures that multiple threads coordinate their activities so that one thread doesn't accidently change data that another thread is working on. This is done by providing function calls that can limit the number of threads that can access some data concurrently.

In the simplest case (a Mutual Exclusion Lock—a *mutex*), only one thread at a time can execute the given piece of code. This code presumably alters some global data or does reads or writes to a device. For example, thread T1 obtains a lock and starts to work on some global data. Thread T2 must now wait (typically it goes to sleep) until thread T1 is done before it can execute the same code. By using the same lock around all code that changes the data, we can ensure that the data remains consistent.

Scheduling

The fundamental scheduling scheme for threads (there are others) is a preemptive, priority-based, non-time-slicing algorithm that allows the highest

---

4. Signals are the kernel's way of interrupting a running process and letting it know that something of interest has happened. It could be that a timer has expired, or that some I/O has completed, or that some other process wants to communicate something.

priority threads to run as long as they need to. This algorithm can operate completely in user mode, not requiring any system calls at all. In practice, scheduling is not generally an issue. Most programs are written in such a way that each thread needs something from the other threads, with the result that when the running thread needs that something (data, or a resource), it will voluntarily stop running and allow other threads to run until that something becomes available.

The Value of Using Threads

There is really only one reason for writing MT programs—you get better programs, more quickly. If you're an ISV, you sell more software. If you're developing software for your own in-house use, you simply have better programs to use. The reason that you can write better programs is because MT gives your programs and your programmers a number of significant advantages over nonthreaded programs and programming paradigms.

A point to keep in mind here is that you are not replacing simple, nonthreaded programs with fancy, complex, threaded ones. You are using threads only when you need them to replace complex or slow nonthreaded programs. Threads are really just one more way you have to make your programming tasks easier.

The main benefits of writing multithreaded programs are:

- Performance gains from multiprocessing hardware (parallelism)
- Increased application throughput
- Increased application responsiveness
- Enhanced process-to-process communications
- Efficient use of system resources
- The ability to make use of the inherent threadedness of distributed objects
- There is one binary that runs on both uniprocessors and multiprocessors
- The ability to create well-structured programs
- There can be a single source for multiple platforms

The following sections elaborate further on these benefits.

Parallelism

Computers with more than one processor provide multiple simultaneous points of execution (Figure 2-6). Multiple threads are an efficient way for application developers to exploit the parallelism of the hardware. Different threads can run on different processors simultaneously with no special input from the user and no effort on the part of the programmer.

A good example of this is a process that does matrix multiplication. A thread can be created for each available processor, allowing the program to use the entire machine. The threads can then compute distinct elements of the result matrix by doing the appropriate vector multiplication (see the example *Matrix Multiplication* on page 159).

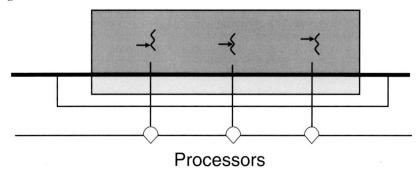

Processors

Figure 2-6   Different Threads Running on Different Processors

Throughput

When a traditional, single-threaded program requests a service from the operating system, it must wait for that service to complete, often leaving the CPU idle. Even on a uniprocessor, multithreading allows a process to overlap computation with one or more blocking system calls (Figure 2-7). Threads provide this overlap even though each request is coded in the usual synchronous style. The thread making the request must wait, but another thread in the process can continue. Thus, a process can have numerous blocking requests outstanding, giving you the beneficial effects of doing asynchronous I/O, while still writing code in the simpler synchronous fashion.

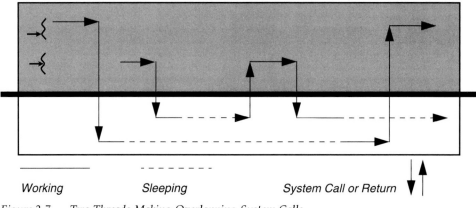

Working   *Sleeping*   *System Call or Return*

Figure 2-7   Two Threads Making Overlapping System Calls

Responsiveness

Blocking one part of a process need not block the whole process. Single-threaded applications that do something lengthy when a button is pressed typically display a "please wait" cursor and freeze while the operation is in progress. If such applications were multithreaded, long operations could be done by independent threads, allowing the application to remain active and making the application more responsive to the user. In Figure 2-8, one thread is waiting for I/O from the buttons, and several threads are working on the calculations.

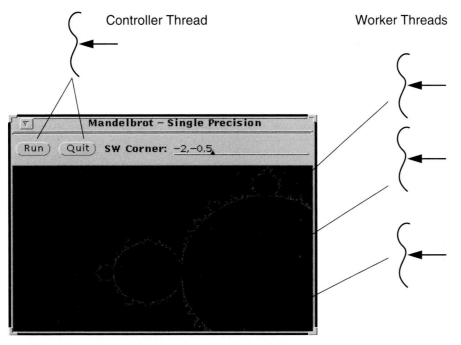

Figure 2-8   *Threads Overlapping Calculation and I/O*

Communications

An application that uses multiple processes to accomplish its tasks can be replaced by an application that uses multiple threads to accomplish those same tasks. Where the old program communicated among its processes through traditional IPC (interprocess communications) facilities (e.g., pipes or sockets), the threaded application can use the inherently shared memory of the process. The threads in the MT process can maintain separate IPC connections while sharing data in the same address space. A classic example is a server program, which can maintain one thread for each client connection (Figure 2-9). This provides excellent performance, simpler programming, and effortless scalability.

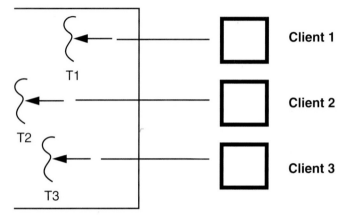

Figure 2-9   Different Client Machines Being Handled by Different Threads in a Server Program

System Resources

Programs that use two or more processes to access common data through shared memory are effectively applying more than one thread of control. However, each such process must maintain a complete process structure, including a full virtual memory space and kernel state. The cost of creating and maintaining this large amount of state makes each process much more expensive, in both time and space, than a thread. In addition, the inherent separation between processes may require a major effort by the programmer to communicate among the different processes or to synchronize their actions. By using threads for this communication instead of processes, the program will be easier to debug and can run much faster.

An application can create hundreds or even thousands of threads, one for each synchronous task, with only minor impact on system resources. Threads use a fraction of the system resources used by processes.

Distributed Objects

With the first releases of standardized distributed objects and object request brokers (coming in 1995), your ability to make use of these will become increasingly important. Distributed objects are inherently multithreaded. Each time you request an object to perform some action, it executes that action in a separate thread (Figure 2-10). Object servers are an absolutely fundamental element in distributed object paradigm, and those servers (as discussed above) are inherently multithreaded.

Although you can make a great deal of use of distributed objects without doing any MT programming, knowing what they are doing and being able to create objects that are threaded will increase the usefulness of the objects you do write.

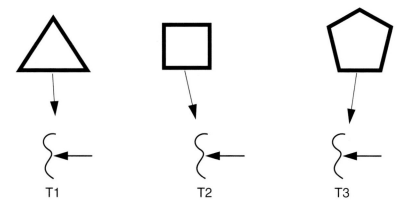

Figure 2-10   Distributed Objects Running on Distinct Threads

Same Binary for Uniprocessors and Multiprocessors

In most older parallel processing schemes, it was necessary to tailor a program for the individual hardware configuration. With threads, this customization isn't required because the MT paradigm works well irrespective of the number of CPUs. A program can be compiled once, and it will run acceptably on a uniprocessor, whereas on a multiprocessor it will just run faster.

Program Structure

Many programs are more efficiently structured with threads because they are inherently concurrent. A traditional program that tries to do many different tasks is crowded with lots of complicated code to coordinate these tasks. A threaded program can do the same tasks with much less, far simpler code. Multithreaded programs can be more adaptive to variations in user demands than single-threaded programs (see Figure 2-11).

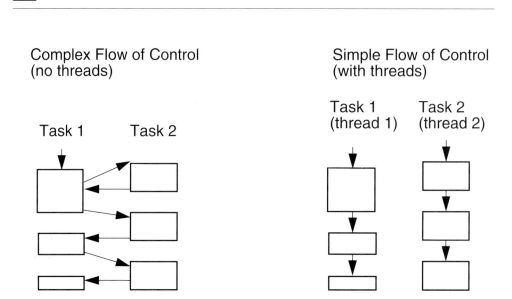

Complex Flow of Control
(no threads)

Simple Flow of Control
(with threads)

Task 1   Task 2

Task 1   Task 2
(thread 1)   (thread 2)

Figure 2-11   Simplified Flow of Control in Complex Applications

Single Source for Multiple Platforms

Many programs must run on numerous platforms. With the POSIX threads
standard (see *Threads Standards* on page 21), it will be possible to write a single
source and recompile it for the different platforms. Most of the UNIX vendors
have signed up to do POSIX threads.

This is quite some set of claims, and a bit of healthy skepticism is called for when
reading things like this. Sure, it sounds good when we say it, but what about
when you try to use it? We cannot guarantee that you will experience the same
wonderful results, but we can point out a number of cases where other folks have
found MT programming to be of great advantage (see *Performance* on page 22).

What Kind of Programs to Thread?

There is a spectrum of programs that one might wish to thread. On one side, there
are those that are inherently MT—you look at the work to be done, and you think
of it as several independent tasks. In the middle, there are programs where the
division of work isn't obvious, but possible. On the far other end, there are those
that cannot be threaded at all.

Inherently MT Programs

The inherently MT programs are ones that are just more easily expressed as numerous threads doing numerous things. Such programs are easier to write using threads, because they are doing different things concurrently anyway. They are generally simpler to write and understand when threaded, easier to maintain, and more robust. The fact that they may run faster is a mere pleasant side effect. For these programs, the general rule is that the more complex the application, the greater the value of threading.

Typical programs that are inherently MT include:

Independent tasks: A debugger needs to run and monitor a program, keep its GUI active, and display an interactive data inspector, dynamic call grapher, and performance monitor. All in the same address space, all at the same time.

Servers: A server needs to handle numerous overlapping requests simultaneously. NFS®, NIS, DBMSs, stock quotation servers, etc., all receive large number of requests that require the server to do some I/O, then process the results and return answers. Doing this by completing one request at a time would be *very* slow.

Repetitive tasks: A simulator needs to simulate the interactions of numerous different elements that operate simultaneously. CAD, structural analysis, weather prediction, etc., all model tiny pieces first, then combine the results to produce an overall picture.

Not Obviously MT Programs

This class comprises those programs that are not inherently MT, but for which threading is reasonable. This is where you take an algorithm that does not have an obvious decomposition and impose threads upon it in order to achieve a speedup on an MP machine. Such a program is (somewhat) harder to write, a bit more difficult to maintain, etc., than its nonthreaded counterpart. But it runs faster. Because of these drawbacks, the (portions of) programs chosen are generally quite simple.

Typical programs in this class include:

Numerical programs: Many numerical programs (e.g., matrix operations) are made up of huge numbers of tiny, identical, and independent operations. They are most easily (well, most commonly) expressed as loops inside of loops. Slicing these loops into appropriate-sized chunks for threads is slightly more complicated, and there would be no reason to do so, save for the order-N speedup that can be obtained on an N-way SMP machine.

Old code: These are the "slightly modified existing systems." This is existing code that makes you think to yourself: "If I just change a few bits here and there, add a few locks, then I can thread it and double my performance."

It's true, it is possible to do this, and there are lots of examples. However, this is a tough situation because you will constantly be finding new interactions that you didn't realize existed before. In such cases (which, due to the nature of the modern software industry, are far too common), you should concentrate on the bottlenecks and look for absolutely minimal submodules that can be rewritten. It's *always* best to take the time to do it right: rearchitect and write the program correctly from the beginning.

Automatic Threading

In a subset of cases, it is possible for a compiler to do the threading for you. If you have a program written in such a way that a compiler can analyze its structure, analyze the interdependencies of the data, and determine that parts of your program could run simultaneously without data conflicts, then the compiler can build the threads for you.

With current technology, the types of programs that avail themselves of this are limited to FORTRAN programs that have time-consuming loops where the individual computations in those loops are obviously independent. The primary reason this is limited to FORTRAN is that FORTRAN programs tend to have very simple structuring, both for code and data, making the analysis viable. Languages such as C, which have constructs such as pointers, make the analysis enormously more difficult.

With the different FORTRAN MP compilers[5], it is possible to take vanilla FORTRAN 77 code, make no changes to it whatsoever, and have the compiler turn out threaded code. In some cases it works very well; in others, not. The cost of trying it out is very small, of course.

Programs Not to Thread

Then there is a large set of programs that it doesn't make any sense to thread. These are programs that either do not lend themselves easily to threading or programs that run just fine the way they are. Some programs simply require separate processes to run in. Perhaps they need to do one task as root, and you don't want to have any other code running as root. Perhaps the program needs to

---

5. Sun® FORTRAN MP, Kuck and Associates FORTRAN compiler, EPC's FORTRAN compiler, SGI's MP FORTRAN compiler.

be able to control its global environment closely, changing working directories, etc. Some programs run quite fast enough as they are and don't have any inherent multitasking, such as an icon editor or a calculator application.

What About Shared Memory?

Right about now you may be asking yourself this question: "What can threads do that can't be done by processes sharing memory?"

The first answer is "nothing." Anything that you can do with threads, you can also do with processes sharing memory. Indeed, a number of vendors implement a significant portion of their threads library in roughly this fashion. If you are thinking about using shared memory in this fashion, you should make sure you have (a) plenty of time to kill programming, (b) plenty more time to kill processing, and (c) lots of money to burn buying RAM.

You see: (a) Debugging cross-process programs is tough, and the tools that exist for this are not as good as those for MT. (b) Things take longer. In Solaris, creating a process is about 30 times slower than creating a thread, synchronization variables are about 10 times slower, and context switching about 5 times slower. (c) Processes eat up lots of kernel memory. Building a few thousand threads is no big deal. Building a few thousand processes is.

You can do everything with shared memory. It just won't be as easy nor run as fast.

Threads Standards

As of the writing of this book (June 1995), the POSIX committee on multithreading standards 1003.1c (formerly 1003.4a) and the IEEE standards board have just ratified the draft standard 10. There is now an official POSIX threads standard.

This standard defines the API[6] and behavior that all the *pthreads* libraries must meet. It is part of the extended portion of POSIX, so it is not a requirement for meeting XPG4, but all major UNIX vendors have committed to meeting this standard. Presumably, a compliant library will be available from every vendor by the end of 1996, although individual plans and release dates may differ.

---

6. "Applications Programming Interface." This is the set of standard library calls that an operating system makes available to applications programmers. For MT, this means all the threads library function calls.

The futures for OS/2 threads and Windows NT threads are probably different. Both implementations contain some fairly radical departures from the POSIX standard—to the degree that even porting from one or the other to POSIX will prove moderately challenging. Neither one plans to adopt the standard (see *Comparisons of Different Implementations* on page 102).

Performance

Even after reading all these wonderful things about threads, there's always someone who insists on asking that ever-so-bothersome question: "Does it work?" For an answer, we turn to some real, live, shipping programs. Some of these are described in greater detail in the MT "Case Studies" available on the SunSoft WWW threads page (see *Threads on the World Wide Web* on page 205).

Solaris 2

Solaris 2 is a large, complex, yet still highly efficient and robust program. Solaris has been in daily use by several hundred thousand users over the past couple of years and has endured the stress put on it by tens of thousands of programmers who are not known for their generosity towards operating systems. SunSoft couldn't have built Solaris 2 without threads. Mach, NT, and OSF/1 are also threaded, and many of the other UNIX vendors are also moving toward a threaded kernel.

NFS

Under Solaris 2.4, both the NFS client and server are threaded. There aren't any standardized benchmarks for the client side, so you'll have to take our word that it's faster. On the server side, however, there is the LADDIS benchmark from SPEC. You'll notice, in Table 2-1, that not only does NFS scale well on multiprocessor machines, but even on a uniprocessor it runs faster than its single-threaded predecessor[7].

Table 2-1   SPEC LADDIS Results

	SS10/41 1 CPU Workstation	SC2000 8 CPU Server
SunOS 4.1	342	N/A
Solaris 2.3	352	2575
Solaris 2.4	N/A	3242

from the December 1994 Newsletter (Bigger is Better)

SPECfp 92

The rules for the SPECfp benchmark are that a compiler is allowed to do pretty much anything it wants to, as long as that same compiler is available to customers and nobody changes the source code at all. The Sun FORTRAN 77 MP compiler automatically multithreads a program with no user intervention, so it's legal. You give the compiler the code, completely unchanged, and it looks to see if there is any possibility of threading it. In 6 of the 14 SPECfp programs, it is possible to automatically thread them. The results are *very* impressive[8].

Table 2-2   SPECfp92 Results

	Tomcatv	Su2cor	Swm256	Hydro2d	ora	nasa7
SS20/61	93.0	108.7	50.6	101.4	192.7	111.6
SS20/612	148.0	191.4	94.9	175.4	360.2	148.0

From the June 1994 and Sept. 1994 SPEC Newsletter (Bigger is Better)

PAR93

SPECfp 92 is a reasonable set of benchmarks for single-CPU machines, but it does not give a very good picture of the performance of multiprocessor machines. SPEC is currently working on producing a set of benchmarks specifically designed to give a better picture of how well MP machines and MP compilers work. This work, currently known as PAR93, is not standardized yet, so caution should be exercised when looking at the numbers below. SPEC does not stand behind them. However, they do give a nice view of how effective MP compilers can be.

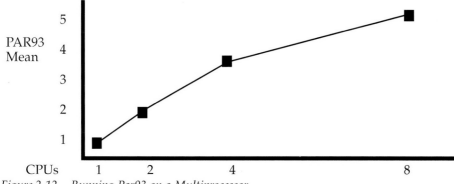

Figure 2-12   *Running Par93 on a Multiprocessor*

---

7. SPEC is very precise about how LADDIS is measured. It's an expensive process, so it's typical to restrict testing to specific machines, hence the N/A. This sometimes makes direct comparisons difficult to obtain. We *can* say that in internal NFS tests (which must not be compared to LADDIS!), Solaris 2.4 on an SS10/41 ran about 50% faster than the same machine under SunOS™ 4.1. SunOS 4.1 does not run on an SC2000.

8. A SPARCstation 20/61 is a single-CPU desktop workstation with a 60 MHz SuperSPARC™ CPU. A SPARCstation 20/612 is a dual-CPU desktop workstation with two 60 MHz SuperSPARC CPUs.

Dakota Scientific Software, Inc.

Dakota Scientific Software offers a multithreaded version of the standard BLAS, FTTPACK, VFTTPACK, LINPACK, and LAPACK libraries for FORTRAN. These libraries consist of sets of highly independent operations that can run in separate threads with very little synchronization required. They see near-linear scaling on MP machines (meaning that a two-CPU machine is almost twice as fast as a one-CPU machine). A huge number of numerical programs make use of these libraries, and they see significant performance improvement on MP machines.

MARC Analysis Inc.

In the arena of finite element analysis, MARC Analysis Inc., one of the premier ISVs, has threaded a section of their solver. This is the portion of the program that does major floating-point matrix operations and eats up approximately 80% of the total processing time. It scales to 80% on an eight-way machine.

Delphax and Uniq Inc.

Delphax is a high-speed printer company that rasterizes PostScript® files for output on very high speed duplex printers (180 impressions a minute). They had the assistance of an Australian consulting firm, Uniq Inc., to multithread their print engine. Uniq claims that threading allowed them to write the program more quickly, more easily, and more robustly, with better performance on a uniprocessor. Delphax has the proof.

Adobe

Adobe has threaded its Photoshop™ application, which is a desktop image processing and publishing application. It makes enormous demands on both the I/O subsystem and the floating-point unit of a system. On uniprocessors, Adobe reports significant improvements in the I/O speed, which directly affects the total speed of the application. On multiprocessor systems, Adobe reports near-linear performance improvements on some tests.

Facet Decision Systems, Inc.

Facet builds the Facet Spatial Spreadsheet, a GIS system based on a spreadsheet paradigm. It is a single application that can draw maps, simulate fluid flow, and model habitats, yet still calculate cash flow. The size and complexity of the spreadsheets involved are enormous, and they can take significant amounts of time to recalculate. By threading the application, Facet obtained enormous speedups on multiprocessing hardware.

The ImagiNation Network

The leader in multiuser gaming software, ImagiNation has some 100 games that users can access from a PC over a modem, and interact with other players. ImagiNation's server software runs all on multiprocessor SPARCservers. "Everything" is threaded. On average, several hundred threads are running at any one time. ImagiNation is expecting to scale to thousands of users with their current design.

Visual Numerics

Application-development tool-supplier Visual Numerics has released a multithreaded version of its IMSL FORTRAN 77 Numerical Libraries for SPARC® workstations and servers. The company claims the MP version of IMSL FORTRAN performs almost four times as fast as the uniprocessor version. IMSL FORTRAN is a collection of user-callable mathematical and statistical subroutines used to speed up the development of software programs and to provide building blocks for the programmer.

Vantage Analysis Systems, A Viewlogic Company

Vantage has a VHDL simulator that models the behavior of complex circuits on computers. Each circuit element has its own inputs and outputs. By having multiple threads perform the evaluations of all the active models of the elements, Vantage has seen speedups approaching a factor of four on an eight-way SMP server.

Landmark Graphics

Landmark Graphics' VoxCube product is their latest 3D visualization software that utilizes threads. VoxCube uses volume rendering to quickly isolate and evaluate seismic attributes contained in seismic data. Threading is used extensively in VoxCube to parallelize the volume rendering process. Landmark has noted a 91% performance improvement for each additional processor added to Sun SPARCstations. They believe that adding multiple processors to Sun desktop workstations plus comprehensive threading support gives users a scalable, high-performance solution.

University of Houston

Researchers in the University of Houston's Biochemical and Biophysical Sciences Department are using the Sun MP FORTRAN compiler to speed their work on the Human Genome Project, which seeks to map the entire genetic complement of a human being. They expect that the application running on a four-processor SPARC system will execute between 3 and 3.5 times faster.

Geophysical Development Corporation

GDC writes code for seismic testing which is used by numerous oil companies, as well as by many other companies. The work is all done in FORTRAN. By using the Sun MP FORTRAN compiler, GDC saw a near-linear speedup in much of their code, cutting analysis runs from days to hours.

InfoGraphix Technologies Incorporated

InfoGraphix develops and markets software for converting PostScript files into rasters (large arrays of pixel values) and then performing various image processing functions on those rasters (a computationally intensive task). In preliminary coding, most images registered a pleasant 20% to 50% speedup on a two-way workstation, after only a few hours of programming work.

Scitex

Scitex, a world leader in pre-press color systems, has used multithreading in its Savanna color publishing system—a high performance graphics workstation. Retouching of raster images has been speeded up by parallelizing key pixel operations such as shape drawing, geometric transformations, filtering, etc., into separate areas, each potentially handled by its own processor. In dual processor desktop systems, the performance of these multithreaded operations has improved between 60% and 98%.

Western Geographical

Western Geographical's TotalNet application solves, in real time, large networks of electronic positioning data. They used threading to improve TotalNet's performance in two ways. First, profiling revealed that 95 percent of the processing time was spent in a single matrix-manipulation routine. By splitting this routine across three threads and performing some hand optimization, they dramatically improved the performance of the application, measuring speed gains of three to four times when running on a 4-CPU SPARCstation. Second, by moving the I/O-bound output stream into its own thread, they improved application performance by an additional 10 to 15 percent.

Foundations 3

In which the reader is introduced to the underlying structures upon which threads are built, the construction of the thread itself, and the operating system support that allows an efficient implementation.

Implementation vs. Specification

When writing a book of this nature, the authors are often faced with a difficult decision: How much should they restrict themselves to the pure specifications, and how much in the way of implementation should they allow to show through? By talking only about the specifications, the reader is given a pure rendition of what the library should do and is not misled into thinking that because a particular implementation did things one way, they have to be like that[1].

Unfortunately, describing only the specification is rather akin to teaching the concepts of mathematics without ever mentioning the existence of numbers[2]. It's clean and pure, but it's terribly difficult to comprehend fully. So we have chosen to bring in implementation details when we think they will aid in comprehension. The implementation we will refer to most is the Solaris one, largely because we know it best.

Please keep in mind that these implementation details are included for your edification, but you should never write programs that depend upon them. They can change at any time, with no notification. Learn from the implementation, write to the specification.

Thread Libraries

There are two fundamentally different ways of implementing threads. The first is to write a user-level library that is substantially self-contained. It will make calls to system routines, and it may depend upon the existence of certain kernel

---

1. A specification is a description of what a program is supposed to do. An implementation is an actual program, which hopefully does what the spec says it should. The U.S. constitution is a specification for a country. The United States is an implementation.

2. Yes, we are members of the "New Math" generation.

features, but it is fundamentally a user-level library and contains no "magic" hooks into secret kernel routines. All of the defining structures and code for the library will be in user space. The vast majority of the library calls execute entirely in user space and make no more use of system routines than does any user-level library.

The second way is to write a library that is inherently a kernel-level implementation. It may define all the same functions as in the first case, but these functions will be completely dependent upon the existence of kernel routines to support them and may well be almost entirely in kernel space. The user-level portion of the library will be relatively small compared to the amount of kernel-level support it requires. The majority of library calls will require system calls.

Both of these methods can be used to implement exactly the same API, and they overlap in the kinds of kernel support they require. The Solaris implementation of the POSIX standard is of the first kind, while we anticipate[3] that most other implementations of POSIX will be of the second kind. Certainly both OS/2 and Windows NT threads (neither of which is POSIX compliant) are of the second type.

In either case, the programmer will use an API that is implemented by a threads library. That library will provide a set of function calls (typically about 50 calls) that is the programmer's sole interface to threads. Everything not provided by those calls must come from the system's other libraries, meaning that 99% of writing a multithreaded program consists of writing regular, old-fashioned code almost the same way as before.

As you read the descriptions of the APIs, you may be struck by the lack of fancy features, especially in the Solaris API. This is intentional. These libraries provide a foundation for writing MT programs, but not every little thing you might like. They provide you the resources with which to build more elaborate functions. Spin locks, priority-inheriting mutexes, deadlock-recovery features, etc., can be built out of these primitives with relative ease. Thus, if you want very fast, minimal functionality constructs, they are provided. If you want the slower, more complex constructs, you can build them.

We begin by talking about the parts of the system that are not inherently related to threads, but that do define a great deal about how threads must work. We use the specific example of how Solaris deals with the issues involved in building a viable interface between kernel-provided functionality and the user-level threads requirements. Other operating systems and other libraries have chosen different

---

3. No one else is quite there and we are not in a place to put words in their mouths.

ways of providing this interface, and we do discuss them in general terms. We believe that by understanding the Solaris implementation in detail, you will acquire the background needed to fill in the gaps for the other implementations.

The Process Structure

The only thing the kernel knows about is the process structure. And the process structure has changed (slightly) since you last looked at it in traditional multitasking operating systems such as SunOS 4.x (see Figure 3-1).

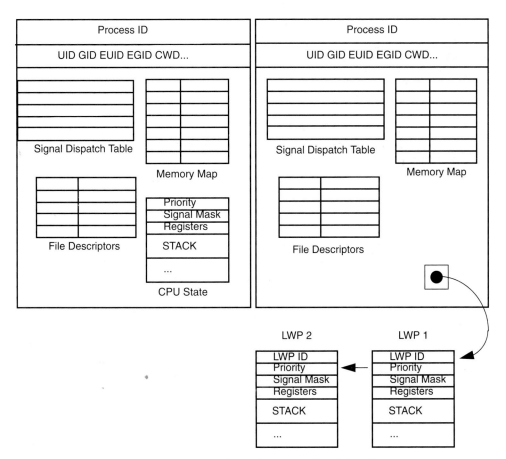

Figure 3-1   The Process Structure in Traditional UNIX and in Solaris 2

It used to contain the memory map, the signal dispatch table, signal mask, user ID, group ID, working directory, etc., along with runtime statistics, CPU state (registers, etc.), and a kernel stack (for executing system calls). In Solaris 2, the last couple bits have been abstracted out and placed into the a new structure called a *lightweight process* (LWP)[4]. So, a process contains all of the above, save for the runtime statistics, CPU state, and kernel stack, which are now part of the LWP structure. A process thus contains some number of LWPs (one for a "traditional" process, more for a multithreaded process). Just as the threads all share the process variables and state, the LWPs do the same.

The Solaris 2 process structure shown in Figure 3-1 is in kernel space—below the solid line in the figures. It is not directly accessible by any user code. User code can only access it via a system call. That restriction allows the kernel to check the legality of the call and prevent user code from doing things it shouldn't, either by intention or mistake. Because a system call is required to access the process structure information, it is a fairly costly operation, compared with a function call.

Lightweight Processes

A lightweight process[5] can be thought of as a virtual CPU that is available for executing code. Each LWP is separately dispatched by the kernel. It can perform independent system calls and incur independent page faults, and multiple LWPs in the same process can run in parallel on multiple processors.

LWPs are scheduled onto the available CPU resources according to their scheduling class and priority, as illustrated later in Figure 3-4. Because scheduling is done on a per-LWP basis, each LWP collects its own kernel statistics—user time, system time, page faults, etc. This also implies that a process with two LWPs will generally get twice as much CPU time as a process with only one LWP. (This is a wild generalization, but you get the idea—the kernel is scheduling *LWPs*, not processes.)

An LWP also has some capabilities that are not exported directly to threads, such as scheduling classes. A programmer can take advantage of these capabilities while still retaining use of all the thread interfaces and capabilities by specifying that the thread is to remain permanently bound to an LWP (discussed further in *Bound Threads and Real-time LWPs* on page 53).

---

4. The other operating systems that support user-level threads have different ways of dealing with the same issue. Some of them copy the entire process structure for each thread, some of them don't do anything. None of the others we know about have quite the same two-level model. The concept of a separate, schedulable entity such as the LWP proves to be an excellent pedagogical concept, and the other designs can be easily described in terms of LWPs.

5. SunOS 4.x had a library known as the LWP library. There is no relationship between Solaris 2 LWPs and SunOS 4.x LWPs.

LWPs are an implementation technique for providing kernel-level concurrency and parallelism to support the threads interface. There is no reason for you to ever use the LWP interface directly. Indeed, you should specifically avoid it. It gains you nothing but costs you your portability.

Because both levels of interface in the architecture are defined, a clear distinction is made between what the programmer sees and what the kernel provides. When it is appropriate to optimize the behavior of the program, the programmer can tune the relationship between threads and LWPs. This capability allows the programmer to structure the application, assuming extremely lightweight threads, while bringing the appropriate degree of kernel-supported concurrency to bear on the computation. To some degree, a threads programmer can think of the LWPs used by the application as the degree of real concurrency that the application requires.

Threads and LWPs

In a typical, traditional, multitasking operating system (MVS, VMS, UNIX, Windows NT, OS/2, etc.), a process comprises memory, the CPU register state, and some system state (file descriptors, user ID, working directory, etc., all stored in the *process structure*). When it's time to context switch two processes, the kernel saves the registers in the process structure, changes some virtual memory pointers, loads the CPU registers with data from the other process structure, and continues.

For unbound threads, a context switch is quite similar. It is performed entirely in user space by the threads library; it consists of saving the registers into one thread structure and replacing them with the saved state from another thread structure. The virtual memory page tables and all the system state remain unchanged. The idea is that you have a single program, in one memory space, with many virtual CPUs running different parts of the program concurrently. It's a user-level version of multitasking.

What actually makes up a thread are (see Figure 3-2): its own stack and stack pointer; a program counter; some thread information, such as scheduling priority, and signal mask, stored in the thread structure; and the CPU registers (the stack pointer and program counter are actually just registers). It is important to realize that the code, just like global data, is not part of the thread. The thread will run the code, it will use the global data, but both of those exist independently of any specific thread and can be used by all of threads. Indeed, it is perfectly normal for several threads to be executing exactly the same section of code simultaneously.

Everything else comes either from the process or (in a few cases) the LWP. The stack is just memory drawn from the program's heap. A thread *could* look into and even alter the contents of another thread's stack if it so desired. (Although you, being a good programmer, would never do this, your bugs might.)

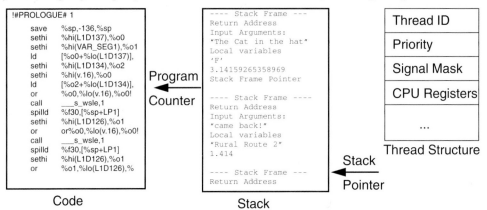

Figure 3-2   The Contents of a Thread

Putting all this together, we end up with a picture such as Figure 3-3. The threads, their stacks, the code they run, and the global data that they share, are all in user space, directly under user control. The thread structures are also in user space, but completely under control of the threads library. There is no legal[6] way for a user program to directly access those structures. The library itself, just like every other system library, is just regular user code that you could have written yourself.

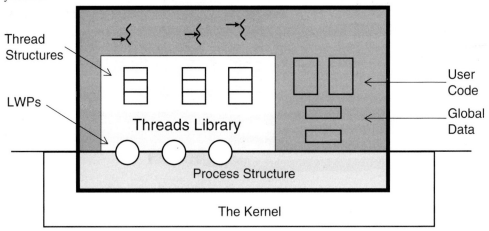

Figure 3-3   How the Threads Library Fits into a Process

6. Because this is in user space, there is no way to prevent you from accessing those structures if you really want to, unlike the process structure, where you cannot do so. But once again, don't! If the API doesn't give you what you think you need, you're probably doing something wrong. Discuss it with someone.

The LWPs are part of the process structure, but we show them crossing the line because this is how we think of their use. They are the main vehicle for processing from the threads library's point of view, so we show them in illustrations crossing that boundary, although they are, strictly speaking, in kernel space. The actual process structure is completely in kernel space.

Notice that *Solaris* threads are completely user-level entities. The kernel doesn't know they exist. This is the major motivating factor for having threads, as opposed to using lots of shared memory processes. They are user-level entities, hence cheap. They require no kernel resources, and basic operations run an order of magnitude faster than basic operations on a process. *Threads are inherently faster to operate on.*

As you can deduce, this definition of threads residing in a single address space means that the entire address space is seen identically by all threads. A change in shared data by one thread can be seen by all the other threads in the process. If one thread is writing a data structure while another thread is reading it, there will be problems (see *Race Conditions* on page 76).

As threads share the same process structure, they also share most of the operating system state. Each thread sees the same open files, the same user ID, the same working directory, each uses the same file descriptors, *including the file position pointer*. If one thread opens a file, another thread can read it. If one thread does an `lseek()` while another thread is doing a series of reads on the same file descriptor, the results may be surprising.

The other important aspect of the threads library being a user-level library is that it doesn't change UNIX at all. *All UNIX semantics are retained*, and old, nonthreaded programs continue to run exactly the same way they always did. The same compilers you're using still work. All the same tools still work the same way[7].

---

7. You may not always like the *results*, however. The data will be the same as before, but with MT programs you
   often discover that what you *really* want is something different. (See Chapter 8, *Programming Tools*.)

≡ 3

Solaris Multithreaded Model

Figure 3-4 illustrates the Solaris two-level multithreaded model in its full glory.

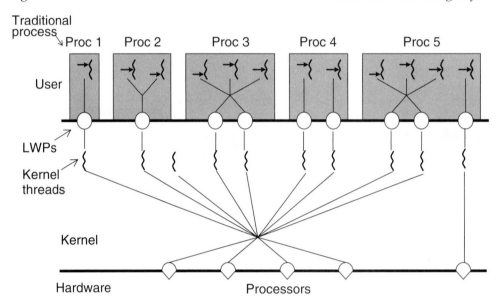

Figure 3-4   The Solaris Multithreaded Architecture

In this model, threads are the portable application-level interface. Programmers write applications using the threads library. The library schedules the threads onto LWPs. The LWPs in turn are implemented by kernel threads in the Solaris kernel. These kernel threads are then scheduled onto the available CPUs by the standard kernel scheduling routine, completely invisibly to the user. At no time will the programmer ever need to go below the public threads interface. Indeed, doing so would seriously compromise the portability and upward compatibility of the program.

The importance of the two-level model lies in its ability to meet the demands of different programming requirements. Some programs require large amounts of concurrency, such as a window system that provides each widget with one input handler and one output handler. Other programs need to map parallel computation onto the actual processors available. Still others need the concurrency provided by being able to have numerous threads involved with blocking system calls simultaneously. In all cases, programs want to have complete access to all system services.

System Calls

A system call is the way multitasking operating systems allow user processes to get information or request services from the kernel. Such things as "Write this file to the disk" and "How many users are on the system?" are done with system calls. We divide system calls into two categories, blocking and nonblocking calls (aka *synchronous* and *asynchronous* I/O). In a blocking call, such as "Read this file from the disk," the program makes the call, the operating system executes it and returns the answer, and the program proceeds. If a blocking system call takes a long time, then the program just waits for it.

In a nonblocking system call such as "Write this file to the disk without waiting," the program makes the call, the operating system sets up the parameters for the write, then returns, and the program continues. Exactly when the disk write actually occurs is not particularly important, and the program is able to continue working. A nonblocking system call may send the process a signal to tell it that the write is completed. Nonblocking I/O is very important for many nonthreaded applications, as it allows the application to continue to work, even while it's waiting for I/O.

When a process makes a system call, the following events occur:

1. The process traps to the kernel.
2. The trap handler runs in kernel mode, and saves all of the registers.
3. It sets the stack pointer to the process structure's kernel stack.
4. The kernel runs the system call.
5. The kernel places any requested data into the user-space structure that the programmer provided.
6. The kernel changes any process structure values affected.
7. The process returns to user mode, replacing the registers, and returns the appropriate value from the system call.

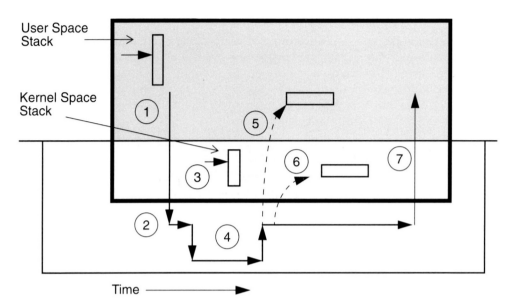

Figure 3-5   The Operation of a System Call

Of course, system calls don't always succeed. They can out-and-out fail (e.g., if you supply an incorrect argument), in which case they return a failure value and set errno (see *Global Variables (errno)* on page 137). Or they can be interrupted by a signal (see *Signals* on page 37), in which case the call is forced out of the kernel, the signal handler is run, and the system call returns EINTR. Presumably the program will see this value and repeat the system call. (As a diligent programmer, you always check for these things, right?[8])

What happens in a process with multiple LWPs? In Solaris, almost exactly the same thing. The LWP enters the kernel, there's a kernel stack for each LWP, all the usual things happen, and the system call returns. And if several LWPs make system calls? They all execute independently and everything works as expected. With the usual caveats.

If several calls affect the same data, things could turn ugly. For example, if two threads issue calls to change the working directory, one of them is going to get a surprise. Or if two threads do independent calls to read(), using the same file descriptor, the file pointer will not be coordinated by either one of them, resulting in one thread reading from a different place than it expected.

---

8. Nor do we. But we know we should.

The really nice thing about different threads being able to execute independent system calls is when the calls are blocking system calls. Ten different threads can issue ten synchronous reads, all of which block, and yet all the other threads in the process can continue to compute. Cool.

Signals

Signals are the mechanism that UNIX uses in order to get asynchronous behavior in a program[9]. How this works is this: Your program is running along normally, minding its own business. Then something (another process or the kernel) sends a signal to your process. The kernel then stops your process in its tracks, and forces it to run some other function (it is probably one you have written). That function runs, doing whatever it wants, then it can either return, and your program will then resume right where it left off; or it can do a `longjmp()`, in which case your program resumes at the `setjmp()` location; or it can just call `exit()`, causing the entire process to exit.

So, a typical program will start up in `main()`, as in Figure 3-6.

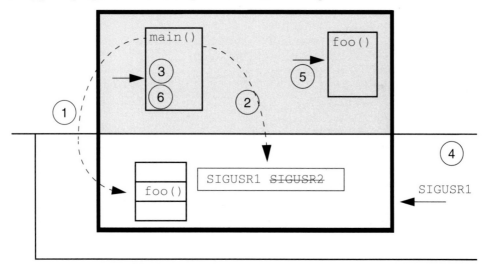

Figure 3-6   The Operation of a Signal

9. Neither NT nor OS/2 implements anything like signals, making asynchronous behavior difficult to achieve.

The program will then call `sigaction()` (1) to declare some function of your choosing to be the *handler* for a given signal[10] (say, function `foo()` will handle `SIGUSR1`). The kernel will put a pointer to that handler into the process structure's signal dispatch table (see Figure 3-1). Next, your program will call `sigprocmask()` (2) to tell the kernel which signals it is willing to accept. Finally your program takes off and starts doing what you wrote it to do (3).

Now, when some other process sends your process `SIGUSR1` (4), your program will stop what it's doing and run the handler code you wrote (5). You have no idea what your program might be doing when the signal arrives. That's the idea with signals, they can be completely asynchronous.When the signal handler is done, it typically just does a return, and your program continues where it left off, as if nothing had happened.

According to the POSIX definition, externally generated signals (the asynchronous ones) are directed to the process (not the LWP, certainly not the thread). As we saw, the process structure contains a single dispatch table, so there can be only one set of signal handlers for the entire process (i.e., one handler for `SIGUSR1`, another for `SIGUSR2`, etc.). Normally, the library simply decides which user thread should receive the signal and arranges for that thread to run the user-installed signal handler. (Any thread in the process can run the signal handler, depending upon the state of its individual signal mask and how attractive it looks in terms of priority level, run-state, etc.)

Each individual thread has its own signal mask, and this is what determines which signals that thread will accept. When you are programming with threads, you will be concerned solely with the thread signal mask, and will never read, change, or even think about the kernel-level signal masks. You cannot control which thread will run the signal handler other than by setting the signal mask. The library will manage those details for you (see Appendix B, *Solaris Signal Implementation*).

For synchronous signals (these are really traps—divide by zero, illegal memory reference, etc.), the library guarantees that the signal will be delivered to the offending thread. (It would be pretty dumb for thread 1 to do a divide by zero and for thread 2 to get the signal.)

As the programmer, you can also send signals. You can even send them directly to individual threads inside your program. These signals will behave exactly as if they had been sent from the outside, save that they are guaranteed to be delivered to the thread chosen. As is consistent with UNIX semantics, if they are masked out at the time, they will be queued as pending until such time as the mask is changed.

10.There are about 40 different signals in UNIX.

Don't Use Signal Handlers!

Now that you understand all the tricky details of how threads can receive signals and run signal handlers, we're going to suggest you avoid it all together. There will be some programs where you will want to have threads handle signals as we've just described, but not very many. What we suggest is that you designate one thread to do all of the signal handling for your program. This will simplify your programming, yet still give you all the functionality you need.

There are two ways of designating a signal-handling thread. You can mask out all asynchronous signals on all threads but one, then let that one thread run your signal handlers. You can just create the thread, and then immediately have it block, trying to decrement a semaphore. Even though it's sleeping, the library will still wake it up to run the signal handler.

The other, more recommended method, is to have this one thread call `sigwait()`. It will then go to sleep waiting for a signal to come in, and when one does, it will return from the `sigwait()` call with the signal, and decide how to act on it. (See the example on page 190.) The call `sigwait()` is a POSIX-defined system call that will be on all POSIX-compliant platforms.

Per-Thread Timers

Sometimes you will find need to have a timer alarm sent to an individual thread. It's not terribly common, but it does happen. The canonical instance is when you have a specific thread doing I/O to an unreliable device, and you want the thread to time out if the device fails. Unfortunately, POSIX does not provide a good solution to this problem.

Some implementations did (or still do!) specify that certain kinds of alarms send their expiration signal directly to the calling thread (or LWP); however, this is not part of the POSIX standard, and it should not be relied upon[11]. So, what's a poor programmer to do?

We recommend that you write a thread-specific timer call-out queue yourself, depending upon the POSIX semantics for SIGALRM. That is, you write code that keeps track of which thread is waiting for the alarm, when that alarm is to go off, and that you take care of delivering it. This is a bit of work, and you may wish to peruse the WWW page to see what we can offer. (See Appendix C, *Threads on the Net.*)

---

11. Solaris implemented SIGALRM in this fashion before POSIX had settled upon the standard. One of the coming versions of Solaris will now implement SIGALRM according to the POSIX standard, so you are best advised not to depend upon the current behavior.

≡ *3*

Scheduling 4 ≣

In which we explain the myriad details of the different scheduling models. After the reader is given a firm grounding in the fundamental concepts, we explain the various alternative choices that could have been made. Finally, the reader is treated to a comprehensive explanation of the intricacies in the life of a thread.

Different Models of Kernel Scheduling

There are three primary techniques for scheduling threads onto kernel resources (and indirectly, CPUs). Two of them involve the use of LWPs (or something similar). These are the techniques from which the designers of the various operating systems had to choose. They wanted a model that would adequately support the complexity of the operating system and still meet the various demands that dedicated programmers would make. All of these three models are perfectly reasonable and give the programmer different sets of trade-offs, while building programs that do exactly the same things with different levels of efficiency.

Historically, and even presently, all three of these models are in use by different vendors.

Many Threads on One LWP

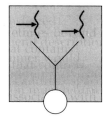

The first technique is known as the "Many-to-One" model. It is also known as "co-routining[1]." Numerous threads are created in user space, and they all take

---

1. The exact use of this term varies from book to book, but in broad terms, this is accurate.

turns running on the one LWP. Programming on such a model will give you a superior programming paradigm, but running your program on an MP machine will not give you any speedup, and when you make a blocking system call, the whole process will block. However, the thread creation, scheduling, and synchronization is all done 100% in user space, so it's fast and cheap and uses no kernel resources. The DCE threads library follows this model on HP-UX.

There is a clever hack that is used for blocking system calls in some threads libraries (e.g., DCE[2] threads) that is worth mentioning. The library puts a "jacket" routine around each blocking system call. This jacket routine replaces the blocking system call with a nonblocking one. Thus, when a thread makes a blocking system call, the library can put that thread to sleep and allow another one to run. When the signal comes back from the kernel, saying that the system call is complete, the library takes care of figuring out which thread made the call, waking up that sleeping thread, and everything proceeds as if the thread had blocked in the first place. It's hassle-free async I/O!

One Thread per LWP

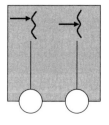

The "One-to-One" model allocates one LWP[3] for each thread. This model allows many threads to run simultaneously on different CPUs. It also allows one or more threads to issue blocking system calls while the other threads continue to run—even on a uniprocessor.

Question 1 – Explain why this model can make MT programs run faster than their single-threaded counterparts on uniprocessor machines[4].

---

2. DCE (Distributed Computing Environment) is a major package which the OSF created. It contains a threading library based on an early draft of POSIX (see *DCE* on page 293). DCE does this for a subset of blocking calls.

3. Remember, when you read about how another vendor implements this model, the vendor will not distinguish between the thread and the (conceptual) LWP. The vendor will simply refer to the thread and expect you to understand that it's a single entity containing everything.

4. Answers to the questions are found in Appendix A, *Answers*.

This model has the drawback that thread creation involves LWP creation, hence it requires a system call, as does scheduling and synchronization. In addition, each LWP takes up additional kernel resources, so you are limited as to the total number of threads you can create. Windows NT and OS/2 use this model.

Many Threads on Many LWPs

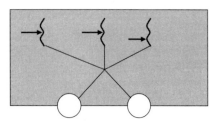

The third model is the "Many-to-Many" model. Any number of threads are multiplexed onto some (smaller or equal) number of LWPs. Thread creation is done completely in user space, as is scheduling and synchronization (well, almost). The number of LWPs may be tuned for the particular application and machine. Numerous threads can run in parallel on different CPUs, and a blocking system call need not block the whole process. As in the Many-to-One model, the only limit on the number of threads is the size of virtual memory[5].

The Solaris Two-level Model

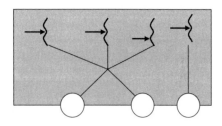

Solaris uses a variation of the Many-to-Many model, better known as the "Two-Level Model." It's a Many-to-Many model with the ability to specifically request a One-to-One binding for individual threads (a somewhat rarely used, but valuable extension).

This model is probably the best of the choices. Currently, Solaris is the only operating system to use this model, although IBM is publicly considering it, and DEC UNIX, with its "lightweight threads" (threads) and "heavyweight threads" (LWPs) certainly has the potential. It's a bit more work for the library writers but gives the programmer the optimal model to work with.

---

5. On a 32-bit SPARC machine, this is roughly 2 GB (total VM) / 8 KB (minimum stack size) = 256,000 threads.

≡ 4

Threads Are Not Always User-level Entities

Looking at the above descriptions, you should realize that implementations of the One-to-One model do not necessarily create both user-level threads and LWPs. So, thread libraries in this class really are kernel-level entities, combining the roles of the thread and the LWP into a single kernel structure. It is legal to implement POSIX threads by using the One-to-One model, and some vendors do so. NT and OS/2 are relatively locked into this model by the nature of their kernel architecture.

Thread Scheduling

There are two basic ways of scheduling threads: process *local* scheduling and system *global* scheduling. Local scheduling means that all of the scheduling mechanism for the thread is local to the process—the threads library has full control over which thread will be scheduled on an LWP. In particular, this implies that no system calls are involved, hence no time-slicing. Global scheduling means that the scheduling is done by the kernel. Hence, time-slicing could be involved. Solaris implements both (via "bound" and "unbound" threads), POSIX allows both (it doesn't require both), while both NT and OS/2 implement only global scheduling.

The whole subject of scheduling is fraught with problems. Both the scheduling of threads, and the scheduling of processes themselves have problems in all operating systems that have never been resolved to everyone's satisfaction. In brief, there are two basic situations in which we find ourselves.

The first case (the "independent" case) is when two processes (or threads) are running almost completely independently—neither ever has anything it wants from the other, and both would happily chew up every CPU cycle they could get. For example, consider two developers working on different projects on the same machine. Time-slicing is necessary for both of them to get a fair share of the machine.

The other situation (the "dependent" case) is when the two processes do depend very directly upon each other. One process needs another to perform some task for it before it can continue—a text editor cannot do anything until the file system has delivered it files to work on, and the file system has nothing to do until the text editor requests some services from it. In such a case, time-slicing is of no use at all. A real machine is typically faced with both situations all the time, along with the judgements of users and system administrators as to the relative importance of the various processes.

We will not attempt to solve these problems here. Suffice it to say that the use of both priorities and time-slicing results in less than perfect scheduling algorithms, but we have done fairly well with them over the past 20–30 years nonetheless.

Thread Scheduling Details

We will now go into some of the gory details of how scheduling is done. The major point that we are going to make is that most threaded programs are of the "dependent" case above, and scheduling is accomplished mainly by dependence upon the program's need for synchronization.

In Solaris threads, global scheduling is accomplished by binding a thread permanently to an LWP. That LWP (and hence the bound thread) is then scheduled by the kernel according to the normal kernel scheduling algorithms. POSIX does much the same thing (although it does not specify how the implementation is to be done). Both OS/2 and NT have only global scheduling, and it is completely handled by the normal kernel scheduler. There are a number of different scheduling classes for the different operating systems (batch, timesharing, interactive, real-time, etc.), but we will not go into those here.

Local scheduling in Solaris is done by the threads library. The library chooses which unbound thread will be put on which LWP. The scheduling of the LWP is (of course) still global and independent of the local scheduling. While this does mean that unbound threads are subject to a sort of funny, two-tiered scheduling architecture, in practice, you can ignore the scheduling of the LWP and deal solely with the local scheduling algorithm.

By some people's definition of the word, unbound threads don't *do* scheduling—meaning that there is no concept of *time-slicing* as in timesharing operating systems. Once a thread starts running on an LWP, it will continue to run, potentially forever. Some portion of the program (in this thread or in another one) must contain code that specifically causes the thread to yield its LWP. It is possible for one thread to completely starve out all others (on this LWP).

There are four means of causing a running thread (say, T1) to context switch. All of them require that the programmer has written code. These methods are largely identical across all of the libraries.

1. **Synchronization**. By far the most common means of being context switched (based on observation of actual code) is for the thread (T1) to request a mutex lock and not get it. If the lock is already being held by another thread (T2), then the calling thread will be placed on the sleep queue, awaiting the lock, thus allowing a different thread to run.

2. **Suspension**. Any thread may call thr_suspend() on T1 (itself included). T1 will be placed on the "stopped" queue and remain there until

`thr_continue()` is called on it (by another thread, of course). Solaris, OS/2, and NT define suspension; POSIX does not.

3. **Preemption**. A running thread (perhaps T1, perhaps another) does something that causes a higher priority thread (T2) to become runnable. In that case, the lowest priority running thread (T1, we'll assume) will be preempted, and T2 will take its place on the LWP. The ways of causing this to happen include releasing a lock, calling `thr_continue()` on a suspended thread, changing the priority level of a runnable thread upwards or of an active thread downwards.

4. **Yielding**. If the programmer puts an explicit call to `thr_yield()`[6] in the code that T1 is running, then the scheduler will look to see if there is another runnable thread (T2) of the *same* priority. If there is one, then that one will then be scheduled. If there isn't one, then T1 will continue to run. Only Solaris and POSIX define yielding.

Question 2 – There cannot be a thread of higher priority on the runnable queue. Prove it.

A bit of reflection will show the reader that three of the methods can be executed entirely in user space, with the thread-level context switch requiring about 20 microseconds on a SPARCstation 10/41. Preemption, however, is a bit more involved and requires a system call to execute (see *Preemption* on page 52).

In actual practice, you, the programmer, will spend very little time thinking about issues of scheduling. When a thread needs a common resource, it uses a synchronization variable. If it doesn't get the synchronization variable, it blocks, and another thread runs. Sooner or later another thread will do something that releases the synchronization variable, and the first thread will become runnable again.

The scheduler for unbound threads has a very simple algorithm for deciding which thread to run. Each thread has a priority number associated with it. The runnable threads with the highest priority get to run. These priorities are *not* adjusted by the threads library. The only way they change is if the programmer writes an explicit call to `thr_setprio()`. This priority is an integer in C. We don't give you any advice on how to choose the value, as we find that we don't use it much ourselves. You probably won't, either.

The natural consequence of the above discussion on scheduling is the existence of five scheduling states for threads. (The astute reader has already figured this all out and may skip this section.)

---

6. Beware of this function. Your program should be designed to run 100% correctly without it. If you find yourself calling it a lot, you're probably doing something wrong.

A thread may be in one of the following states:

Active: Meaning that it is on an LWP[7].

Runnable: Meaning that it is ready to run, but there just aren't enough LWPs for it to get one. It will remain here until an active thread loses its LWP or until a new LWP is created.

Sleeping: Meaning that it is waiting for a synchronization variable.

Stopped: Meaning that a call to `thr_suspend()` has been made. It will remain in this state until another thread calls `thr_continue()` on it.

Zombie: Meaning that it is a dead thread and is waiting for its resources to be collected.

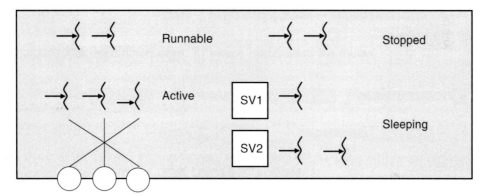

Figure 4-1   Some Threads in Various States

In Figure 4-1, we see a process with ten unbound threads and three LWPs. Five of the threads want to run, but only three can do so. They will continue to run as long as they want or until one of them makes a threads library call that changes conditions, as noted above. The two runnable threads are of equal or lower priority than the three active ones, of course. Should one of the sleeping or stopped threads be made runnable, then whether they actually become active will be a question of priority levels. If the newly runnable thread is of higher priority than one of the active threads, then it will displace the lowest priority thread. If it is of lower priority than all of them, then it won't. If it is of *equal* priority, then we make no guarantees. You should not write a program assuming anything about this condition.

POSIX defines three different scheduling algorithms. One is exactly the Solaris local model—a strict priority-based scheme. The second is a true time-sliced model[8], where all threads in a priority class get the same time quota, exactly the

7. Whether or not the LWP is on a CPU is irrelevant.

way Solaris schedules LWPs in the timesharing class. The third is a priority-based FIFO scheme. The only difference between the first and third is that you are assured of the order in which the threads will become active. POSIX also defines something that is effectively the same as bound threads by defining scheduling *scopes*, where `PTHREAD_SCOPE_SYSTEM` is the equivalent of bound threads and `PTHREAD_SCOPE_PROCESS` is the equivalent of unbound threads.

Suspension has proven to be of value in only two places. It is used at creation time, when you create the thread suspended and then alter some attribute[9] of it before it starts running (an issue for Solaris only). The other situation is when you are writing a garbage collector and must halt all of the other threads to let the GC thread do its work. Suspension is not in the POSIX definition, so consider carefully before you use it.

The LWPs that are to be used by the unbound threads are set up in a pool and are identical in all respects. This setup allows any thread to execute on any of the LWPs in this pool. You should not change any of attributes of these LWPs, as you don't know which thread will be running on them at any given time. Should you want a special LWP, you'll want a bound thread to run on it. (See *Bound Threads and Real-time LWPs* on page 53.)

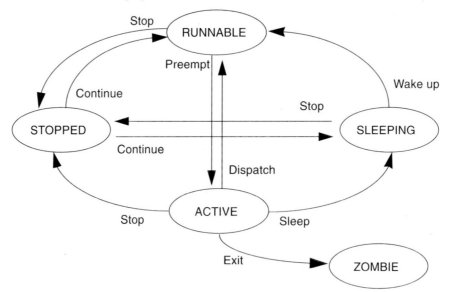

Figure 4-2   Simplified View of Thread State Transitions

8. Hence, expensive! Every thread context switch requires a system call.
9. POSIX creates threads by setting the desired attributes first, so this is not an issue for POSIX.

When an unbound thread exits, goes to sleep, or suspends, and there are no more runnable threads, the LWP that was running the thread goes to sleep in the kernel. When another thread becomes runnable, the idling LWP wakes up and runs it. Should an LWP remain idle for an extended length of time (currently five minutes), the threads library will kill it.

When a bound thread blocks on a process-local synchronization variable, its LWP must also stop running. The LWP does so by making a system call that puts it to sleep. When the synchronization variable is released, the bound thread must be awakened. This is done by making a system call to wake up the LWP. The LWP then wakes up, and the thread resumes running. Much the same thing happens when an unbound thread blocks on a cross-process synchronization variable. In both cases the LWP goes to sleep in the kernel until the synchronization variable is released. This description is pretty much the same for POSIX, NT, and OS/2. Only the names are different.

Context Switching

Context switching is a rather complicated concept and has many details of significance, so it is difficult to explain in just a few paragraphs. Nonetheless, we shall try. If you don't feel that you have a firm grasp of how it works, you should go bug a friend to explain all of the subtle nuances. Threads or no threads, you should understand this concept thoroughly.

A context switch is the act of taking an active thread off its LWP and replacing it with another one that was waiting to run. This concept extends to LWPs and traditional processes, also. We will first describe context switching in LWP/CPU terms, then in thread/LWP terms.

The state of a computation is embodied in the computer's registers—the program counter, the stack pointer, general registers, along with the MMU's (Memory Management Unit) page tables. These, plus the memory contents, disk files, and other peripherals, tell you everything about the computer. When it's time to context switch two traditional processes, all the register state must be changed to reflect the new process that we wish to run. It works approximately like this:

All the current registers (including page tables[10]) are stored into the process structure for P1 by the CPU.

All the stored register values from the process structure for P2 are loaded into the CPU's registers.

10. In any real machine there are lots of clever hacks that allow the kernel to avoid much of the page table switching in the normal cases.

The CPU returns to user mode, and voila! P1 is context switched out and P2 is context switched in and running.

All the other data in the process structure (working directory, open files, etc.) remains in the process structure where it belongs. If a process wishes to use that data, it will reference it from the process structure.

When two LWPs in the same process context switch, all of the above happens in much the same fashion, save that the page tables don't have to be changed. (As an applications-level programmer, you will never notice this unless you do some very careful timings.)

Notice also that a context switch must be done by the CPU itself. One CPU cannot do the context switch for another. CPU1 can send a signal to CPU2 to let it know that it should context switch, but CPU1 cannot actually change the registers in CPU2. CPU2 has to want to context switch[11].

Finally, context switching for threads involves much the same procedure. A thread (T1) decides that it has to context switch (perhaps it is going to sleep on a synchronization variable). It enters the scheduler. The CPU stores its register state into the thread structure for T1, then it loads the registers from another thread (T2) into the CPU and returns from the scheduler as T2. No system calls are involved. It happens 100% in user space and is very fast.

As a direct consequence of this, an unbound thread *cannot* keep runtime statistics, as just asking the operating system for runtime would involve a system call and slow the operation down.

It may be a bit unclear what the role of the LWP is when threads context switch. The role is invisible. The threads save and restore CPU registers with no regard to the LWP at all. The threads scheduler does not do anything to the LWP structure. Should the operating system decide to context switch the LWP, it will do so completely independently of what the LWP happens to be doing at that time. Should two threads be in the middle of context switching when the kernel decides to context switch the LWP, it still makes no difference. The threads' context switch will just take a little longer.

Consider the case in Figure 4-3. Three threads are runnable on two LWPs at time 0. Thread T1 holds a mutex, M. Clearly, T1 and T2 will be the active threads, as they have the highest priorities. We'll imagine that T1 is on LWP1, and T2 on LWP2, while T3 is on the runnable queue.

---

11. How many Californians does it take to change a light bulb?

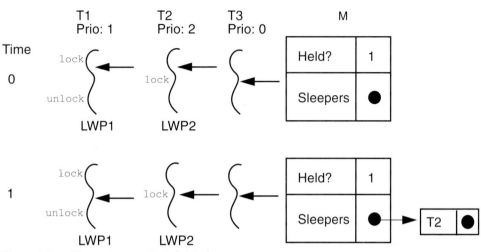

Figure 4-3   How a Context Switch Works

Approaching time 1, T2 attempted to lock M and failed. So, as part of the code for `mutex_lock()`, T2 put itself onto the sleep queue for M, then called the scheduler. The scheduler code ran (still as T2) and decided to run T3. This is the situation at time 1. Next, the scheduler stores away the CPU registers into T2's thread structure and loads the registers from T3's. (At this particular instant, it's not defined what thread is running on LWP2, and it's not important, either.)

The scheduler code finishes its work and returns with T3 running on LWP2. At time 2, T1 releases the mutex. As part of the code for `mutex_unlock()`, it takes the first thread off of M's sleep queue (T2) and makes it runnable. Then it actually releases the mutex. Finally, it calls the scheduler.

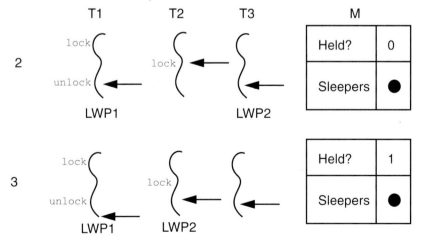

The scheduler notices that there's a runnable thread (T2) that has a higher priority than one of the active threads (T3). The scheduler then sends a signal in order to preempt the thread on LWP2. Now the scheduler has done its work. It returns, and T1 continues to run. This is the state of the world at time 2 (with a signal pending).

For some short period of time, T3 continues to run. When the signal arrives from the kernel, T3 is interrupted and forced to run the signal handler. That, in turn, calls the scheduler, which context switches T3 out and T2 in. And that's it! At time 3, T1 and T2 are both active, T3 is runnable, and T2 holds the mutex.

There are a couple things to notice here. There's no guarantee that T2 will get the mutex. It's possible that T1 could have reclaimed it; it's even possible that T3 could have snatched it away just before the signal arrived. If either of these events occurred, the net result is that a bit of time would have been wasted, but they would both work perfectly. This scenario works as described, irrespective of the number of CPUs. If this runs on a multiprocessor, it will work exactly the same way as it does on a uniprocessor, only faster.

Preemption

Preemption is the process of rudely kicking a thread off its CPU so that some other thread can run instead. For globally scheduled threads, preemption is all handled in the kernel by the kernel scheduler. For locally scheduled threads, it is done by the thread library. Preemption is accomplished by sending the LWP in question a signal specifically invented for that purpose[12]. The LWP then runs the handler, which in turn realizes that it must context switch its current thread and does so. (You will notice that one LWP is able to direct a signal to another specific LWP in the case where they are both in the same process. You should never do this yourself. You may send signals to threads, but never to LWPs.)

Preemption requires a system call, so the kernel has to send the signal, which takes time. Finally the LWP, to which the signal is directed, has to receive it and run the signal handler. Context switching by preemption is more expensive than context switching by "voluntary" means.

How Many LWPs?

The Solaris threads library has a call, `thr_setconcurrency()`, which tells the library how many LWPs you'd like to have available. If you set the number to 10, and you have nine threads, then when you create a tenth thread, you'll get a tenth LWP. When you create an 11th thread, you won't get another LWP. You can also specifically request that a new LWP be created when you call `thr_create()`

12.In Solaris, it's SIGLWP. This is a kernel-defined signal that requires a system call to implement.

with the `THR_NEW_LWP` flag. Now the caveat. This is a *hint* to the library as to what you'd like. You may not get what you ask for! Your program must run correctly without all the LWPs you want, though it may run faster if it gets them. In practice, this is an issue only when your system is supporting a lot of LWPs.

You've got the power, but how do you use it wisely? The answer is totally application dependent, but we do have some generalities. (N.B.: *Generalities*. If you need a highly tuned application, you've got to do the analysis and experimentation yourself.) We assume a dedicated machine.

If your program is completely CPU-bound, then one LWP per CPU will give you maximum processing power. Presumably you'll have the same number of threads.

If your program is highly CPU-bound *and* you do some I/O, then one LWP per CPU and enough to cover all simultaneous blocking system calls[13] are called for.

If your program is only I/O bound, then you'll want as many LWPs as simultaneous blocking system calls.

In one respect, Solaris will help you. If all of your LWPs are in blocking system calls, then Solaris will send your process a `SIGWAITING` signal. The threads library's handler for this signal will then look at the queue of runnable threads. If there are any, then it will create a new LWP and schedule the highest priority thread on it. This allows your program to still make progress computing, even when many threads are blocked, allowing you to get reasonable concurrency without doing extensive timing and experimentation. This is strictly an implementation detail to improve efficiency.

Bound Threads and Real-time LWPs

A bound thread is nothing more than a typical thread that is permanently tied to a specific LWP. The LWP runs only that thread and that thread runs only on the LWP. (In POSIX-lingo, it's a globally scheduled thread.) This means that this thread is never merely runnable. It is either sleeping on a synchronization variable, suspended, or active. It is never prevented from getting time (that is, "virtual time"—time on an LWP) when it wants it.

So, when do you want to use bound threads? The answer is very rarely—basically, only when an event outside the process requires immediate processing by that particular thread or when you want global scheduling. If you use globally scheduled threads everywhere, your program will use a lot more kernel resources than it presumably needs.

---

13. Blocking system calls include all calls to the usual system calls such as `read()`, but also any thread that blocks on a cross-process synchronization variable should be counted. Bound threads are independent of this, as they each have their own LWP.

Just because a thread is bound to an LWP does not imply that the LWP is going to be scheduled on a CPU immediately. Depending upon the nature of your application requirements, you may need to alter the kernel-level scheduling priority of that LWP. If you merely need to ensure that it gets a CPU within a second, then relying upon the normal time-slicing scheduler is probably sufficient. If response is required on the order of 100 ms, then simply raising the timesharing class priority of the LWP is probably sufficient.

It's when you require response in the 2–100 ms range that things get interesting. You'll need to put the LWP into the real-time scheduling class. You'll want to do all of the typical real-time tricks—meaning no blocking system calls, probably no I/O[14], no paging (you'll need to lock down all the memory that your thread will use: functions, stack, data.), etc. ("Etc." means that there is plenty more involved that we haven't thought about, but that you'd better. Real-time processing is a tricky thing; be very careful!) Both NT and OS/2 have real-time scheduling classes.

One place where you might require a bound thread is when you have the undivided attention of a user and are doing constant updating (e.g., mouse tracking, video or audio playback). Another place would be where you are doing machine feedback and control (e.g. autonomous vehicle navigation, robotics). Other places include where you are doing real-time data collection with analysis.

Places you might think you need it, but don't, include updating displays with the *divided* attention of a human (if I'm 100 ms late in seeing the latest from the stock ticker, no big deal). *Avoid using the real-time class if you possibly can.*

Binding LWPs to Processors

It's possible to ensure that a given LWP will always run on a selected processor via the system call `processor_bind()`. It's also possible to ensure that a given LWP will run to the exclusion of all other LWPs in all processes by putting it into the real-time class. Doing both effectively binds the processor to the LWP so long as the LWP wants to run.

The question of when these things are useful has a somewhat tricky answer, and it changes with new operating system releases. If schedulers worked perfectly and had ESP, you would never bind an LWP to a CPU. In practice, it's *sometimes* otherwise.

---

14. For I/O, you'd typically set up the buffers in the real-time thread but then allow a normal thread to execute the I/O call on those buffers.

Happiness Is a Warm Cache

The main issue is that of cache memory latency. The current batch of PCs and workstations have external caches of significant size (the SS10, SS20, and SS1000 have 1 megabyte, the SC2000 has 2 megabytes). To completely replace the contents of such a cache can take a very long time (upwards of 100 ms, depending upon individual architecture). If an LWP was running on CPU 0 and it was context switched off for a short time, then the vast majority of that cache will still be valid. So, it would be much better for that LWP to go back onto CPU 0.

The normal scheduler in Solaris endeavors to do precisely that via *processor affinity*. It will delay running an LWP on CPU 1, should that LWP have previously been on CPU 0. If CPU 0 becomes available relatively quickly (currently, 30 ms—three clock ticks), then that LWP will be put back on CPU 0. If CPU 0 does not become available within that time frame, then the LWP will be scheduled on whatever CPU is available. It is possible for this scheme to go awry under some odd circumstances. (If LWP 1 and LWP 2 both got started on CPU 0, CPU 1 could end up completely idle.) It is unusual, but possible, for things to go wrong like this, especially in later releases of Solaris.

We know of some instances where it has proven valuable to do processor binding of LWPs. If you are considering this, test first. *You should not even consider processor binding unless you already know that there's a clear problem of this nature.* And you must be aware that everything may be different on a different architecture or different OS release.

When Should You Care About Scheduling?

There are times when you will want to deal with scheduling directly, but those times are few and far between for any of the libraries. If you find yourself thinking about this a lot, you're probably doing something wrong. Some examples:

It is possible to design a server program where each thread runs forever, picking up requests off the net, processing them, and returning for more. It is possible for an unbound thread to get starved out in this situation. Here you would want to add LWPs for the purpose of effecting a time-slicing scheme.

A program that used a set of threads to produce data, and another single thread to push that data out to some device in real time, would need to ensure that the output thread got to run when it needed to. Here a higher priority would be in order. In the Delphax/Uniq case study (See *Delphax and Uniq Inc.* on page 24), they found it worthwhile to make a bound thread and put the LWP into the real-time class.

≡ 4

Scheduling is not a topic you will spend much time thinking about. In spite of all the attention we just paid to explaining it, you will not write much (if any!) code to deal with it. If the library writers did their job well in writing the library, everything will "just work," without any effort on your part at all. In most MT programs, the different threads all depend upon one another, and it doesn't really matter which one runs first. Sooner or later, the running threads will need something from the other threads, and they will be forced to sleep until those other threads have produced that something.

Thread Creation and Destruction

At thread creation time, you get to establish the nature of your thread. Threads will differ in the way that they exit, get garbage collected, are scheduled, how much stack space they use, and of course, what they do.

In the simplest case in Solaris, you can call `thr_create()` with a function to run and an argument for the function to run on. Everything else will then take default values. Should you desire to pass your start routine more than a single argument, you must create a structure and pass the multiple arguments in that. As you can see from the code fragments below, all of the libraries have very similar creation functions and operate in very similar fashions.

Code Example 4-1   A Simple Call to Create a Solaris Thread

```
(void *) foo(int arg);
int arg;
thr_create(NULL, NULL, foo, (void *) arg, NULL, NULL);
```

Code Example 4-2   A Simple Call to Create a POSIX Thread

```
(void *) foo(int arg);
int arg;
pthread_create(NULL, NULL, foo, (void *) arg);
```

Code Example 4-3   A Simple Call to Create an OS/2 Thread

```
VOID foo(ULONG arg);
ULONG arg;
TID ThreadID;
ULONG stacksize = 0x500;
DosCreateThread(&ThreadID, (PFNTHREAD) foo, arg, NULL, stacksize);
```

Code Example 4-4   A Simple Call to Create an NT Thread

```
DWORD foo(DWORD arg);
DWORD ThreadID;
DWORD arg;
CreateThread(NULL, NULL, (LPTHREAD_START_ROUTINE) foo,
(LPVOID) arg, NULL, &ThreadID);
```

The default stack size for each Solaris thread is one megabyte, plus a *guard* page. A guard page is a page that is mapped invalid and will cause a SEGV when the stack overflows onto it. One megabyte is a huge stack and gives you plenty of room to do just about anything you want. Because it has mapped-in MAP_NORESERVE, none of the pages actually use any physical memory or swap space unless they are accessed[15]. Should you decide that you need more or less room for your stack, you may pass in an integer, and the threads library will create for you a stack that size, plus guard page. It's up to you to figure out how much stack space you'll need. Window system calls can get nested pretty deep, and if your thread might run a signal handler, you'll need room for that too.

It is possible for you to manage the stack yourself. You can allocate the memory, create a guard page, then garbage collect the stack when the thread exits. We have not yet found any instances where we would want to do this.

To make a bound thread, you include the flag THR_BOUND to the creation call. The library will then create a bound thread, along with the LWP to bind it to.

Solaris threads can be designated as *daemons* at creation time by use of the THR_DAEMON flag. These are threads that are intended as background tasks, and they shouldn't be considered when counting up user threads. Should the number of nondaemon user threads fall to zero, then the library will call exit(). Daemon threads are not part of POSIX, NT, or OS/2, and if portability is an issue for you, you won't want to use them.

Returning Status and Memory

Sometimes you specifically want to wait for a thread to exit. Perhaps you've created 20 threads to do the 20 pieces of a task and you can't continue until they are all finished. To do this, you can call thr_join() on each of the desired thread IDs. The caller will block until each of the specified threads has exited.

---

15. This also leads to a tricky little bug, should you not have sufficient virtual memory (see *Insufficient Swap Space* on page 210).

4

In addition to waiting for the threads to exit, the caller can receive a status from the exiting threads. The exiting thread calls thr_exit() and supplies the return value as an argument. To ensure no deadlocks occur, it makes no difference if the waiting thread calls thr_join() first or if the exiting thread calls thr_exit() first. POSIX, NT, and OS/2 have similar calls.

Not all threads can be joined. At creation time, you can specify that you intend *not* to join on a thread by supplying the THR_DETACHED flag, creating a so-called *detached thread*. You can specify that you *do* intend to do a join by not supplying that flag, creating a *nondetached thread*. Any thread can call thr_join() on any other nondetached thread, but the exiting thread can be joined only once. It is also possible to request a join on "any thread" by passing NULL instead of a thread ID. This will join on the very next nondetached thread to exit. The initial thread (the one running main()) is a nondetached thread, so it can be joined. NT and OS/2 do not have this concept.

That's Not a Bug, That's a *Feature*!

Nondetached threads are not the most common case, but they are the default. You have to be careful with this, because it bites. If you try to join on a detached thread, it will return an error—that's simple. If you forget to join on a nondetached thread, however, it will simply not free its storage, and you will have a very big memory leak. (This is actually a good thing, because it's easy to find.)

You see, a detached thread will clean up after itself upon exit, returning its thread structure, TSD array, and stack to the heap for reuse. A nondetached thread will clean up after itself *only* after it has been joined[16]. And as you create and exit more threads, your application will use up more and more of your address space, and finally die a slow and horrible death, for which you will bear sole responsibility.

Exiting the Process

The UNIX semantics of exit() are retained in MT programs. When any thread in a process calls exit(), the process exits, returning its memory, system resources, process structure, all LWPs, etc. If main() "falls off the bottom" of the initial thread, it makes an implicit call to exit(), also killing the process.

16.Sure, it could clean up some of its structures at thr_exit() time, but that would imply that we expect programmers to make this mistake. By doing it this way, it's actually simpler, because big memory leaks are much easier to find than small ones.

When any other thread falls off the bottom of its initial function, it implicitly calls thr_exit(), exiting only that one thread. In the special case where the initial thread (i.e., main()) calls thr_exit() directly, that thread exits but does not call exit(), and the process continues. This is true for all the libraries.

Finally, should all nondaemon threads exit, the thread library will detect this and call exit() itself. This situation is not typical, however, as you will generally be aware of when it's time to exit your process, and you should call exit() explicitly.

Question 3 – Someone always asks something like: 'If the process exits and there are still threads running, will they continue to run?' What's the answer?

Cancellation

Sometimes you have reason to get rid of a thread before it has completed its work. Perhaps the user changed her mind about what she was doing. Perhaps the program was doing a heuristic search and one thread found the answer. Under Solaris threads you could either have the threads check some global variable periodically to see if they should quit, or you could send a signal to the threads to kill them.

The first solution is a pain in the neck and requires you to accurately analyze your code so that you don't leave a big hole where it never checks. The second is also fraught with danger. What if the thread to be liquidated happens to be holding a lock? If you kill the thread, the lock won't be released and you'll never see it unlocked again!

Only POSIX threads has a formal solution to this problem, *cancellation*. It comes in two variants.

In one variant, you bracket sections of your code with calls that enable and disable cancellation. Should another thread attempt to cancel this thread, it will be put off long enough for the thread to arrive at an allowable point before it dies.

In the other variant, a thread establishes *cancellation points*—places where it's safe to die, and a cancellation will be delayed until one of these points is reached (see *Cancellation* on page 112). In addition, POSIX provides for a stack of cleanup handlers—functions that will get called upon cancellation. So, if you allocate some resource, you can push a function to release that resource onto the stack. Should a cancellation occur, the function will be run and the resources freed. Should you later release that resource yourself, you can pop the function off the stack and discard it.

No matter how you choose to deal with the issues of cancellation, be it in OS/2, NT, Solaris, or POSIX threads, the primary issues remain the same. You must ensure that any thread that you are going to kill is able to release any locks it might hold, free any memory it may have allocated for its own use, and that it leaves the world in a consistent state.

Question 4 – Could you create cancellation in Solaris threads? If so, how?

Synchronization 5≣

In which the reader is led on a hunt for the intimidating synchronization variables and discovers that they are not actually as frightening as had been thought. After the hardware and software issues surrounding them are explained, the reader is shown the trade-offs involved in selecting the proper one to use. The chapter concludes with an explanation of thread-specific data.

Synchronization Issues

In order to write any kind of concurrent program, you must be able to reliably synchronize the different threads. Failure to do so will result in all sorts of ugly, messy bugs. Without synchronization, one thread will start to change some data just as another thread is reading it. The reader will get half old data and half new data. To avoid this disaster, threads must be able to reliably coordinate their actions.

Memory Model

It is important to realize that on modern computers, the order of loads and stores is not guaranteed. Just because your program wrote X first and Y second doesn't mean that that's what the other processors on the system will see. Even storing a single data structure[1] could be done "out of order." Therefore, *all use of shared data*[2] *must be locked.* Even when you think you don't have to, it still can surprise you. Typically, the bug will show up just after you've released your product at your most important customer site.

One side effect of using a synchronization variable is that it executes a "flush" instruction that ensures all data in the CPU's buffers is written out to where the

---

1. 64-bit numbers are an obvious example, but on some architectures even different parts of a 32-bit word can be stored independently and, possibly, out of order. Many machines do not have byte load/store instructions, so storing a single byte is accomplished by loading the entire 32-bit word, replacing the byte in question, then storing the word back.

2. Shared data is any data that more than one thread uses. Typically, such data includes all global variables, all statics, and any data structures they point to.

other CPUs can see it. Some CPUs have "store buffers," which are like a miniature, internal data cache for writes. These buffers are not written back to cache with any definable regularity, so data can reside there for extended periods of time without any other CPU being aware of it being changed.

On a V8 SPARC machine (such as a SPARCstation 20), the flush is caused by the atomic instruction `ldstub`, and it flushes the CPU's store buffer out to external cache. Sun's SPARC MP machines all have an active *bus snooper* for each CPU, which will see that data moving to external cache and invalidate any information in its own cache. On other architectures the details vary, but the results are the same.

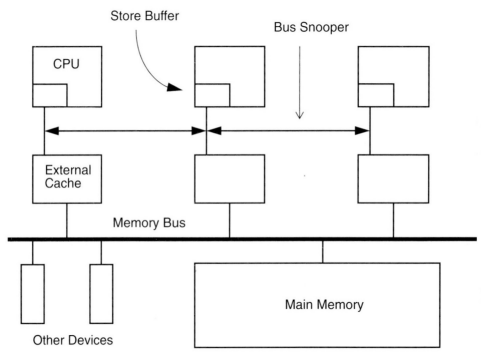

Figure 5-1   A Typical Design for an SMP Machine

Question 5 – Clearly, if some data were in use by CPU 2 when CPU 1 flushed that data from its store buffer, it would be a formula for disaster. This never happens. Why?

Implementation of synchronization variables requires the existence of an atomic *test and set* [3] instruction in hardware. This is true for uniprocessor systems as well as MP machines. Because threads can be preempted at any time, between any two instructions, you must have an atomic test and set instruction. Sure, there might be only a 10 nanosecond window for disaster to strike, but you still want to avoid it.

Critical Sections

A critical section is a section of code that must be allowed to complete atomically with no interruption that affects its successful completion or the data it is working on. Such things as context switching a thread or updating a record in a database are critical sections. Other things may go on at the same time, and the thread that is executing in the critical section may even lose its processor, but no other thread may do anything that affects the critical section. Should another thread want to execute that same critical section, it is forced to wait until the first thread finishes.

Critical sections are typically made as short as possible and often carefully optimized because they can significantly affect the concurrency of the program.

Lock Your Global Variables!

All shared data must be protected by a synchronization variable. Failure to do so will result in truly ugly bugs. Keep in mind that all means *all*. Global variables are the obvious example[4]. Data structures that can be accessed by multiple threads are included. *Static variables* are included.

Statics are really just global variables that can be seen by only one function or functions in one file. It was somewhat convenient to use these in the single-threaded programs of yore, but in MT programs they are disaster waiting to strike. You should reconsider your use of statics very carefully. If you do use 'em, lock 'em first!

Synchronization Variables

Synchronization is provided by a set of synchronization functions that manipulate special variables in user memory. Solaris implements four *synchronization variables* and the function `thr_join()` to provide this functionality. POSIX provides three of the four, along with `pthread_join()`. The fourth is easily built from the first three. Windows NT and OS/2 both

---

3. A *test and set* instruction tests (or just loads into a register) a word from memory and sets it to some value (typically 1), all in one instruction with no possibility of anything happening in between the two halves (e.g., an interrupt or a write by a different CPU). If the value of the target word *was* 0, then it gets set to 1 and you are considered to have ownership of the lock. If it already was 1, then it gets set to 1 (i.e., no change) and you don't have ownership. All synchronization variables are based upon the existence of this instruction.

4. It is, of course, possible to have global variables that are not shared, but this would be rather unusual. Be very careful if you think you have one. If you're wrong, you're going to be very unhappy when something breaks.

5

provide 3-1/2 synchronization variables of a slightly different nature. In all libraries, these provide the only reliable means you have to coordinate the interactions of your threads. There are other tricky things you can do to try to coordinate your threads, but they won't work reliably. If you find yourself thinking along these lines, you would do well to ask a friend to peruse your work, because you're doing something wrong!

Mutexes

The mutual exclusion lock is the simplest and most primitive synchronization variable. It provides a single, absolute owner for the section of code that it brackets between the calls to mutex_lock() and mutex_unlock(). The first thread that calls lock on the mutex gets ownership, and any subsequent calls to lock will fail, causing the calling thread to sleep. When the owner calls unlock, one of the sleepers will be awakened, made runnable, and given the *chance* to obtain ownership. *It is possible that some other thread will call mutex_lock() and get ownership before the newly awakened thread does.*

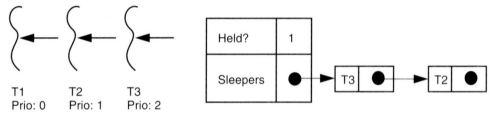

Figure 5-2   A Mutex with Several Threads Sleeping on It

In Figure 5-2, three threads all need a mutex. They have different priorities, which determine the order in which they go onto the sleep queue[5]. The threads have requested the lock in the order: T1, T2, T3. Being the first to try, T1 owns the lock, and T3 will be awakened as soon as T1 releases it, even though T2 requested the lock before T3. Note that the mutex *doesn't* know who owns it. The code fragment below shows the only proper way to use mutexes.

Code Example 5-1   Using a Mutex

```
Thread 1                        Thread 2
mutex_lock(&m);                 mutex_lock(&m);
global++;                       local = global;
mutex_unlock(&m);               mutex_unlock(&m);
```

5. This a very minor point. If you find yourself thinking about this for more than a minute while writing a program, you're doing something wrong. Trust the mutex, Luke!

For the (rare) situation when you really don't want to block, a `mutex_trylock()` function is included in the API. It returns 0 if you get the lock, and EBUSY if you don't. If you get EBUSY, you'll have to figure out something else to do, as entering the critical section anyway would be highly antisocial. You will probably never need this function, so if you think you do, look very carefully at what you're doing!

It is important to realize that although locks are used to protect data, what they *really* do is to protect that section of code that they bracket. There's nothing that forces another programmer (who writes another function that uses the same data) to lock his code. Nothing but good programming practice.

Question 6 – When a thread tries to obtain a lock and fails, it is put on the mutex's sleep queue. The mutex is a shared data item, of course, as is its sleep queue. How do we ensure the integrity of that sleep queue? What happens when two threads both decide to sleep on a mutex at exactly the same time?

POSIX mutexes are virtually identical. NT provides a similar mutex, along with a *critical section*, which is pretty much the same, save with some different features. OS/2 calls mutexes *mutex semaphores*, but defines much the same behavior (there are a bunch of added bells and whistles). Both NT and OS/2 mutexes are recursive—meaning that the same thread can lock the mutex multiple times. By its very definition, a recursive mutex must be several times slower than a simple mutex, as it does several levels of locking. Recursive mutexes are easily built from Solaris and POSIX primitives.

Reader/Writer Locks

Sometimes you will find yourself with a shared data structure that gets read often, but written only seldom. And the reading of that structure may require a significant amount of time (perhaps it's a long list through which you do searches). It would seem a real waste to put a mutex around it and require all the threads to go through it one at a time when they're not changing anything. Hence, reader/writer locks.

With a reader/writer lock, you can have any number of threads reading the data concurrently, whereas writers are serialized. The only drawback to reader/writer locks is that they are more expensive than mutexes. So, you must consider your data structure, how long you expect to be in it, how much contention you expect, and choose between a mutex and a reader/writer lock on that basis.

As a rule of thumb, a simple global variable (an int, char, real, etc.) will always be locked with a mutex, while searching down a 1000-element, linked list will often be locked with a reader/writer lock.

≡ 5

Question 7 – The decision of when to use a reader/writer lock is tricky to calculate. Produce a first-order estimate and defend it.

The first reader that requests the lock (`rw_rdlock()`) gets it. Subsequent readers also get the lock, and all of them are allowed to read the data concurrently. When a writer requests the lock (`rw_wrlock()`), it is put on a sleep queue until all the readers exit. A second writer will also be put on the writer's sleep queue in priority order. Should a new reader show up at this point, it will be put on the reader's sleep queue until all the writers have completed. Further writers will also be placed on the same writer's sleep queue as the others (hence, in front of the waiting reader), meaning that writers are always favored over readers.

The writers will obtain the lock one at a time, each waiting for the previous writer to complete. When all writers have completed, the entire set of sleeping readers are awakened and can then attempt to acquire the lock. Readers' priorities are not used.

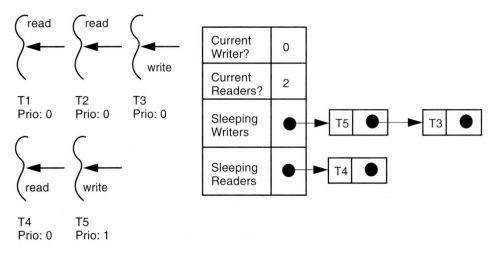

Figure 5-3   How Reader/Writer Locks Work

In Figure 5-3, five threads all need a reader/writer lock. They have different priorities, which determine the order in which they go onto the *writers'* sleep queue. The threads have requested the lock in the order: T1, T2, T3, T4, T5. T1 and T2 own the lock, and T5 will be awakened as soon as they both release it, even though T3 and T4 requested the lock before T5.

You will be disappointed to discover that only Solaris implements reader/writer locks. However, all is not lost. They can be built out of the primitives already available to you—mutexes, lists, etc.[6]

Condition Variables

Sometimes you want to work with complex situations. Perhaps you want a thread
to execute some code only if X > 17, Y is prime, and grandmother is visiting next
Thursday. As long as you can express the condition in a program, you can use it
in a condition variable (CV). A condition variable creates a safe environment for
you to test your condition, sleep on it when false, and be awakened when it
might have become true.

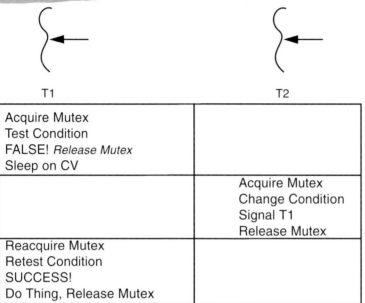

T1	T2
Acquire Mutex Test Condition FALSE! *Release Mutex* Sleep on CV	
	Acquire Mutex Change Condition Signal T1 Release Mutex
Reacquire Mutex Retest Condition SUCCESS! Do Thing, Release Mutex	

Figure 5-4   Classic Operation of Condition Variables

It works like this (Figure 5-4): A thread obtains a mutex (CVs always have an
associated mutex) and tests the condition under the mutex's protection. No other
thread should alter any aspect of the condition without holding the mutex. If the
condition is true, your thread completes its task, releasing the mutex when
appropriate. If the condition isn't true, the mutex is released *for you*, and your
thread goes to sleep on the CV. When some other thread changes some aspect of
the condition (e.g., it reserves a plane ticket for granny), it calls `cond_signal()`
and wakes up your thread. Your thread then reacquires the mutex[7], reevaluates
the condition, and either succeeds or goes back to sleep, depending upon the

---

6. As a matter of fact, we've already done so! See *The SPILT Package for Solaris/POSIX Compatibility* on page 205 to
   find out where to obtain the SPILT package.

7. Obviously, when a thread sleeps on a CV, the mutex must be released (so other threads can acquire it) and
   reacquired upon waking. All of this is handled for you by `cond_wait()`.

outcome. You *must* reevaluate the condition! Even if the condition was true when the signal was sent, it could have changed before your thread got to run.

Should you desire, the thread that changes the condition may awake all sleepers via `cond_broadcast()`. This may cause some contention for the mutex, but that may be OK.

CVs also allow you to limit the sleep time. By calling `cond_timedwait()`, you can arrange to be awakened after a fixed amount of time, in case you're the impatient type. You generally use this directly in conjunction with the condition you're concerned about. Should you know the condition ought to change within some time frame, you can wait for that amount of time, then go out and figure out what went wrong. You can also use it simply as a thread-specific timer.

```
              Thread 1                           Thread 2
 mutex_lock(&m);
 while (!my_condition)
 while(cond_wait(&c, &m) != 0) ;
                                    mutex_lock(&m);
                                    my_condition = TRUE;
                                    cond_signal(&c);
                                    mutex_unlock(&m);
 do_thing();
 mutex_unlock(&m);
```

Figure 5-5   The Code for Using a Condition Variable

An important detail about condition variables is that `cond_wait()` and `cond_timedwait()` are allowed to return under unusual circumstances without holding the mutex. Should a signal be handled by the thread or should another thread call `fork()`, then they will both return with the value `EINTR`. Should the timer expire, `cond_timedwait()` will return with the value `ETIME`. In both cases, they will return without holding the mutex. Hence, that funny extra `while` loop in Figure 5-5.

Neither NT nor OS/2 implements condition variables, and, unfortunately, they are rather difficult to implement from the primitives provided. The basic CV is simple enough, but `cond_timedwait()` requires functionality that the two operating systems simply do not have.

Semaphores

In the 19th century, when trains were still advanced technology and railroad tracks were exotic and expensive, it was common to run single sets of tracks and restrict the trains to travel in only one direction at a time. *Semaphores* were invented to let the trains know if other trains were on the rails at the same time. A semaphore was a vertical pole with a metal flag that was adjusted to hang at either 45 or 90 degrees to indicate the existence of other trains.

In the 1960s, E. W. Dijkstra, a professor in the Department of Mathematics at the Technological University, Eindhoven, Netherlands, extended this concept to computer science. A *counting semaphore*[8] (aka *PV semaphore*) is a variable that you can increment arbitrarily high, but decrement only to zero. A `sema_post()` operation (aka "V" –*verhogen* in Dutch) increments the semaphore, while a `sema_wait()` (aka "P" – *Proberen te verlagen*) attempts to decrement it. If the semaphore is greater than zero, the operation succeeds; if not, then the calling thread must go to sleep until a different thread increments it.

A semaphore is useful for working with "train-like" objects, that is, objects where what you care about is whether there are either zero objects or more than zero. Buffers that fill and empty are a good example. Semaphores are also useful when you want a thread to wait for something. You can accomplish this by having the thread call `sema_wait()` on a semaphore with value zero, then have another thread increment the semaphore when you're ready for the thread to continue.

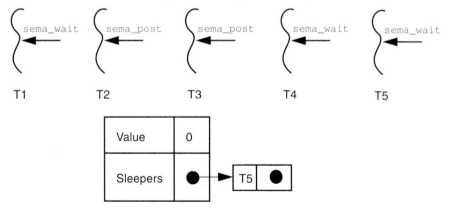

Figure 5-6   How a Semaphore Operates

---

8. The word semaphore has come to take on other meanings in computer science. System V semaphores, for example, are much more elaborate objects than counting semaphores.

In Figure 5-6, the semaphore started with a value of zero. The threads have executed their respective operations in the order: T1, T2, T3, T4, T5. After T1 executed its `sema_wait()`, it had to wait (as the value was zero). When T2 did the `sema_post()`, T1 was awakened, and continued. T3 did a `sema_post()`, so the value was 1 when T4 did its `sema_wait()`. Thus, T4 could continue without waiting at all. Finally, T5 called `sema_wait()`, and it is still waiting.

Semaphores are unique among synchronization variables in one particular fashion: They are *async safe*, meaning that it is legal to call `sema_post()` from a signal handler (see *Async Safety* on page 95). No other synchronization variable is async safe. So, if you want to write a signal handler that causes some other thread to wake up, this is the way to do it.

If you look at the definition of semaphores, you will also notice that, like condition variables, a semaphore may return from a wait with a legal, non-zero value, `EINTR`. This means that the semaphore was interrupted by a signal or a call to `fork()` and it did not successfully decrement.

Correct usage of a semaphore requires that it be executed in a loop:

```
while (sema_wait(&s) == EINTR) {<probably do nothing>}
do_thing();              /* NOW the semaphore has been decremented! */
```

If you block out all signals and never call `fork()`, then, and only then, can you use semaphores (and `cond_wait()`) outside a loop.

NT, OS/2, and POSIX all implement counting semaphores with very similar definitions.

Barriers

A barrier allows a set of threads to sync up at some point in their code. It is initialized to the number of threads to be using it, then it blocks all the threads calling it until it reaches zero, at which point it unblocks them all. The idea is that you can now arrange for a set of threads to stop when they get to some predefined point in their computation and wait for all the others to catch up. If you have eight threads, you initialize the barrier to eight. Then, as each thread reaches that point, it decrements the barrier, and hence goes to sleep. When the last thread arrives, it decrements the barrier to zero, and they all unblock and proceed.

Barriers are not part of any of the libraries, but they are easily implemented. They are also implemented in the SPILT package.

Event Semaphores

Both NT and OS/2 define event semaphores (called *event objects* in OS/2), which block all threads calling them until some other thread signals that event. Event semaphores are easily built from condition variables.

OS/2 Critical Sections

OS/2 defines a rather extreme version of synchronization under the name *critical section*. Between calls to `DosEnterCritSec()` and `DosExitCritSec()`, all other threads are stopped. It is possible to build such calls from Solaris primitives, but it does not seem a terribly good idea.

Spin Locks

Normally, you should hold a lock for the shortest time possible, to allow other threads to run without blocking. There will occasionally be times (few and far between) when you look at the blocking time for a mutex (about 48 μs on an SS10/41, see Appendix D, *Timings*) and say to yourself "48 μs?! The other thread is only going to hold the mutex for 5 μs. Why should I have to block, just cause I stumbled into that tiny window of contention?"

You don't. You can use a *spin lock* and try again. It's simple. You initialize a counter to some value (say, 30), and do a `mutex_trylock()` — that takes about 2 μs. If you don't get the lock, decrement the counter and loop. Another 2 μs. Repeat. When the counter hits zero, then give up and block. If you get the mutex, then you've saved a bunch of time. If you don't get it, then you've only wasted a little time (if you chose 30, then 30 * 2 = 60 μs).

In Code Example 5-2, we show the construction of a simple spin lock. Although this is a good description of a spin lock, it's actually a poor implementation, as the repeated calls to `mutex_trylock()` will saturate the memory bus. A better implementation of a user-level spin lock is available on the WWW.

Code Example 5-2   A Simple Spin Lock

```
spin_lock(mutex_t *m)
{int i;
   for (i=0; i < SPIN_COUNT; i++)
      {if (mutex_trylock(m) != EBUSY)
          return; }            /* got the lock! */
   mutex_lock(m);              /* give up and block. */
   return; }                   /* got the lock after blocking! */
```

Spin locks can be effective in very restricted circumstances. The protected section *must* be short, you *must* have significant contention for the lock, and you *must* be running on more than one CPU. If you do decide that you need a spin lock, test that assumption. Set the spin time to 0 and time your standardized, repeatable test (you must have one!). Then set the spin time to a realistic value (100 is about the maximum), and time the test again. If you don't see a significant improvement, go back to regular mutex locks. Spin locks are almost always the *wrong* answer, so be careful!

Question 8 – Why must a spin lock critical section be short, have contention, and be on a multiprocessor machine?

Spin locks are not part of any of the libraries, but they are easily built in both POSIX and Solaris. Neither NT nor OS/2 has the required trylock primitives

Adaptive Locks

A refinement of spin locks, called *adaptive locks*, is used in the Solaris kernel. The current definition of both Solaris and POSIX threads does not allow for their use, but you might be interested in knowing what they are.

If you could find out whether the thread holding the desired mutex was in fact currently running on a CPU, then you could make a more reasoned judgement as to whether or not to spin. This is what an adaptive lock does: If the mutex owner is running, then the requestor spins. If the owner isn't, then the requestor doesn't.

Unfortunately, in the user-level threads library, you cannot find out which thread holds a mutex, and even if you could, the system call required to find out whether the thread in question was on a CPU would be more expensive than just blocking.

Cross-process Synchronization Variables

Threads in different processes can synchronize with each other via synchronization variables placed in shared memory. This kind of synchronization works in all four libraries, even though threads in different processes are invisible to each other, as shown in Figure 5-7.

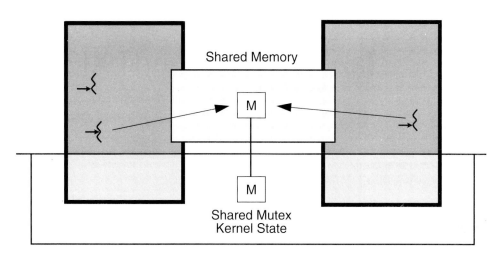

Figure 5-7   Synchronization Variables in Shared Memory

Both processes must know about the synchronization variable, and (exactly) one of them must initialize it to be cross-process. Then, both processes (or possibly more) can use it as a normal synchronization variable. The only difference between a single-process synchronization variable and a shared memory synchronization variable occurs when an attempt to acquire it fails. Then, the shared memory version will simply take longer (see Appendix D, *Timings*). There is no requirement that the processes themselves be multithreaded.

The implementation of blocking involves the unsuccessful thread making a system call, which then goes to sleep in the kernel. Thus, one LWP is effectively removed from the pool during this time. When the owner of the mutex releases it, the sleeping LWP is awakened. Once again, there is no *guarantee* that the newly wakened thread will be the one that acquires the synchronization variable, but the odds favor it.

Synchronization variables can also be placed in files and have lifetimes beyond that of the creating process. For example, a file can be created that contains database records. Each record can contain a mutex lock variable that controls access to the associated record. A process can map the file into its address space. A thread within this process can directly acquire the lock that is associated with a particular record that is to be modified. If any thread within any process that maps in the file attempts to acquire this lock, then that thread will block until the lock is released. Obviously, a process cannot be allowed to exit while it is still holding such a shared lock. All the libraries allow shared memory synchronization variables.

Synchronization Variable Initialization and Destruction

All synchronization variables have both initialization and destructor functions. The initialization functions take care of initializing the memory that the synchronization variables use, along with setting up kernel state should the synchronization variable be defined to be cross-process. The initialization functions are called once before the first use of the synchronization variable, and never again. You cannot use them to "reinitialize" a synchronization variable. The Solaris definition of synchronization variables does not *require* that statically allocated local synchronization variables be initialized, whereas the POSIX definition does. Dynamically allocated ones must always be initialized. Just do it: You will probably move your Solaris code to POSIX someday.

The destructor functions mark the synchronization variables as being unusable. They do not do any kind of garbage collection. For dynamically allocated synchronization variables, using destructor functions is a good and useful programming practice that allows you to indicate that the synchronization variable in question is not to be used any more. Destruction of a synchronization variable is not strictly required, unless you plan to free its memory. If you do build one from malloc'd memory, you probably will want to free it. If you do free it, you *must* call destroy first.

Destroying a synchronization variable and freeing its memory can be a bit tricky, as you must ensure that no thread ever accesses that variable again. Either you must know that no other thread still has a pointer to it, or you must maintain some kind of list of valid dynamic synchronization variables. There are no particular differences between freeing memory used by synchronization variables and freeing memory used for other things. You just have to be careful in both cases.

Synchronization Problems

A number of things can go wrong when you try to coordinate the interactions of your threads. Not using synchronization variables is the most obvious and most common. But even when you've been careful to lock everything is sight, there are still other problems you may encounter. All of them have a solution, none of them have a perfect solution.

Deadlocks

A deadlock is a kind of a Catch-22, where one thread needs another thread to do something before it proceeds, and the other thread needs something from the first. So they both sit there, doing nothing, waiting for each other, forever. This is generally a bad thing.

A typical deadlock occurs when thread T1 obtains lock M1, and thread T2 obtains lock M2 (see Figure 5-8). Then thread T1 tries to obtain lock M2, while thread T2 tries for lock M1. Although typically a two-thread kind of problem, deadlocks can involve dozens of threads in a circle, all waiting for one another. They can involve a single thread that tries to obtain the same mutex twice, and they can involve a thread that holds a lock dying while another thread is waiting for it.

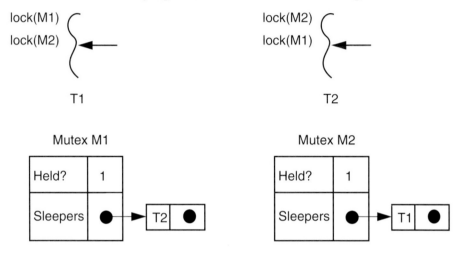

Figure 5-8   A Typical Deadlock

The other typical deadlock is the recursive one, when one thread tries to lock the same mutex twice. The most insidious version of this is when a thread is in the middle of some function that requires a mutex (say, `malloc()`), and just as that function has obtained the mutex, a signal interrupts that thread. The thread runs the signal handler, and, lo and behold, the signal handler calls `malloc()`. Deadlock[9]. Be aware of these possibilities, and avoid them (see *Async Safety* on page 95).

Deadlocks can often be avoided simply by careful programming practices. If you always acquire locks in the same order—A before B before C, etc.—then there is no chance of a deadlock. In instances where you cannot avoid out-of-order locking, you can use the trylock functions to see if you can get all the locks you need, and if not, then release them all and try again later.

---

9. Of course, doing dynamic memory allocation (e.g., calling `malloc()`) in a signal handler is a bad thing to do.

☰ 5

Race Conditions

Races are instances of indeterminacy in otherwise deterministic programs. The result a program will give in a race condition depends upon the luck of the draw—which thread happens to run first, which LWP happens to get kicked off its processor by the page daemon, etc. Race conditions are generally bad things, although there are situations where they are acceptable. Certainly one would be upset if 1414.60/2.414 came out to be 586 on one run of a program, and 586.001 on the next.

Most commonly, race conditions come around in programs where the programmer forgot to write proper locking protection around some shared data. But it is certainly possible to write code that is perfectly correct, yet suffers from races. Consider Code Example 5-3, where thread 1 is to lock a mutex around global variable v, double it, then release the lock, while thread 2 is to lock the same mutex, subtract 1 from v, and then release it. If v starts with the value 1, then the result will either be 1 or zero, depending upon which thread runs first.

Code Example 5-3   A Simplistic Race Condition

```
Thread 1                    Thread 2
mutex_lock(&m)              mutex_lock(&m)
v = v - 1;                  v = v * 2;
mutex_unlock(&m)           mutex_unlock(&m)
```

It is worth noting that some instances of indeterminacy in a program are acceptable. If you write a program that searches for a solution to a chess problem by creating lots of threads to consider lots of different possible moves, then you may get different answers depending upon which thread completes first. As long as you get one good answer ("Checkmate in three!"), you don't really care if you move your pawn first or your rook.

Recovering from Deadlocks

A common question is "What if a thread that is holding a lock dies? How can I recover from this?" The first answer is "You can't." If a thread was holding a lock, then it could legitimately have changed portions of the data that the lock protected in ways impossible to repair. If it was in the midst of changing the balance of your bank account, there is no inherent way for you to know if it had credited the deposit it was working on or not. This, of course, is a very bad thing. Neither Solaris nor POSIX makes any provision for this situation. Only the owner of a mutex can release it, and should that owner die, the mutex will never be released. Period.

You can, however, build arbitrarily complex "recoverable" locks from the primitives in all of the libraries. Using them properly is the trick. NT mutexes do allow recovery, should the owner thread die. This is nice functionality if you need it, but it makes mutexes more expensive to use when you don't.

In a single, multithreaded program, recovering from deadlocks is not too much of a problem, as you have complete control over your threads, and if your process dies, all the threads die with it. In a shared memory, multiple-process program, it is more problematic, as it is more common for one process to die, while leaving others running. Once again, there is no way to guarantee recovery.

It is somewhat reasonable to consider recovering from a deadlock in the case of a process (or thread) dying unexpectedly. In other deadlock situations, where threads are waiting for each other, you really shouldn't be looking at recovery techniques. You should be looking at your coding techniques.

System V shared semaphores do make provision for recovery, and they may prove to be the solution to your problem. They provide room for a system-maintained "undo" structure, which will be invoked should the owner process die, and they can be reset by any process with permission. They are expensive to use, though, and add complexity to your code.

Still, just having undo structures that can reset semaphores does not solve the real problem. The data protected may be inconsistent, and this is what you have to deal with. It is possible to build arbitrarily complex undo structures for your code, but it is a significant task that should not be lightly undertaken. Database systems do this routinely via "two-phase commit" strategies, as they have severe restrictions on crash recovery. Essentially, what they do is (a) build a time-stamped structure containing what the database will look like at the completion of the change, (b) save that structure and begin the change, (c) complete the change, (d) update the time stamp on the database, (e) delete the structure. A crash at any point in this sequence of events can be recovered from reliably.

Be very, very careful when dealing this problem!

Priority Inversion

Should a high-priority thread (T2 in Figure 5-9) be blocked, waiting for a lock that is held by another thread of lower priority (T1), it may have to wait a longer time then seems reasonable, because a third thread (T3) of middling priority might be hogging the CPU. In order to do justice to overall system performance, it would be reasonable to elevate the scheduling priority of the owner to the level of the blocked thread. This is not done in the Solaris user-level library, so user programs may suffer from priority inversion. The Solaris kernel threads do take this into account. In POSIX, priority inheritance is an option during initialization. It is not terribly difficult to build priority-inheritance mutexes in the other libraries, but it's not often of much value. Think carefully before you decide you need it.

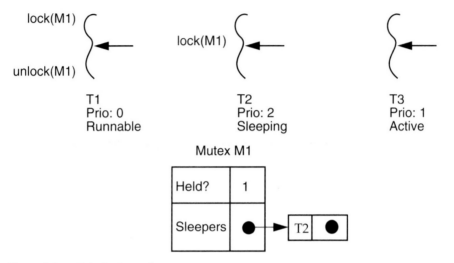

Figure 5-9   Priority Inversion

FIFO Mutexes

Every now and then, you come upon a program where you want to ensure that the thread that is blocked on a mutex is the next owner of the mutex—something which is not in the definition of simple mutexes. Typically, this situation occurs when two threads both need some mutex to do their work, they hold the mutex for a significant length of time, they do their work independently of each other, and they have very little to do when they don't hold it. Thus, what happens is that thread 1 grabs the mutex and does its work, while thread 2 tries for the mutex, and blocks. Thread 1 then releases the mutex and wakes up thread 2. Before thread 2 manages to obtain the mutex, thread 1 reacquires it! In Figure 5-10, this is illustrated in case 2, where Wo is work being done when the thread is not holding the mutex (outside the critical section), and Wi is work being done when the mutex is being held (inside the critical section).

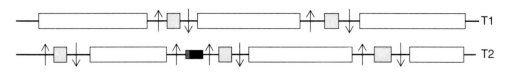

1: The common case: Very little contention, normal mutexes work well.

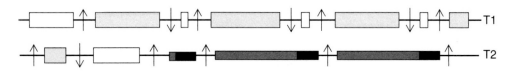

2: The uncommon case: T1 keeps reacquiring the mutex.

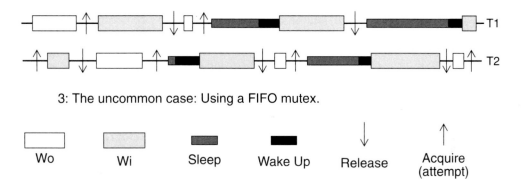

3: The uncommon case: Using a FIFO mutex.

| Wo | Wi | Sleep | Wake Up | Release | Acquire (attempt) |

Figure 5-10   When FIFO Mutexes Are Valuable

Case 3 assumes that you have implemented FIFO mutexes, where the owner of the mutex automatically hands ownership over to the first waiter when releasing the mutex.

This is a rare situation, and it merits you reconsidering your algorithm before dealing with it. (If you contrast case 2 and case 3 against case 1, you will notice that the two threads are spending a lot of time sleeping on the job.) But should you find yourself stuck with this kind of problem, it is a simple programming effort for you to implement guaranteed FIFO mutexes yourself. Try it, then compare your implementation to the one we have on the threads page (see Appendix C, *Threads on the Net*).

Thread-specific Data

Sometimes it is useful to have data that is globally accessible to any function, yet still unique to the thread. The example of errno comes to mind, not to mention things that the programmer might wish to define. It sure would be a bummer if one thread made a system call, got an error, and just before it got the chance to look at errno, another thread also got an error on a system call and changed the value of errno (a race condition!).

TSD provides this kind of global data by means of a set of function calls. Essentially, this is done by creating an array of "key" offsets to "value" cells, attached to each thread structure.

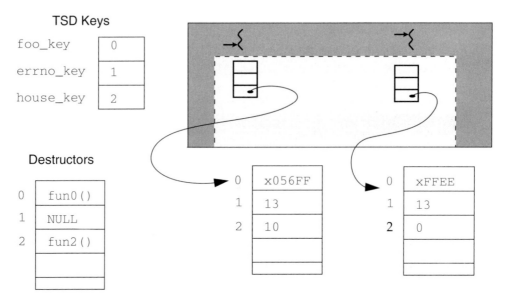

Figure 5-11   Thread-specific Data

To use TSD, you first create a new key, which is then added to the TSD arrays for all threads. Keys are just variables of type thread_key_t (which are really integers), and key creation ("initialization" would be a more descriptive term) consists of setting the value of the key to the next integer. Once the key has been created, you can access or change the value associated with the key via calls to thr_getspecific() and thr_setspecific(). These will access and change the value associated with that key for each thread.

Question 9 – We have just explained the functionality of TSD by showing you an implementation. There is nothing that says TSD has to be implemented by using offsets to arrays hanging off the thread structure. Give some different possible implementations.

For those cases when the data you want to be thread specific is a structure, array, object, or anything larger than one word, you'll need to `malloc` the storage for that structure and place a pointer to it in the TSD array. To ease your programming burden when deleting the thread, a destructor function is provided for each keyed item. At key creation time, you can include a function that will be run on that item when the thread exits.

The typical usage of TSD is to declare all the keys globally, initialize (er, "create") them in `main()`, set them to initial values, then start the program for real (see Code Example 5-4). If you are creating some TSD in a library, you must arrange for that library to do the initialization before use[10].

Code Example 5-4   Usage of TSD

```
extern thread_key_t house_key;

foo()
{float n;
    thr_getspecific(house_key, (void **) &n);
...
}

main()
{...
    thr_keycreate(&house_key, NULL);
    thr_setspecific(house_key, (void *) 3.14159265358979);
    thr_create(NULL, NULL, foo, NULL, NULL, NULL);
...}
```

So, how does `errno` work? It's a hack. Essentially, it is a thread-specific data item. In multithreaded programs, all system calls change the TSD value instead of the global value. Then, when you reference `errno` in your program, there is a `#define` in the `errno.h` header file that conditionally redefines `errno` to be a call to `thr_getspecific()`[11]. Clever, eh?

---

10. SVR4 libraries have ".ini" sections in which you can define functions to be called before `main()` starts.

Question 10 – As it is possible to add new keys dynamically, what happens when the array fills up?

POSIX TSD is identical. NT also defines a very similar kind of TSD (called *dynamic thread local storage*). OS/2 does not.

TSD is simple but somewhat expensive when compared to accessing a global variable. Each call to a TSD function requires a function call, then a series of offsets: first to the array pointer in the thread structure, then from the array to the key value. It requires about 40 instructions, while a simple global reference requires just one load instruction. It is a useful feature, but you clearly want to restrict its use to where you need it.

The best answer to the problems of TSD is to write good, clean code that eschews the excessive use of globals. Unfortunately, far too many programs have preexisting conditions, and they seem to demand TSD. It is worthwhile to consider a couple of tricks to avoid excessive use of TSD. *Don't even consider any of this stuff until you are sure you have a problem!*

One thing you can do is to cache TSD data in a local block of its own, where you know it's safe.

Not this:

Code Example 5-5   Normal Use of TSD

```
{for (i ...)
    {thr_getspecific(v_key, &v);
    s+=f(v);
    }
```

but rather:

Code Example 5-6   Cached Use of TSD

```
{thr_getspecific(v_key, &v);
    for (i ...) s+=f(v);
}
```

---

11. Actually, POSIX defines the implementation slightly differently. If you look at errno.h, you'll see that the definition of errno is ___errno(). The effect is the same as if TSD had actually been used.

The other thing you can do is to create your own personal version of lexical scoping. Create a structure that contains all the data you wish to be thread specific and pass that structure to every function that is going to access it.

Code Example 5-7   Passing Structures Instead of Using TSD

```
struct MY_TSD
{   int a
    int b;
}

start_routine()
{struct MY_TSD *mt;
   ...
   mt = malloc(sizeof(MY_TSD));
   mt->a = 42; mt->b = 999;
   foo(x, y, z, mt);
   bar(z, mt);
   ...
}

void foo(x, y, z, struct MY_TSD *mt)
{int answer = mt->a;
...}
```

No, this isn't pretty. However it is clean, safe, and relatively efficient.

Thread Local Storage

TLS is an alternate method of providing the functionality of TSD. It allows you to declare a set of global variables to be "thread local." These variables can then be treated exactly like normal global variables (except that you don't have to lock them). Unfortunately, TLS has a number of severe limitations. It requires either a change to the compiler or some tricky memory map manipulations, it cannot dynamically allocate new keys—the TLS segment is fixed at link time—and it is not portable.

Both POSIX and Solaris concluded that TLS wasn't worth it, and chose to specify TSD instead. NT implements TLS in addition to TSD. It's called *static TLS*, and it does indeed require changes to the compilers.

▦ 5

Global Variables, Constants, and Cheating

Now a little detail to consider: a TSD key is a shared global variable. We say you should always lock shared data when using it. Here's the exception. If you can *guarantee* that a global will never be changed (and changing the value of a key would be a *bad* idea), then you can safely get away with putting a lock around the initialization only. This guarantee effectively means that the key is really being treated like a constant, not a variable.

The same is true for any globally declared variable that is used as a constant. If you are doing this kind of "cheating," you must be certain that you set the variable exactly once from the initial thread. You must do so before creating any other threads. It absolutely must be used as a constant and *never* changed. Any deviation from this will cause you no end of problems.

The other time when you may wish to deal with shared data outside a critical section is when you don't need the value to be correct. If you are content to test a variable, then do something on the basis of its *probably* being correct, then you can do so. The actual definition of spin locks in the kernel is like this. We test the mutex *without* using `mutex_trylock()` (thereby not saturating the memory bus), and then call `mutex_trylock()` as soon as it looks like it's clear. We'll be correct 99.99% of the time, and when we're wrong, we just restart the test loop. This kind of "cheating" is a very rare thing to do, and it's easy to do it wrong.

Comparing the Four Libraries

If we look at the specifications of the different libraries, we find a number of distinctions in their design philosophies, their functionalities, and some factors that affect the maximal efficiency of the implementations.

The Solaris thread specification is the most "primitive" of the libraries in the sense that it provides all of the base functionality but requires the programmer to construct the fancy stuff on top. This is good because these primitives are much faster than the fancy stuff, but it does require a bit more programming work in some cases. Of course, it also means that you are able to build exactly what you want.

The POSIX specification is largely based on Solaris but includes a modest number of more complex primitives. The additional functionality costs in efficiency but reduces the programming load in those cases where it is required.

OS/2 and NT both have much heavier libraries, containing more complex primitives. This is good where that functionality is required, but your programs pay for it dearly in efficiency when it's not used. OS/2 contains a built-in interdependency between windows and threads. Not just any thread can construct and use windows. OS/2 also has a system-wide limit of 256 on the total number of threads. NT threads require changes to the compiler, so not just any old compiler will do.

Table 5-1   Comparing the Different Thread Specifications

Functionality	Solaris Threads	POSIX Threads	NT Threads	OS/2 Threads
Design Philosophy	Base Primitives	Near-Base Primitives	Complex Primitives	Complex Primitives
Scheduling Classes	Local/Global	Local/Global	Global	Global
Mutexes	Simple	Simple	Complex	Complex
Counting Semaphores	Simple	Simple	Complex	Complex
R/W Locks	Simple	Buildable	Buildable	Buildable
Condition Variables	Simple	Simple	Impossible	Impossible
Multiple-Object Synchronization	Buildable	Buildable	Complex	Complex
Other Complex Synchronization	Buildable	Buildable	Complex	Complex
Thread Suspension	Yes	Impossible	Yes	Impossible
Cancellation	Buildable	Yes	Difficult	Difficult
Thread-specific Data	Yes	Yes	Yes	Difficult
Signal-Handling Primitives	Yes	Yes	n/a	n/a
Compiler Changes Required	No	No	Yes	No

In Table 5-1 we give a simple comparison of the four specifications. By "simple," we mean that the object is just about as small and fast as is possible to implement the functionality, whereas "complex" implies that it has other functionality that makes it more useful in limited circumstances, but also slower. "Buildable" means that such functionality is not part of the specification but is fairly simple to construct. "Difficult" means that it is humanly possible to construct from the supplied primitives but involves some tricky programming. It may not be possible to build all of that functionality, and it may require all programmers to do extra work, such as calling initialization functions when starting a thread. "Impossible" means just that.

From our own, biased point of view, we find the simplicity and inherent speed of the Solaris threads specification most attractive. POSIX is a bit more complicated, but acceptable. We think NT and OS/2 are excessively complex and slow, contain unreasonable limitations (the compiler and window system dependencies), and in general do not seem to be as well thought-out as other parts of those systems.

Nonetheless, we recognize that you, the programmer, do not have a great deal of choice in the matter and must use the libraries supplied. To the largest degree, you can write any program with any of the libraries. For the most part, even the design and construction of the programs will be identical. They have more in common than they have that which is different.

Operating System Issues 6

In which we explore a variety of operating systems issues that bear heavily upon the usability of the threads library in actual programs. We also examine a set of general operating system functions and their value.

Multithreading is a fine and wonderful programming paradigm as we have described it thus far. However, it's not worth too much if it doesn't have the operating system support to make it viable. Most of the major operating systems are in a state of significant flux, so it would be difficult for us to say much about all of them. Instead we will stick with the issues that need to be considered and describe where Solaris is with respect to them. A bit of this may sound rather like an advertising pitch and, in a way, it is. But for each bit of advertisement, there's a very real issue behind it, and you should examine your operating system of choice with respect to it.

The Solaris Threads Library

The Solaris threads library is an integral, bundled part of the operating system. It is there in every Solaris 2 configuration, so you can write your program and not worry about whether the dynamic library will be there when you need it. It will be. So long as you write your programs legally, you will be able to move them across different machines and across different versions of the operating system without any problems at all.

All the system files you require in order to write and ship MT programs are bundled with Solaris. The threads library is just a normal system library, so any legal SVR4 compiler can be used, and there are plenty of them out there. Any legal SVR4 debugger will work, although a debugger with MT extensions is to be vastly preferred. (As of this writing, we are aware of only two, one from SunSoft and one from Centerline.)

Solaris Multithreaded Kernel

The Solaris kernel itself is implemented using threads. It uses generally the same API that you have access to. There is no inherent connection between the kernel being multithreaded and the existence of a user-level MT library. SunSoft programmers could have written the user-level library without the kernel being threaded, and they could have threaded the kernel without supplying you a user-level library. They could have even built LWPs, made Solaris real time, SMP, and preemptable without the use of threads. Theoretically.

In practice, the same things that make MT so attractive to you also make it attractive to the kernel hackers. Because the kernel implements all internal schedulable entities as threads, it is much easier to implement SMP support, real-time scheduling, and make the kernel preemptable. So, LWPs are built on top of kernel threads. Interrupts are built with kernel threads. Preemption of kernel threads works much the same way as preemption of user-level threads.

Concurrency vs. Parallelism

Concurrency means that two or more threads (or processes for the general case) can be in the middle of executing code at the same time; it could be the same code, it could be different code (see Figure 6-1). They may or may not be actually executing at the same time, but they are in the middle of it (i.e., one started executing, it was interrupted, and the other one started). Every multitasking operating system has numerous concurrent processes, even though only one may be on the CPU at any given time.

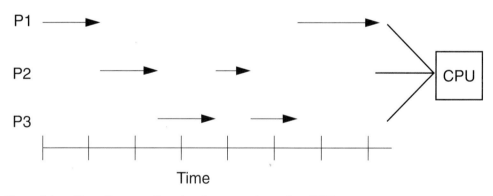

Figure 6-1   Three Processes Running Concurrently on One CPU

Parallelism means that two or more threads actually run at the same time on different CPUs (see Figure 6-2). On a multiprocessor machine, many different threads can run in parallel. They are, of course, also running concurrently.

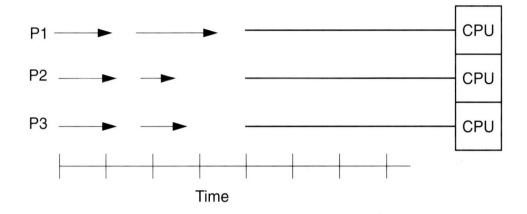

Figure 6-2   Three Processes Running in Parallel on Three CPUs

The vast majority of timing and synchronization issues in MT are issues of concurrency, not parallelism. Indeed, the threads model was designed to avoid your ever having to be concerned with the details of parallelism. Running an MT program on a uniprocessor does not simplify your programming problems at all. Running on a multiprocessor doesn't complicate them. This is a good thing.

Question 11 – Actually, there are a few parallelism-only issues that you can choose to address. Some are mentioned in this book. What are they?

In Figure 6-3, we illustrate the various degrees to which a kernel can support concurrent system calls.

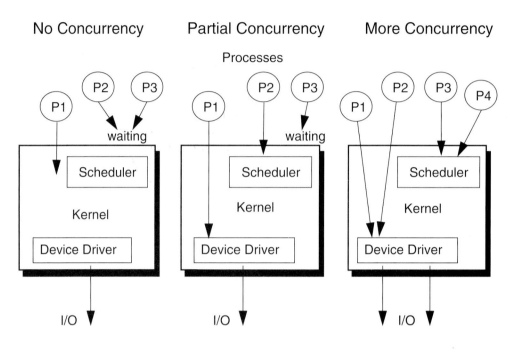

Figure 6-3   Concurrency Within the Kernel

In the first case (which is like SunOS 4.1.3 and most other operating systems), only one process can be in the midst of executing a system call at any one time. In the second case, locks are put around each major section of code in the kernel, so several processes can be in the midst of executing system calls, as long as the calls are to different portions of the kernel. In the third case (like Solaris 2), the granularity of the locks has been reduced to the point that many threads can be in the midst of executing the same system calls.

Now, if you take these diagrams and substitute "processor" for "process," you will get a slightly different picture, but the results will be largely the same. If you can execute several things concurrently, with arbitrary context switching, then you can execute them in parallel. A slightly different, but perfectly valid way of looking at this is to consider it in terms of critical sections. In the "no concurrency" case, the critical section is very large—it's the whole kernel. In the "more concurrency" case, there are lots of little critical sections.

One point of complexity is the issue of blocking versus nonblocking system calls. A blocking system call is a call that enters the kernel, does all its work, then returns. In the case of I/O, a blocking system call might end up waiting around in the kernel for a long time, with nothing to do, until the disk completes a revolution or the user types a key. While this call is blocking, all the kernels will, of course, schedule some other process to run.

In order to keep traditional processes busy, *nonblocking system calls* were introduced into UNIX. A nonblocking system call is one in which the call starts the kernel working on a request and then returns to the user process directly. The process is then free to do other work while waiting for the disk to spin. When the data requested is ready, the kernel will send the user process a signal to let it know. Nonblocking system calls (aka asynchronous I/O—nonblocking calls are all I/O calls, though they don't *have* to be) provide a method of getting better performance from traditional processes, but they involve a significant amount of extra, complicated programming.

In SunOS 4.x, and indeed all UNIX systems, nonblocking system calls could always be executed concurrently, even though they couldn't be executed in parallel. This behavior occurred because the kernel was not subject to arbitrary context switching. It could determine for itself when it would context switch, so it could always ensure that it waited until all the data was consistent before it would allow any other process to run. In a multiprocessor system, this determination isn't possible in the same fashion, and it takes a lot more work to make the operating system function correctly.

Solaris Symmetric Multiprocessing

SMP merely means that all processors are created equal and endowed by their designers with certain inalienable functionalities. Among these functionalities are shared memory, the ability to run kernel code, and the processing of interrupts. The ability of more than one CPU to run kernel code simultaneously is merely an issue of concurrency—an important issue, of course, but not a defining one. SunOS 4.1.3 was an SMP operating system that operated by putting one big lock around the kernel and allowing only one CPU in at a time. It worked, but it wasn't real fast.

Solaris 2 was designed to run on uniprocessor systems and tightly coupled, shared memory multiprocessors. The kernel assumes all processors are equivalent. Processors run kernel threads from the queue of runnable kernel threads (just as in user code). If a particular multiprocessor implementation places an asymmetric load on the processors (e.g., if interrupts are all directed to a single CPU), the kernel will nonetheless schedule threads to processors as if they were equivalent, not taking this asymmetry into account.

In general, all processors see the same data in memory. This model is relaxed somewhat, in that memory operations issued by a processor can be delayed or reordered when viewed by other processors (a *store buffer*[1] is an example of the former, while *out-of-order execution*[2] and *partial store order*[3] are examples of the latter). In such an MP environment, shared access to memory must also force memory coherency in order to operate correctly. This is done by *barrier* instructions, which force store buffer flushes and all pending writes to be completed. A side effect of the synchronization primitives is that memory coherency is enforced.

Kernel Scheduling

In addition to symmetric multiprocessing and two-level thread control, Solaris contains the real-time extensions of UNIX SVR4, with additional enhancements from SunSoft. These capabilities make Solaris ideal for applications that depend on split-second response, such as on-line transaction processing. These features include the following:

- Fixed priority real-time processes (also in standard UNIX SVR4)

  Solaris allows processes (actually, LWPs) to be classified as real time. These LWPs have fixed priorities that are not affected by the system's heuristic priority adjustment algorithm. The real-time scheduling class sits above both the timesharing and the system classes, ensuring that real-time LWPs always get time when they want it.

- User LWP priority manipulation (also in standard UNIX SVR4)

  Users can increase or decrease the priority of LWPs by issuing a system call `priocntl()`. This feature gives the user control over system response.

- High-resolution timers (also in standard UNIX SVR4).

  The timers in Solaris can be programmed to provide nanosecond granularity notifications. This feature is particularly useful for monitoring real-time events.

- Completely preemptive scheduling (Solaris value-added)

  The Solaris kernel has also been made completely preemptive, meaning that any thread can be interrupted at almost any point. Since all critical data structures are protected by locks, interrupts can be serviced as soon as they occur, and, if necessary, scheduling can be initiated immediately after the

---

1. A store buffer caches writes out to memory, allowing writes to happen at CPU speeds.

2. In out-of-order execution, instruction 2 is allowed to complete before instruction 1, as long as they aren't interdependent.

3. Partial Store Order allows memory writes to occur in different order than the order of the instructions.

interrupt is processed. By contrast, nonthreaded kernels are generally not preemptive. It's just too difficult to keep track of the state of computation without threads.

- Process priority inheritance (Solaris value-added)

  To avoid priority inversion (see *Priority Inversion* on page 77), Solaris kernel threads make low priority threads inherit the higher priority of waiting threads until they exit the critical section.

- Deterministic and guaranteed dispatch latency (Solaris value-added)

  Solaris provides deterministic scheduling response and guarantees various dispatch latencies on different hardware platforms. On a SPARCstation 1, the guarantee is a dispatch latency of 2 ms.

Are Libraries Safe?

Just because you write perfectly safe code that will run in a multithreaded environment with no problems doesn't mean that everyone else can. What would happen if you wrote a wonderful MT program, but then called a library routine that used a bunch of global data and didn't lock it? You'd lose. So, you must be certain that if you call a routine from multiple threads, it's *MT safe*. MT safe means that a function must lock any shared data it uses, it must use the correct definition of `errno`, and it must only call MT-safe functions.

Well, even programmers with the best of intentions find themselves with conflicting goals. "Make it fast," "Retain UNIX semantics," and "make it MT safe" don't always agree. Some routines in some libraries, (even in Solaris libraries!) will not be MT safe. It's a fact of life, and you have to deal with it. The manual page for each Solaris library call indicates its level of "MT safeness."

Libraries themselves are not safe or unsafe, per se. The *functions* in them are. Just to confuse things, there are libraries that contain some functions that are safe and some functions that aren't safe. This isn't as nutty as it might sound. The function `getc()`, for example, was actually implemented as a little macro. It ran very fast because it didn't even have to make a subroutine call. When the system programmers made it MT safe, they had to put a mutex lock around every call, and `getc()` became painfully slow[4]. So they created a fast, unsafe version also, called `getc_unlocked()`[5], and now you can take your choice of which to use in a threaded program.

There are also functions that are defined to return global data. The function `getctime()` for example, puts its data into a predefined location. There is no way to make this MT safe while retaining its semantics. (Even if we put a lock around the call, as soon as it returned and you tried to use the data, some other thread could have snuck in and changed it. It's like the `errno` problem.) In this case, a new library call was written: `getctime_r()`, which operates just like `getctime()`, save that you must create a structure to pass along with the call. The results will be stored in this structure. This is probably how `getctime()` should have been defined in the beginning, but it's too late to change it now (too many programs depend upon its current behavior).

The calls `read()` and `write()` are technically MT safe, but in practice, if you do concurrent operations from different threads on the same file descriptor, you're bound to get very confused. For these, there is a pair of calls: `pread()` and `pwrite()`, which operate just the same way, except that you have to pass an explicit file position pointer along with them.

XView™ is one of the most important libraries that is not MT safe. The amount of global state associated with the windows, the widgets, etc., made it absurdly difficult to sanitize. Because XView is designed around the concept of having an "event loop" waiting for window events, the only way to use it in an MT program is to execute all XView calls from one thread and have it dispatch work to other threads that it will subsequently collect for display[6]. As XView is not one of the toolkits of the future, there are no plans to ever make it MT safe. The future of X Window System™ toolkits is CDE™ (See *CDE* on page 292) and these libraries will be made MT safe, presumably in the near future.

On top of all these details, there's the question of whether a library contains calls that are even consistent with an MT environment. Remember `errno`? And how there is a `#define` to turn it into a call to `thr_getspecific()`? Well, it would be a disaster if some library were used in an MT program that didn't know about this trick. Even if it were only called from one thread, it would still be incorrect[7].

---

4. For unthreaded programs, a clever `#ifdef` retains the original version of `getc()`.

5. This is exactly what `getc()` used to be. There is nothing wrong with using it in an MT program; it simply requires that you, the programmer, ensure proper synchronization. You may choose to access a file descriptor from only one thread, or you may wish to place locks around your calls yourself.

6. True X hackers know about this part already. For non-X hackers, this collection of results can be accomplished by either (a) pretending to send an X event, which will cause the event loop to run whatever code you have set up to be run for that particular event (see `XCreateEvent()` in an X programming manual), or (b) opening a pipe down which the worker thread will send notification, also causing the event loop to run the code for that pipe. (There is a short example of this on the WWW.)

This and several similar #define calls are enabled by the -D_REENTRANT flag to the compiler. All libraries that will be used in an MT program *must* be compiled with this flag. One hundred percent of the Solaris libraries are.

Whew! That gives us five categories for library calls:

Table 6-1   Categories of MT Library Calls

Category	Meaning
MT safe	A function may be called concurrently from different threads.
MT hot	An MT safe function that is also "fast" (perhaps it spawns threads, perhaps it uses no global data, perhaps it just uses a tiny bit of global data, reducing locking contention).
MT unsafe	A function that is legal in an MT program but cannot be called concurrently.
Alternative	A function that is MT unsafe, but there is an MT safe equivalent function that you can use.
MT illegal	A function that wasn't even compiled with -D_REENTRANT and should not be used from any thread other than thr_main().

Of these, only the terms MT safe and MT unsafe are ever used in the literature.

Async Safety

Just as you thought you had it all figured out, there's one more little detail. This is not an MT issue per se, but it bears mention here. Imagine you have just called malloc() from your thread, and a signal came in. Now imagine that the signal handler also called malloc(). Well, the current implementation of malloc() requires it to lock some global data. If your thread's call to malloc() happened to hold that lock just when the signal came in, then trouble would be brewing. When the signal handler's call to malloc() tried to grab that same lock, it wouldn't get it. Deadlock! So, there's also an orthogonal category known as *async safe*. The library routine malloc() is not async safe, nor for that matter are very many of the routines in any of the libraries.

---

7. That is, unless the implementors were very clever and chose to make the global location for errno coincide with one of the thread specific errno locations. In Solaris, the main thread does just this, so it is possible to call unrecompiled functions from the main thread. But you should really recompile those libraries as soon as you can.

Conclusion? Look at the manual page for every library call that you are planning to use. That will tell you if it's safe, if there's an alternate call to use, or if you have to do some hacking yourself. In practice, this will not be a very big issue for you, if you take our very good advice and use `sigwait()` instead of installing signal handlers[8].

New Semantics for System Calls

Several of the UNIX system calls have new semantics when used in a multithreaded program. The choices of how to handle these new semantics are not uniform between Solaris and POSIX, although in any realistically normal program, the differences will not be noticed. Solaris will adopt the POSIX definition when it becomes an approved standard. (None of the other UNIX implementations are sufficiently advanced to have had to deal with this problem!)

Forking New Processes

According to the old definition of `fork()`, the kernel is to duplicate the entire process completely. One could reasonably conclude that calling `fork()` in a multithreaded program would duplicate everything, including the threads and LWPs. This is what Solaris does in every operating system up to 2.4. The problem is that it is highly unlikely that you would ever write a program in which you actually intended to use all of those threads and LWPs. The most common usage of `fork()` is to follow it immediately with a call to `exec()`. The result of this is that by doing "the right thing," you end up wasting time duplicating threads and LWPs that you will never use.

Solaris dealt with this problem by introducing a new system call, `fork1()`, which only duplicates the calling thread and its LWP. Almost all of the time, this is what you really want. POSIX, which came to this problem well after Solaris had been in the field for some time, made the same kind of choice, only they made it mandatory! In POSIX, `fork()` for a multithreaded program is defined to have the same semantics as `fork1()` in Solaris. When POSIX is ratified, the Solaris implementation of POSIX threads will rename the current `fork1()` to `fork()`, and there will be no "fork all." The Solaris implementation of Solaris threads will retain the current definitions.

---

8. This is one of those rare instances where we actually take our own advice!

Should you use `fork1()` and not immediately call `exec()`, you should be cautious about touching any locks that might be held by threads that do not exist in the child process. A deadlock would be very easy to arrive at. Even just calling `printf()` from the child can cause a deadlock. So, if you're doing this stuff, be very, very careful!

As with `fork1()`, `vfork()` duplicates only the one thread that called it. All of the same caveats apply.

Executing a New Program

The call `exec()` does exactly what it did before—it deletes the entire memory mapping for the calling process and replaces it with one appropriate for the new program. A program with multiple threads that calls `exec()` will have all of those threads (and any LWPs) terminated, and the only thing left will be the new program.

The New System Call `sigwait(2)`

Both Solaris and POSIX define a new system call that is designed to handle signals in a new fashion. A thread calls `sigwait()` with a set of signals to wait for. It will block until one of those signals is sent to the process, then it will return with that signal number. You can write code that will execute a case statement based on that signal number. As with signal handlers, the code can do whatever you wish. Unlike signal handlers, the code you write need not be async safe! As it is not running asynchronously, there are no limitations on what the code may do. This is a great thing—you get an asynchronously aware program that is written completely synchronously.

The Solaris Operating Environment

If you are going to be writing threaded code, chances are you are going to be using Solaris. (a) Because there's more of it than anything else that has threads (IDC claims 60% of all UNIX software development is done on Solaris). (b) Because it has by far the most advanced library, tool set, and general MT programming environment. (c) Because SunSoft is putting so much support behind it (like letting us write this book!). So, a description of Solaris is in order.

Solaris 2 is way-cool because it is a fully SVR4 compliant, real-time, fully preemptive, SMP operating system that allows dynamically loadable kernel modules, including user-defined system calls, device drivers, and even scheduling classes. On startup it does auto-configuration for all self-identifying devices, it supports dynamically loadable, shared memory modules with memory-mapped files and optimized swap space requirements. It supports

Transport-Layer Interfaces for networks, and ISV-defined, dynamically loadable, graphics hardware pipelines. As the Cose effort comes to fruition, Solaris will implement that, too. And we didn't even mention the Cache File System, Federated Naming Service, Network Information Service Plus, CDE, and the coming Project DOE (Distributed Objects Everywhere).

And it supports standards. One of the truly impressive things about Sun is its dedication to open standards. Sun took a lot of flak for "giving away the family jewels" by publishing the specifications for its interfaces and for constantly adopting standards where other companies chose to lock users in with proprietary implementations. Solaris supports more standards than does any other system.

Well, that was a nice pile of buzzwords. Here's what all of that means and why it's significant.

SVR4 and SPEC 1170 Compliant

While SVR4 consolidates the leading versions of UNIX—Xenix®, BSD, Solaris, and System V—Solaris 2 goes beyond SVR4 capability by introducing this extensive new functionality. As SPEC 1170 (now known as the *Single UNIX Specification*) is finalized and adopted by all the major UNIX vendors, your code becomes portable over a wide range of platforms, not even requiring recompilation for different implementations of UNIX on the same architecture!

And if another operating system vendor that you port to doesn't offer it? You just have a lot more porting to do.

Real-Time, Fully Preemptable Kernel

Because any call in the kernel can be preempted at just about any time, it is possible to guarantee system response time to outside events. By placing an LWP into the real-time class, you can be certain that it will get CPU time as soon as it needs it, for as long as it wants.

And if another operating system vendor that you port to doesn't offer it? You cannot do real-time tasks.

SMP

Solaris is able to schedule any LWP (or any kernel thread) on any CPU, and any number of them can be in the kernel simultaneously, so your programs can run faster.

And if another operating system vendor that you port to doesn't offer it? You could just get machines with very, very fast CPUs. Or you may be stuck with poorer response.

Dynamically Loadable Kernel Modules

The raw Solaris kernel occupies approximately 900 Kbytes (that's small!). All the code for device drivers, file systems, scheduling classes, etc., are loaded into kernel only when they are needed. So you pay only for what you use.

And if another operating system vendor that you port to doesn't offer it? Buy more memory.

Auto-Configuration

When you boot the machine with the `-r` flag, Solaris will look out on the bus, figure out which devices are there, and configure itself for them. Adding a new device? No kernel recompile! You don't even have to reboot, you can run the command `drvconfig`.

And if another operating system vendor that you port to doesn't offer it? You will just have to tell your customers to do a manual reconfiguration. Now when I was young, that meant hours of work. On these new, superfast workstations, it should take less than an hour per attempt. (Uh, er, *successful reconfiguration.*)

Dynamically Loadable, Shared Memory Modules

All of the Solaris libraries are dynamically loadable, so you can compile your program once, then move it from Solaris release to Solaris release without having to recompile. With each new set of bug fixes and performance improvements SunSoft makes, your program improves, at no cost to you! And because modules are shared, you save in the total amount of RAM you need.

And if another operating system vendor that you port to doesn't offer it? You just have to do a recompile for each operating system release. And buy lots of memory.

Memory-Mapped Files

This feature allows for simple, fast file I/O and a simplified model for shared memory.

And if another operating system vendor that you port to doesn't offer it? You use `read()`, spend some more time hacking your code, and buy a faster machine.

Optimized Swap Space

Solaris considers RAM to be part of your swap space, so you don't need to have as much disk to provide backing store. Memory-mapped files constitute their own backing store, so you need less there, too.

And if another operating system vendor that you port to doesn't offer it? You buy lots of disk.

Transport-Layer Interfaces

Sockets, Novell network stacks, ISO, etc., are all abstracted into a single interface. You no longer have to specify your choice of transports at coding time.

And if another operating system vendor that you port to doesn't offer it? You have to restrict your network choices.

Cache File System and Auto File System

CacheFS is the ability of the operating system to cache files that you often read over the network via NFS on a local disk. This means that you have many of the positive effects of having your data local, while it actually resides on a server. AutoFS is the ability of the system to know how to find files out across the network that are not NFS-mounted.

And if another operating system vendor that you port to doesn't offer it? You suffer the same slow access times for remote files that you're used to, while spare local disk goes unused. And you also must specify each and every file system that you want mounted.

Interactive Scheduling Class

The interactive scheduling class raises the priority of the process for the window that the user is currently typing to, giving superior interactive response.

And if another operating system vendor that you port to doesn't offer it? You suffer slower response times.

In-kernel `rlogin`/`telnet`

`rlogin` and `telnet` have been moved into the kernel to provide faster server response and the ability to support larger numbers of user.

And if another operating system vendor that you port to doesn't offer it? You suffer slower response times and support fewer users.

Wabi and MAE

Wabi™ and MAE are translation programs that allow a UNIX user to run MS-Windows and Macintosh programs under UNIX. Not only do the programs run (sometimes faster than on the native platform, with identical hardware!), but they also run under X windows. So you can run MS-Windows programs remotely!

And if another operating system vendor that you port to doesn't offer it? You'll just have to buy another machine if you want to play "Space Slime Invaders."

Network Information Service Plus

NIS+™ is a distributed, hierarchical method of keeping administrative control over your network. It allows a system administrator to configure network-wide entities, such as users, printers, workstations, aliases, etc., that will be distributed across networks of arbitrarily large size. A single administrator can control an enormous network with NIS+ and delegate restricted levels of authority to other, lower-level administrators.

And if another operating system vendor that you port to doesn't offer it? You hire more administrators and spend more time hassling with network problems.

CDE

CDE is the Common Desktop Environment that almost all of the major UNIX vendors have agreed to support. By providing this common desktop, code can be much more easily ported from one vendor's system to another's.

And if another operating system vendor that you port to doesn't offer it? You do more porting.

Project DOE

Distributed Objects Everywhere is Sun's vision of the future of computing. SunSoft believes that in the next few years, this paradigm will become dominant. It allows a simpler, vastly more efficient, and wider use of networks than was possible ever before. It allows users to view their computing resources in terms of "the network" instead of "the computer."[9]

And if another operating system vendor that you port to doesn't offer it? You don't get to make much use of networks.

Multiple Hardware Architectures

Solaris is the underlying operating system for both the current, and the next generation of SPARC, 80x86, and (soon) PowerPC™ microprocessor-based systems. You can write one piece of source code and recompile it for all three platforms with no changes whatsoever.

And if another operating system vendor that you port to doesn't offer it? You just do two extra ports.

---

9. It also allows for the old slogan "The Network is the Computer"™ to be recycled—very ecological.

Solaris Threads Debugging Interface

If you are not involved in writing a debugger or some other related tool for threads, then this section is not interesting. You will never use any of this information in an end-user MT program. You may be interested in knowing that it exists, however. This is a Solaris implementation only; there is no POSIX standard for a debugging interface.

Basically, the debugging library, libthread_db.so, provides an interface to the internals of the threads library. With it you can do all sorts of things that you can't do otherwise, such as look at the scheduling queues, lists of extant threads, synchronization variable sleep queues, TSD data arrays, and current LWP lists and their internal states. You can also "reach in" and alter these things directly, look at and change the individual thread's stack, etc. The library gives you all the power you need to implement a debugger, a garbage collector, or other kinds of tools.

So, if you're an implementor of MT tools, this is interesting. If not, not.

Again: Do not even *think* of writing an MT program that depends upon anything in this library. Use the standard API for everything. And if you think there's something that's missing, tell us. A lot of very smart people spent a lot of time putting together the user-level threads library. They spent years programming with it. And while they *may* have missed some vital feature, it's not very likely. Ask first.

Comparisons of Different Implementations

We now touch an issue that is slightly dicey for a book like this, especially considering that we work for Sun. Comparisons of different implementations are not difficult to do, but they are difficult to do 100 percent correctly and without bias. We contacted each of the different vendors and asked them about their current status and their plans. We present the answers below without further comment.

Table 6-2   Implementation Comparison of Different Operating Systems

Feature	Solaris	DCE	OS/2	NT	DEC	HP-UX	SGI	AIX
Multithreaded Kernel	Yes	n/a	No	Yes	Yes	No	Yes	Yes
SMP Support	Yes	n/a	No	Yes	Yes	Yes	Yes	Yes
User Threads Libraries	Yes	Yes	Yes	Yes	Yes	Yes	Yes	Yes

Table 6-2   Implementation Comparison of Different Operating Systems (Continued)

Feature	Solaris	DCE	OS/2	NT	DEC	HP-UX	SGI	AIX
Current POSIX Library (draft level)	Yes 10	Yes 4	Never	Never	Yes 6	Yes 4	Future	Yes 7
Architecture	M:M	M:1	1:1	1:1	M:1	M:1	1:1	1:1
Automatic Threading Compilers	FORTRAN Ada	No	No	No	FORTRAN	No	FORTRAN Ada, C	No

Architecture refers to the scheduling model (see *Different Models of Kernel Scheduling* on page 41), where M:M is Many-to-Many, M:1 is Many-to-One, and 1:1 is One-to-One.

This chart is based on publicly available information and individual calls to each of the companies.

IBM is publicly considering the adoption of a Solaris-like, two-level model (they don't call it that). We noticed that DEC also has the machinery in place to do the same, although they have not declared their intentions.

The major point of this chart is not that one vendor is so much better than any other, but rather that all major vendors are actively working on some sort of threads library, and all the libraries are based on the same paradigm. In spite of the differences we have noted throughout this book, all the libraries are actually very similar, and knowing how to write a program in one gives you just about everything you need to write in another.

6

Threads Primer

POSIX Threads (pthreads)　　　7

In which the details of the POSIX concepts are explained and contrasted to those of Solaris. A brief consideration of the issues of moving from Solaris threads to POSIX threads concludes the chapter.

Pthreads Introduction

Pthreads is a new standard POSIX API that provides library routines used for the development of multithreaded programs. The pthreads API used in this book is based on Draft 10 of the POSIX 1003.4a standard.

Pthreads and the Solaris threads API are similar in many ways. They both have similar library interfaces, including the actions performed by the library and the syntax of the calls. In many cases, the POSIX API and the Solaris API share identical library calls where only the name of the call is different. The POSIX API uses the prefix `pthread_` before each library call, whereas the Solaris API uses the prefix `thr_`. In all cases of similar calls between the pthreads interface and the Solaris interface, the function argument types will be different.

Although the pthreads and Solaris threads APIs are similar, they do not match exactly. The pthreads API has some functionality that is not available in the Solaris API, and the Solaris API has some functionality that is not available in pthreads.

It is important to understand that the POSIX specification is a general description of an API that should provide pretty much everything a programmer would want. Because of its generality, the pthreads standard permits certain portions of the specification *not* to be implemented. In such cases, the function must return the value `ENOTSUP`, which indicates that the POSIX function is not supported.

Figure 7-1 shows the areas that pthreads and Solaris threads share and those areas in which the APIs are unique.

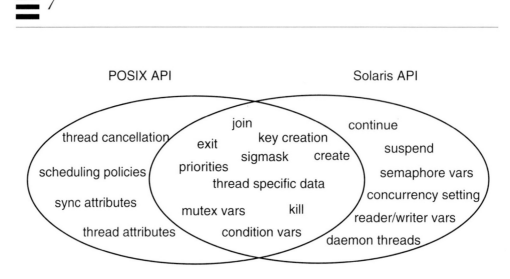

POSIX API   Solaris API

Figure 7-1   POSIX and Solaris API Differences

As you can see from Figure 7-1, Solaris threads and pthreads share a majority of
the functionality. However, there are differences between the two APIs.

Solaris threads have the following features not found in pthreads:

- Reader/writer locks (many readers, single writer)
- Ability to suspend and continue a given thread
- Ability to create daemon threads (THR_DAEMON)
- Ability to set and get a level of concurrency

Pthreads have the following features not found in Solaris threads:

- Cancellation semantics (ability to cancel threads)
- Attribute objects (threads and synchronization attributes)
- Scheduling policies

Attribute Objects

The pthreads API permits the programmer to create threads and synchronization
variables in many different states. For example, a thread can be created bound or
unbound, a mutex variable can be interprocess or intraprocess. Solaris controls
these states by using flags when creating the thread or the synchronization
variable. Pthreads uses a different approach to setting states. The pthreads API
uses the notion of attribute objects. Attribute objects are created and then used as
arguments to creation or initialization functions to define the state of threads or
synchronization variables, respectively.

The state information defined in the attribute object is used only on the creation or initialization of the thread or synchronization variable. Once a thread or synchronization variable is created or initialized by use of an attribute object, a change in the attribute object will not affect the state of the thread or synchronization variable.

There are two major advantages to using attribute objects. The first advantage is the capability for attribute objects to be implemented on many different systems. The attribute object defines the state that a thread or synchronization variable should use. It does not define how the state is implemented. This capability allows flexibility in designing and implementing attributes on different operating systems. You may have guessed that pthreads on Solaris is implemented using the Solaris threads library; you're right!

The other major advantage in using attribute objects is the readability of application code. A programmer can define all the attribute objects used in an application in one location. This allows all the initialization and state information for all the threads and synchronization variables in your application to reside in one piece of code. This idea also provides an easy way to modify the behavior of all the threads and synchronization variables in just a few lines of code.

Although attribute objects provide an easy way to initialize threads and synchronization variables, they require memory to hold state information. This memory must be managed by the programmer. The memory is allocated when the attribute object is initialized, using the appropriate init function. This memory can be released by means of the related destructor function.

Threads and Attribute Objects

The attribute object used in creating a thread contains all the information needed to define the state of the new thread. This state information includes:

- The thread's scope
- The thread's detach state
- The thread's stack address
- The thread's stack size
- The thread's scheduling information

The attribute object is created and then modified to define a custom attribute object. This object can then be used by any `pthread_create()` call to define the state of the new thread. The advantage of the attribute mechanism is its simplicity. The thread attribute objects can be created and defined in one section of code and then used throughout the application. For example, an attribute object can be created that defines the stack size to be 256 Kbytes. If all the threads in the application are created with this attribute object, then to change the stack size for all the threads in the application, all you need to do is change the one attribute object. (See Appendix H, *Pthreads API (POSIX 1003.1c)* for more information regarding attribute objects.)

Thread attribute objects are broken down into five areas: scope, detach state, stack address, stack size, and scheduling policy.

Scope

The scope determines whether the thread has a process-wide or system-wide scope. You can think of this as how the thread is seen by the kernel. If the thread is defined to have a scope of PTHREAD_SCOPE_SYSTEM, then the thread is bound and the kernel can "see" the thread. If the thread is defined to have a scope of PTHREAD_SCOPE_PROCESS, then the thread is unbound and the kernel does not see the thread. Using PTHREAD_SCOPE_SYSTEM is identical to using the THR_BOUND flag in Solaris threads. If the thread was created with the THR_BOUND flag, then it is bound to an LWP, which is visible to the kernel.

The scope for a thread attribute object can be set by the pthread_attr_setscope() call. The scope of an existing object can be retrieved by the pthread_attr_getscope() call. Both of these calls require that an attribute object be created first.

The default value for the scope of a thread is defined as PTHREAD_SCOPE_PROCESS (unbound thread).

Detach State

The detach state determines whether the thread will be joinable from another thread. This determines whether the threads exit status and resources will be discarded when the thread terminates. If the thread is defined to have a detach state of PTHREAD_CREATE_DETACHED, then when the thread terminates, all of its resources and exit status will be discarded immediately. If the thread is defined to have a detach state of PTHREAD_CREATE_JOINABLE, then the thread exit status and resources will be retained until the thread is joined by another thread. This procedure is identical to Solaris threads' use of the THR_DETACHED flag in thread creation.

The detach state for a thread attribute object can be set and retrieved by the pthread_attr_setdetachstate() and pthread_attr_getdetachstate() calls, respectively. Both of these calls require the attribute object to be created first.

The default detach state for a thread is defined as PTHREAD_CREATE_JOINABLE (nondetached thread).

Stack Address

The stack address specifies the base address (starting address) of the stack for the thread. This address is specified in the attribute object for the thread. If the value for the stack address is non-null, then the system will initialize the threads stack, starting at the given address.

Although the need to specify a stack address is rare, some care must be taken when a specific address is used. For example, if you create an attribute object for a thread with a non-null stack address, then this attribute object should be used to create only one thread. The attribute object must not be reused without a change to the stack base; otherwise, all the threads would be using the same stack address base.

The base stack address can be set and retrieved from an attribute object by `pthread_attr_setstackaddr()` and `pthread_attr_getstackaddr()` calls, respectively.

The default value for a thread stack address is `NULL`, which means the systems assigns a stack base for the thread.

Stack Size

The stack size in the attribute object defines the size of the stack, in bytes, for a thread. If the size of the stack is non-null, then the thread will use the stack size given in the attribute object. If a stack size is given, then it must be at least `PTHREAD_STACK_MIN` bytes in size. If the size of the stack is null, then the system default stack size will be used.

The stack size can be set and retrieved from an attribute object by the `pthread_attr_setstacksize()` and `pthread_attr_getstacksize()` calls, respectively.

The default value for the stack size is `NULL`, which sets the stack size to the system default.

Scheduling Policy

The scheduling parameters for a thread are defined in the attribute object associated with the thread. The scheduling parameters define how the thread is scheduled and set the priority for the thread. The Solaris implementation of pthreads currently only supports setting a priority for a thread. Future implementations will define other scheduling policies for the thread attribute object.

The priority of a thread can be set and retrieved from an attribute object by the `pthread_attr_setschedparam()` and `pthread_attr_getschedparam()` call, respectively.

The default scheduling priority for a thread is defined as NULL, by which the thread will inherit the priority from the threads creator.

Default Thread Attributes

When an attribute object is created, it is defined with a default state. The default state for a thread attribute object is defined in Table 7-1.

Table 7-1   Default Settings for Thread Attribute Objects

Attribute	Default Setting	Description
Scope	PTHREAD_SCOPE_PROCESS	Unbound thread
Detach State	PTHREAD_CREATE_JOINABLE	Nondetached thread
Stack Address	NULL	System-assigned base address
Stack Size	NULL	System default stack size
Priority	NULL	Inherit priority from creator

Synchronization Variables and Attribute Objects

Synchronization variables in pthreads use attribute objects to define the scope of the variable. When a synchronization variable is initialized, an attribute object, which will define how the variable will behave, can be passed to the initialization routine. The only option currently supported in the attribute object is the definition of the synchronization variables scope. The synchronization variable can have a scope that is private to the process. or it can have a scope that is shared among other processes. This concept is identical to the way the Solaris API uses the USYNC_THREAD and USYNC_PROCESS flags when creating synchronization variables.

Each type of synchronization variable has a unique attribute object. The attribute objects must be created before any of the attributes of the object can be modified. Once the attribute has been created, it can be used in the initialization of one or more synchronization variables of the same type. The attribute objects can be initialized and defined in one central location and then used throughout the application code. This feature makes it easy to manage how the synchronization variables will behave from one location in code.

In pthreads, all synchronization variables must be initialized before use.

Mutex Variables

The attribute object used with mutex variables defines whether the mutex variable is shared with other processes. If the attribute object is defined to be PTHREAD_PROCESS_SHARED, then a mutex initialized with this attribute object will be shared among other processes in the system. This attribute object method is identical to using the `USYNC_PROCESS` flag when creating mutex variables in the Solaris threads API. If the attribute object is defined as `PTHREAD_PROCESS_PRIVATE`, then a mutex created with this attribute object will be private to the current process.

The attribute object can be created and destroyed by the `pthread_mutexattr_init()` and `pthread_mutexattr_destroy()` calls, respectively. The scope of the mutex can be set and retrieved by the `pthread_mutexattr_setpshared()` and `pthread_mutexattr_getpshared()` calls, respectively. A mutex attribute object must be created before the scope or the attribute for the mutex is modified.

The default scope of a mutex variable and attribute object is defined as `PTHREAD_PROCESS_PRIVATE`.

Condition Variables

The condition variable attribute object is similar to the mutex attribute object. The attribute object used with condition variables defines whether the variable will be shared among other processes in the system. If a condition variable is created with an attribute object that is defined as `PTHREAD_PROCESS_SHARED`, then the condition variable will be shared among other processes; if the attribute object is defined as `PTHREAD_PROCESS_PRIVATE`, then the variable will be private to the current process.

The condition variable attribute object can be created and destroyed by the `pthread_condattr_init()` and `pthread_condattr_destroy()` calls, respectively. Once the attribute object has been created, the scope of the object can be set or retrieved by the `pthread_condattr_setpshared()` and `pthread_condattr_getpshared()` calls, respectively.

The default scope of a condition variable and attribute object is defined as `PTHREAD_PROCESS_PRIVATE`.

Semaphore Variables

Semaphore variables are not officially part of the pthreads specification; they are actually part of the POSIX real-time specification. However, their use in mutithreaded programs is important.

The scope of a semaphore variable can be set to be shared among other processes or can be private to the process. POSIX semaphore synchronization variables do not use an attribute object to define the scope of the variable. When the semaphore is created by means of the `sem_init()` call, it can be given a flag to define the scope of the variable. If the *pshared* flag is non-zero, then the semaphore will be shared among other processes; otherwise, the semaphore will be private to the processes. This mechanism is identical to the way the Solaris threads API sets a semaphore variables scope.

Cancellation

POSIX threads introduces the concept of thread cancellation. Thread cancellation should be used when the further execution of a thread is no longer required. It provides a way to terminate one or more threads at a known position within each thread. An example of the use of cancellation is in an application that creates multiple threads to search for an item. When one of the threads finds the item, the other threads are no longer needed in the search. The thread that found the item would then cancel the other threads.

Cancellation provides a way of controlling where and when a thread can be cancelled, allowing the thread to clean up any resources used and return to a known state. There are dangers associated with terminating a thread at an undetermined point in its execution. Without cancellation, if a thread is terminated while holding a lock, a possible deadlock situation could arise. Another problem could arise if the thread has allocated some dynamic memory. If the thread is terminated without freeing the memory, then a memory leak exists in the application.

The pthreads API provides a way to programmatically permit or disallow cancellation from anywhere within a thread. The programmer can determine where and when a thread is allowed to be cancelled. The pthreads API also provides a scope for cancellation handlers that provide cleanup and termination services that run only when they are intended to run. This allows cancellation routines to run when the thread is cancelled and before the thread terminates.

The cancellation of a thread can take place under one of the following conditions:

- Asynchronously—The thread can be cancelled (terminated) asynchronously at any point within the execution of the thread.

- Standard execution points—The thread can be cancelled at certain POSIX standard predefined locations with the execution of the thread.

- Discrete points—The application programmer can set up specific locations where a thread can be cancelled.

In each of these cancellation locations, care must be taken to ensure that the thread restores any held resources and returns the thread to a known state.

To cancel a thread, a call to pthread_cancel() must be made with the thread ID of the target as an argument. How the target thread handles the cancellation depends on the cancellation state and type set for the target thread.

Cancellation State and Type

The cancellation state of a thread can exist in two conditions: PTHREAD_CANCEL_DISABLE and PTHREAD_CANCEL_ENABLE. If the target thread has the cancellation state in a disabled mode, then all cancellation requests are held in a pending state. The thread will not be cancelled if the cancellation state for the thread is disabled. However, if a thread has cancellation disabled and later enables cancellation, then any pending cancels will be acted upon as defined by the cancellation type of the thread.

The cancellation type of a thread defines how the thread will act when a cancellation request is delivered. The cancellation type can be defined as either PTHREAD_CANCEL_ASYNCHRONOUS or PTHREAD_CANCEL_DEFERRED.

If the cancellation type is set to asynchronous, then upon receiving a cancellation request, the thread will perform an immediate cancellation. This type of cancellation is dangerous in that the programmer must guarantee that no resources or locks are held when the cancellation request arrives. This can be difficult to determine because the execution state of a thread is not usually known at any given time.

If the cancellation type is set to deferred, then the thread will act upon the cancellation request only at set cancellation points. The POSIX standard defines a set of cancellation points and can be defined by the programmer, who can create a cancellation point by inserting a call to pthread_testcancel() in the threads code. This call will check to see if a cancellation request is pending. If a request is pending, then pthread_testcancel() will not return at all, and the thread will simply be killed. Otherwise, it will return, and the thread will continue.

In addition to the programmatically defined points, the POSIX library provides some additional cancellation points. The current standard cancellation points include:

- A thread blocked in a pthread_cond_wait() call
- A thread blocked in a pthread_cond_timedwait() call
- A thread waiting for the termination of another thread in a pthread_join() call
- A thread blocked in a sigwait() call
- In general, any pthread call that may cause a thread to block is a cancellation point. An exception to this is the pthread_mutex_lock() call, because the cost to check for thread cancellation before each mutex lock would be too costly.

If a cancellation request arrives and the thread has the cancellation state enabled and the type deferred, then the thread will be cancelled at any standard or user-defined cancellation point.

The cancellation state and type for a thread can be set by the `pthread_setcancelstate()` and `pthread_setcanceltype()` calls, respectively. For more information, see Appendix H, *Pthreads API (POSIX 1003.1c)*.

Cancellation Cleanup Handlers

When a thread is cancelled, pthreads provides a way to clean up the thread's state. This is done through a set of cleanup handlers that are called upon cancellation of a thread. There are two calls associated with the cleanup handlers: `pthread_cleanup_pop()` and `pthread_cleanup_push()`. The `pthread_cleanup_push()` call pushes a cleanup handler (a function with one argument) onto the cleanup stack. This stack contains the cleanup routines that are called when a thread is cancelled. The cleanup stack is also used when a thread explicitly or implicitly calls `pthread_exit()`.

The cleanup handlers can also be taken off the stack by the `pthread_cleanup_pop()` call. If the `pthread_cleanup_pop()` call is invoked with a non-zero argument, then the first handler function is popped off the stack and executed. If the `pthread_cleanup_pop()` call is invoked with a zero argument, then the first handler is removed from the stack and is discarded. When a thread is cancelled or exits, a call to `pthread_cleanup_pop()` is effectively made with a non-zero argument. Each handler that was on the cleanup stack at the time of the threads cancellation will be removed from the stack and executed.

Figure 7-2 illustrates the cleanup handler functions.

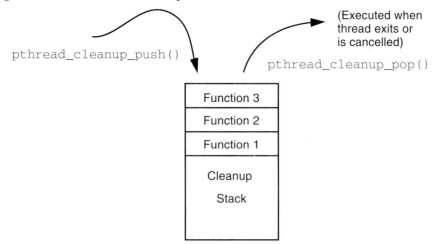

Figure 7-2   Cancellation Cleanup Handler Functions.

The `pthread_cleanup_pop()` and `pthread_cleanup_push()` calls must be placed at the same lexical level within the source code. If the two calls are not at the same lexical level, the program will not function correctly. For an example of the use of these calls, see the *POSIX Cancellation* example on page 182.Care must be taken when using cleanup handlers. The placement of the cancellation points must be based on the underlying application to ensure that the cleanup handlers execute at a known state. Consideration must also be given to restoring cancellation state or type when returning from nested cancellation states. The `pthread_setcanceltype()` and `pthread_setcancelstate()` provide a way of setting the cancellation type and state, respectively.

The general idea for cancellation is that programmers will write their programs such that sections of code that allocate resources, obtain locks, etc., are immediately preceded (or followed) by cleanup handler pushes. These sections of code are performed atomically with respect to cancellation (i.e., the thread cannot be cancelled in the middle). Then, the body of the code that uses that resource is run with cancellation allowed. Upon completion, cancellation is once again disabled while the resource is freed and the handler popped off the stack.

For more information about cancellation cleanup handlers, see Appendix H, *Pthreads API (POSIX 1003.1c)*.

Thread Scheduling

Pthreads offer a flexibility in scheduling threads onto processors, giving the programmer more options on how a thread will be handled by the operating system. In pthreads, two major controls are used for scheduling. The first control is the scheduling scope of an individual thread. The scope of a thread is discussed on page 108 of this chapter. The second control used in scheduling is the scheduling policy defined for a given domain.

Threads that have a scope that is internal to the process (`PTHREAD_SCOPE_PROCESS`) will all share a single scheduling policy within the given process. All other processes running in the system can each conform to their own scheduling policy. Threads that have a scope that is shared system wide (`PTHREAD_SCOPE_SYSTEM`) will share a single scheduling policy with all other system-wide scope threads. Threads with different scheduling states can coexist with threads in the same system and even in the same thread.

Three different scheduling policies are defined in POSIX threads:

- SCHED_FIFO
- SCHED_RR
- SCHED_OTHER

7

The SCHED_FIFO policy defines a simple first in, first out scheduler. Each priority that can be assigned to a thread is associated with a FIFO queue. As each thread becomes runnable, it is added to the associated priority queue. As the thread in a given priority moves to the head of the queue, it is scheduled on the next available processor.

The SCHED_RR policy defines a round-robin scheduling algorithm. The round-robin policy is similar to the SCHED_FIFO policy, except for the addition of a time quota associated with each thread. As the thread for a given priority is running, if its time quota is used up, it is put back on the tail of the associated queue. This scheduling policy is similar to the way UNIX handles timesharing among processes.

The SCHED_OTHER policy is the same default scheduling policy now supported in Solaris threads. This is the only policy that Solaris supports at this time because Solaris threads does not offer multiple scheduling policies. For more information about Solaris's default scheduling policy, see Chapter 4, *Scheduling*.

POSIX threads provide the ability to deal with priority inversion in the SCHED_FIFO and SCHED_RR scheduling classes. Priority inversion refers to the situation in which a high-priority thread is blocked, waiting on a lock held by a lower-priority thread. This problem can be resolved by escalating the priority of the thread holding the lock to the priority of the thread requesting the lock. The pthreads API resolves this problem by defining three different scheduling classes for mutex locks:

- PTHREAD_PRIO_NONE
- PTHREAD_PRIO_INHERIT
- PTHREAD_PRIO_PROTECT

A mutex variable that is created with a scheduling class of PTHREAD_PRIO_NONE will ignore any thread priorities. This is the default for Solaris. Solaris does not yet support mutex priorities.

The PTHREAD_PRIO_INHERIT class will cause a mutex variable to upgrade its priority. If a high-priority thread is blocking, waiting on a mutex lock, then the lower-priority thread that holds the lock will have its priority changed to match the higher-level thread. This change in priority is only temporary. The thread will return to its original priority after the inversion is corrected.

The PTHREAD_PRIO_PROTECT class sets a fixed mutex priority. Any thread that locks the mutex will inherit the priority of the mutex if the priority of the thread is lower than that of the mutex. If the thread holds more then one mutex, it will inherit the highest priority in the set of mutexes.

Moving Between the Two APIs

As mentioned before, Solaris and POSIX are virtually 100% functionally equivalent. We expect Solaris programmers to continue to write programs using Solaris threads until POSIX threads is voted as a standard and is available. At that point, we expect Solaris programmers to make a choice.

If Solaris is your sole platform or if you are willing to do system ports, then we suggest that you use Solaris threads. As new features are conceived, Sun will be able to offer them on Solaris threads long before POSIX can even consider them.

If you are inherently a multiplatform vendor, then we suggest that you begin to write POSIX threads programs. However, since pthreads is not yet a standard, using Solaris threads in your programs will speed the learning of POSIX; any programs written can be easily translated into POSIX.

The following is a list of recommendations that you may want to follow for the development of threaded applications.

- *Solaris implements "Suspend" and "Continue"; POSIX doesn't.* Don't use them if you plan to move to POSIX.

- *Solaris implements* `thr_setconcurrency`; *POSIX doesn't.* This is strictly an efficiency issue. You may wish to use an `#ifdef` to allow the Solaris threads call.

- *Solaris implements reader/writer locks; POSIX doesn't.* These locks are very useful. You can either implement them yourself or use the SPILT package available from Sun.

- *Solaris implements daemon threads; POSIX doesn't.* Don't use them if you plan to move to POSIX.

- *POSIX implements cancellation; Solaris doesn't.* Any routines that you invent to do careful thread-killing in Solaris will remain valid in POSIX. You can continue to use your home-grown methods, or you can replace your methods with POSIX cancellation.

- *POSIX has more scheduling policies than Solaris.* POSIX will give you a little more variety than Solaris. The additional scheduling policies will not affect your Solaris code in any case.

- *POSIX uses "attribute objects," whereas Solaris passes flags to creation/initialization functions.* The mapping from one to the other is obvious.

≡ 7

Moving between the two different libraries should in most cases be a simple matter of changing the name of the library call. Programmers familiar with the Solaris threads API should have no problems moving to the POSIX threads API. So, using the Solaris API, you can learn about threaded programming today and then move to the POSIX API as implementations emerge.

Programming Tools 8

In which we consider the kinds of new tools that a reader would want
when writing an MT program. Details of the Solaris tool set are
discussed in the context of working with actual programs.

Programming with threads adds new challenges to the development tools that
you use. A "normal" debugger in most cases will not work well with threaded
programs, because most development tools were designed and developed to be
used with programs that have a single thread of execution. Most debuggers have
the ability to follow multiple execution streams, but only in processes via a
fork(). Since threads can create multiple streams of execution in the same
process, most debuggers and development tools need to be redesigned.

SunSoft has designed and developed products to be used with multithreaded
programs. SunSoft not only provides multithreaded debuggers but also has
several tools for enhancing and analyzing multithreaded programs.

This chapter focuses on some of the current tools that SunSoft provides for the
development of multithreaded programs. All the following tools are part of the
SPARCworks/iMPact™ multithreaded development kit available from SunSoft.

LockLint

LockLint verifies consistent use of mutex and read/write locks in multithreaded
ANSI C programs. LockLint performs a static analysis of the use of mutex and
read/write locks and looks for inconsistent use of these locking techniques. In
looking for inconsistent use of locks, LockLint detects the most common causes of
data races and deadlocks. LockLint can generate many different types of reports:

- Locking side effects of functions. Unknown side effects can lead to data
  races and/or deadlocks.

- Variables that were not consistently protected by at least one lock or that
  violate assertions made about which locks are supported to protect them.
  This information can point to a potential data race.

- Cycles and inconsistent lock order acquisitions. This information can
  prevent potential deadlocks.

- Which lock(s) were consistently used to protect a variable. This information can assist in judging the appropriateness of the chosen granularity of locks.

LoopTool

LoopTool, along with its sister program LoopReport, profiles loops for FORTRAN programs; it provides information about programs parallelized by SPARCompiler™ MP/FORTRAN.

LoopTool displays a graph of loop runtimes, shows which loops were parallelized, and provides compiler hints about why a loop was not parallelized.

LoopReport creates a summary table of all loop runtimes correlated with compiler hints about why a loop was not parallelized. This information can aid in the determination of which loops would benefit from parallelization.

SPARCworks Debugger

The SPARCworks Debugger used in Solaris, with the iMPact tools installed, extends debugging capabilities to support the development of threaded programs. SPARCworks Debugger allows threaded C, C++, and FORTRAN programs to be used in application development. The debugger can control single threads of execution within a process.

SPARCworks Debugger not only allows control and inspection of threads in a program but also provides the standard fix-and-continue capabilities and runtime error checking that are available for nonthreaded programs.

Thread Analyzer

The Thread Analyzer is a graphical tool that displays and analyzes program information on a per-thread basis. The Thread Analyzer uses tables and graphs to display `gprof` and `prof` profile information for each thread. You can use the Thread Analyzer in the same way you would use `gprof` and `prof` to determine if your program has any bottlenecks.

Thread Analyzer can be used with C, C++, and FORTRAN 77 programs.

Examples of Using the Tools

This section presents some examples showing how some of these tools can be used:

- Example One—A look at a Mandelbrot program, a C program that can be made to run much faster by being multithreaded. We analyze the program with the Thread Analyzer to see where performance bottlenecks take place, then thread it accordingly.

- Example Two—Uses LockLint to check the Mandelbrot program's use of locks.

- Example Three—Shows LoopTool being used to parallelize portions of a library.

- Example Four—Shows how SPARCworks Debugger can be used with multithreaded programs.

Example One: Threading the Mandelbrot Program

This example uses a well-known program that plots vector values in the plane of complex numbers. This produces the distinctive Mandelbrot pattern (see Figure 8-1).

The goal of this exercise was to thread the Mandelbrot program so that portions of the program could execute in parallel. The details of this effort are not shown; the analysis of the problem is our focus.

Mandelbrot produces its pattern according to the equation

$$z_n = \sqrt{z_{n-1}^2 + c}$$

When the magnitude of z is greater than 2, Mandelbrot plots z_0's position on the screen. Mandelbrot assigns a different color to each drawing element according to the number of iterations (up to 1000) needed for z to become greater than 2; the more iterations needed to reach 2, the darker the point. The darker the region, the longer it takes to display.

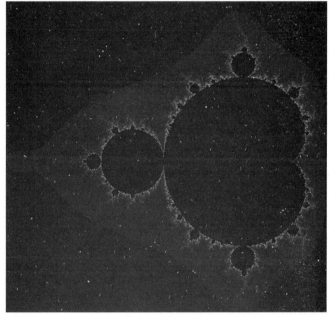

Figure 8-1   Mandelbrot Display

The nonthreaded version of the Mandelbrot program simply repeats the following series:

- calculate each point
- display each point

Obviously, on a multiprocessor machine this is not the most efficient way to run the program. Since each point can be calculated independently, the program is a good candidate for parallelization, using threads.

The program was threaded so that it would execute in parallel. A number of threads were created, one for each processor, that would each execute a portion of the Mandelbrot set. Each thread would independently calculate a row of the set and then display that row.

Thread One	Thread Two	Thread Three
Calculate row	Calculate row	Calculate row
Display row	Display row	Display row

After the program was threaded, it was executed to determine the amount of speedup gained. The threaded version did run faster than the nonthreaded version but not as fast as we expected.

To find out why this might be, we turned to the Thread Analyzer to see why the program was not executing as expected. The program was recompiled with the -Ztha option to instrument the executable for use with the Thread Analyzer. The Thread Analyzer was then started, and the program was loaded into it. The main window of the Thread Analyzer, shows a hierarchical view of the programs threads and the procedures that they call (see Figure 8-2).

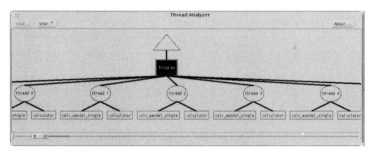

Figure 8-2   Thread Analyzer Main Window (Partial)

The Thread Analyzer can create many different performance-related reports on a per-thread basis. One of these reports is a mutex profile report that displays the amount of time each thread has spent waiting for a mutex lock. Since the threaded Mandelbrot program used mutex locks, we displayed the mutex profile report. To do this, we selected a thread node from the main window, then selected *Mutex Wait* from the *Sorted Metrics* menu.

The mutex profile is presented in Figure 8-3.

Threads Primer

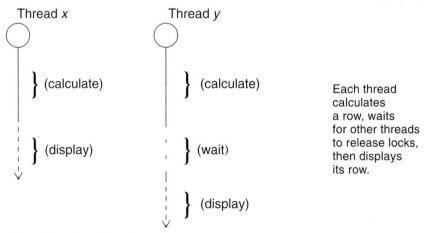

Thread-level Profile Mutex		
Thread	Value	Percent
Total	1.930	
thread 3	0.680	35%
thread 1	0.350	18%
thread 4	0.340	18%
thread 5	0.190	10%
Mandel	0.160	8%
thread 2	0.160	8%
thread 0	0.050	3%

Figure 8-3   Thread Analyzer: Mutex Wait Time

Figure 8-3 shows that the various threads spend a lot of time waiting for the other threads to release the mutex lock. Thread 3's excessive waiting time was random, we found. When we ran the program several times, the wait times varied among the threads. Since the display routine in the program is a serial resource, the threads must wait for each other to finishing displaying before another thread can begin, indicating that the threads are spending too much time waiting for the display mutex lock.

Figure 8-4 shows how the programs works. Each thread can perform the calculations in parallel, but only one thread can be displaying at any given time. This forces other threads to wait until another thread has finished displaying.

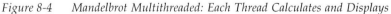

Figure 8-4   Mandelbrot Multithreaded: Each Thread Calculates and Displays

To solve this problem, we changed the code so that the calculations and the displaying are entirely separate. In this version, we have several threads simultaneously calculating rows of points and writing into a buffer, while another thread reads from the buffer and displays rows (see Figure 8-5).

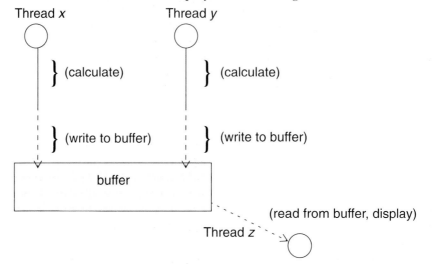

Figure 8-5   Mandelbrot Threaded: Separate Display Thread

After we implemented this change, the calculation threads no longer have to wait for other threads to finish displaying. Now, the display thread waits for the current line of the buffer to be filled. While it waits, other threads can be calculating and writing, so that little time is spent contending for the mutex locks.

This result can be confirmed by rerunning the program and then using the Thread Analyzer again to look at the mutex profile information. Figure 8-6 shows that the program now spends almost all its time in the Mandel loop and much less time waiting for mutex locks. Consequently, the Mandelbrot program runs much faster.

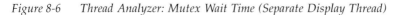

Figure 8-6   Thread Analyzer: Mutex Wait Time (Separate Display Thread)

We used only one of the reports that the Thread Analyzer creates. Many others are just as useful in determining possible performance problems with threaded code.

Example Two: Checking a Program with LockLint

A program such as the Mandelbrot program used in Example One may execute correctly but still contain potential problems. A common problem with threaded programs is the shared access of resources. To control shared access, synchronization variables are commonly used. Synchronization variables that control access to shared data can produce some of the following problems:

- Deadlocks—When two threads are waiting for the other to release a lock before releasing their own.
- Data races—When two or more threads have overlapping read/write access to data, causing unexpected data values.

The SPARCworks/iMPact LockLint tool addresses these potential problems by verifying consistent use of mutex and read/write locks in multithreaded ANSI C programs.

LockLint performs a static analysis on the use of mutex and read/write locks and looks for inconsistent use of these locking techniques. In looking for inconsistent use of locks, LockLint detects the most common causes of data races and deadlocks.

Code Example 8-1   Program to Demonstrate Use of LockLint (`11_examp.c`)

```
#define _REENTRANT
#include <stdio.h>
#include <time.h>
#include <thread.h>

long count;
long initial;

void *printer(void *);
void set_initial();

main(int argc, char **argv)
{
struct timespec ts;

ts.tv_sec = 0;
ts.tv_nsec = 250000000;


set_initial();
```

Code Example 8-1   Program to Demonstrate Use of LockLint (`11_examp.c`) (Continued)

```
printf("Initial count = %ld\n", initial);

count = initial;

thr_create(NULL, 0, printer, 0, THR_DETACHED, NULL);

while (1) {
  count++;
  nanosleep(&ts, NULL);
  }

return(0);
}


void *printer(void *arg)
{
struct timespec ts;


ts.tv_sec = 1;
ts.tv_nsec = 0;

while (1) {
  printf("The value of count = %ld\n", count);
  nanosleep(&ts, NULL);
  }

return((void *)0);
}


void set_initial()
{
initial = (long) time(0);
}
```

To demonstrate the use of LockLint, we started by compiling the `11_exam.c` program (Code Example 8-1) with the `-Z11` flag (see Code Example 8-2). This flag instruments the program with information used by LockLint. Then we ran the program and began the analysis. Figure 8-7 shows the steps used in performing the analysis.

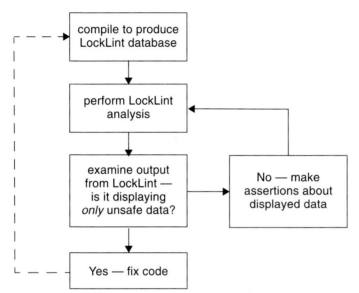

Figure 8-7   Steps in LockLint Usage

LockLint was then used to display the variables in the program that did not have locks consistently held on them while they were accessed (indicated by the empty braces in Code Example 8-2). This was done by using the vars subcommand in LockLint, which displays information about the variables used in the program. The asterisk next to the variable indicates that variable has been written to and that LockLint assumes it is unsafe.

Code Example 8-2   lock_lint Example of vars Subcommand

```
> cc -Zll ll_exam.c
> lock_lint start
> lock_lint load ll_exam
> lock_lint analyze
> lock_lint vars -h
:count      *held={ }
:initial    *held={ }
```

The *initial* variable in the output in Code Example 8-2 does not *need* to be protected because the variable is only written to before any threads are created. Variables that aren't written to except when they're initialized don't need to be protected (see *Global Variables, Constants, and Cheating* on page 84). We can exclude some data from consideration by LockLint and then repeat the analysis. Doing so will enable us to find only the unprotected variables that interest us.

We can also tell LockLint to ignore certain functions in the program if we know that they are safe. In this case, we know that set_initial is safe via inspection of the code, Code Example 8-1. Code Example 8-3 shows how the function "ignores" can be specified.

Code Example 8-3   lock_lint Example, Specifying "ignores"

```
> lock_lint start
> lock_lint load ll_exam
> lock_lint ignore set_initial
> lock_lint analyze
> lock_lint vars -h
:count      *held={ }
:initial    held={ }
```

After making the function "ignores," we reran the variable analysis on the program. As shown in Code Example 8-3, the initial variable is now reported as safe. Now the only variable that is reported as being unsafe is the *count* variable. The example could easily be modified to include a lock around the *count* variable, which would make it safe.

You can see how useful LockLint can be in determining if your program is using locks in a consistent manner and determining the variables that are left unprotected. All the commands that we issued to LockLint from the command line could just as well been put in a script file, which could then be called from your program's Makefile to perform LockLint analysis on every build of your program. We have shown only a very small subset of the commands that are available for LockLint. For more information, refer to the LockLint User's Guide.

Example Three: Parallelizing Loops with LoopTool

This example uses a routine from a popular math library, IMSL, to demonstrate how LoopTool can be used to identify time-consuming loops in application code.[1] The routine selected for this example, 12trg.f written in FORTRAN, computes an LU factorization of a single-precision general matrix.

We first compiled the FORTRAN program without any parallelization, and then we timed the execution of the program (see Figure 8-8).

```
$ f77 12trg.f -cg92 -O3 -limsl
$ /bin/time a.out
real      44.8
user      43.5
sys       1.0
```

Figure 8-8   Original Times for 12trg.f *(Not Parallelized)*

---

1. IMSL is a registered trademark of IMSL, Inc. This example used with permission.

We then recompiled the program with the $-Z1p$ option, which instruments the
executable for use with LoopTool. The program was run again to produce the
LoopTool information.

```
$ f77 l2trg.f -cg92 -O3 -Zlp -limsl
```

LoopTool was then started and the `l2trg.f` program was loaded. Figure 8-9
shows the display of the `l2trg.f` program.

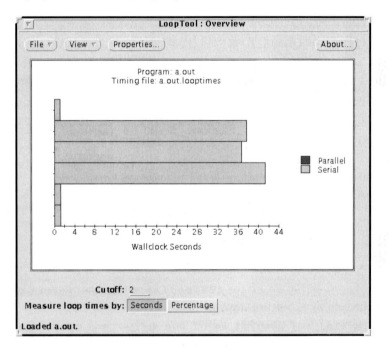

Figure 8-9   LoopTool View Before Parallelization

Each loop in the program is represented by a horizontal bar indicating the
amount of time the loop has consumed. Moving the cursor over a bar displays the
line number of the loop, and clicking on the bar brings up a window that displays
the loop's source code (see Figure 8-10).

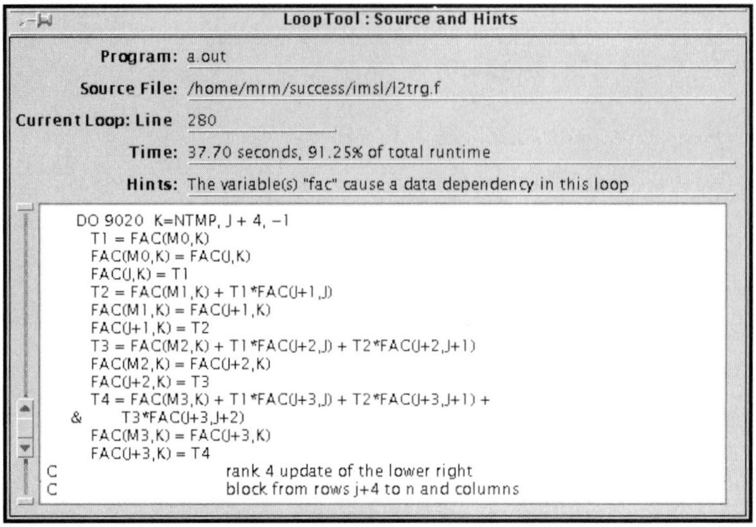

```
 .-|u|                          LoopTool : Source and Hints

           Program: a.out
                                                                          
       Source File: /home/mrm/success/imsl/l2trg.f

 Current Loop: Line  280

              Time: 37.70 seconds, 91.25% of total runtime

             Hints: The variable(s) "fac" cause a data dependency in this loop
 ┌──┐
 │  │    DO 9020 K=NTMP, J + 4, -1
 │  │      T1 = FAC(M0,K)
 │  │      FAC(M0,K) = FAC(J,K)
 │  │      FAC(J,K) = T1
 │  │      T2 = FAC(M1,K) + T1*FAC(J+1,J)
 │  │      FAC(M1,K) = FAC(J+1,K)
 │  │      FAC(J+1,K) = T2
 │  │      T3 = FAC(M2,K) + T1*FAC(J+2,J) + T2*FAC(J+2,J+1)
 │  │      FAC(M2,K) = FAC(J+2,K)
 │  │      FAC(J+2,K) = T3
 │  │      T4 = FAC(M3,K) + T1*FAC(J+3,J) + T2*FAC(J+3,J+1) +
 │  │    &     T3*FAC(J+3,J+2)
 │  │      FAC(M3,K) = FAC(J+3,K)
 │  │      FAC(J+3,K) = T4
 │  │  C                        rank 4 update of the lower right
 │  │  C                        block from rows j+4 to n and columns
 └──┘
```

Figure 8-10   LoopTool Hint About Parallelization

The loop consuming the most time was selected and the source was displayed. Along with the source, hints are given about the selected loop. In this case, LoopTool gave the message

```
The variable "fac" causes a data dependency in this loop
```

After performing some analysis, we determined that the loop could be parallelized. The loop did not contain any dependencies on previous loop calculations, so the loop is safe for the parallelization.

We inserted the MP/FORTRAN directive, C$PAR DOALL before the target loop in the code. This directive tells the MP/FORTRAN compiler to divide the loop into multiple threads of execution, thus enabling parallelization.

The program was then compiled with the -explicitpar option, which instructs the compiler to parallelize only the loops prefaced with the C$PAR DOALL directive. We also made sure the PARALLEL environment variable was set to the number of processors on which we want to run the program. Then, we executed the program to see if it executed any faster. Figure 8-11 shows the results.

```
$ setenv PARALLEL 2                  (2 is the # of processors on the machine)
$ f77 l2trg.f -cg92 -O3 -explicitpar -imsl
$ /bin/time a.out
real      28.4
user      53.8
sys        1.1
```

Figure 8-11   Post-Parallelization Times for l2trg.f

The program now runs over a third faster than the original execution time (see Figure 8-8). The higher number for the `user` time reflects the fact that the program is now running on two processors.

We can verify the results by reloading the `l2trg.f` program into LoopTool. As shown in Figure 8-12, the loop is displayed as being parallelized.

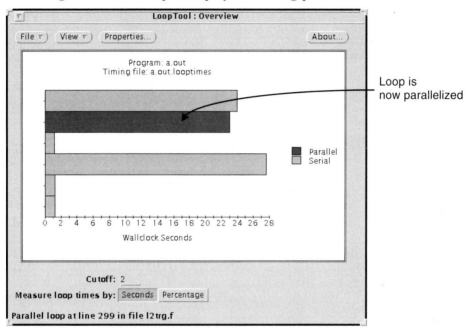

Figure 8-12   LoopTool View After Parallelization

Example Four: Using the SPARCworks Debugger

The SPARCworks Debugger is an excellent tool for debugging multithreaded programs. The problem with most debuggers is that they are not thread aware. This means that they cannot recognize threads of execution within a process. The SPARCworks Debugger is thread aware and provides all the same debugger capabilities that are available for nonthreaded programs.

SPARCworks Debugger is based on the standard UNIX `dbx` debugger. If you are familiar with `dbx`, then you should have no problems using SPARCworks Debugger. SunSoft expanded on the standard `dbx` commands to provide some of the thread capabilities in the debugger. For more information about these additional `dbx` commands see Appendix F, *Compile and Debug Specifics* or the SPARCworks User Manual.

This example uses SPARCworks Debugger to take a look at an example that basically creates and joins some threads. Take a minute and familiarize yourself with the example; it's described in *Using thr_create() and thr_join()* on page 147.

We started by loading the program into the SPARCworks Debugger and then setting a breakpoint at the start of the program. Then, we executed the program and displayed the process inspector and the stack inspector, which provide information about the individual threads and their related stacks, respectively (see Figure 8-13).

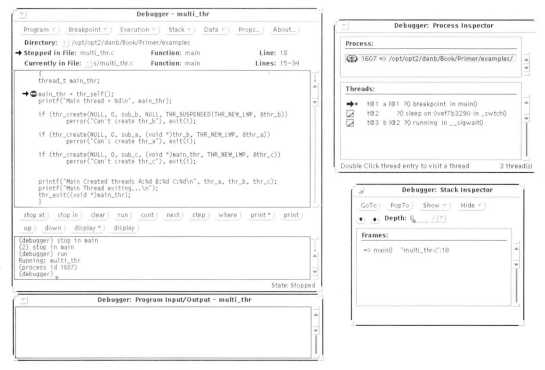

Figure 8-13   SPARCworks Debugger (Program Stopped at main*)*

Notice that the program is stopped at the first executable line of the program, but the process inspector shows that three threads are active in the process. How can that be? The program has not yet reached the `thr_create()` calls in the `main()` thread. Thread IDs 2 and 3 (`t@2`, `t@3`) are always created by the process when it starts. These threads perform certain tasks that we need not account for here; they are essentially managed by the operating system and have no effect on your programs.

It is also important to notice that the `main()` thread is always thread ID 1 (`t@1`). You can see from the process inspector window that the main thread is stopped at a breakpoint in `main()`.

Next, we set a breakpoint at the first print statement after the `thr_create()` calls in the main routine. Then, we instructed the debugger to continue the program. A number of things happened as the program continued. First, the main routine began its execution by creating three more threads. You can see that the threads were created by looking at the process inspector window (see Figure 8-14).

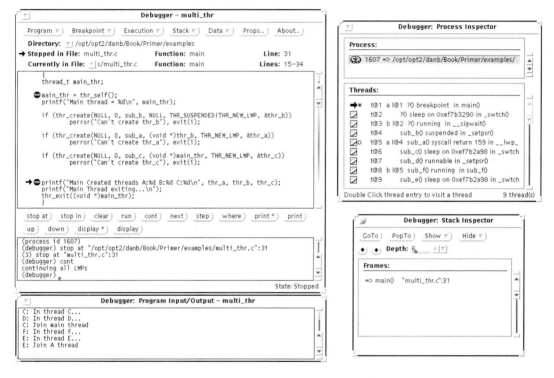

Figure 8-14   SPARCworks Debugger (Program Stopped at Breakpoint)

Notice that six more threads were created. This occurred because the main thread created three threads and those threads also created other threads. When the main thread reaches the breakpoint at the `print` statement, it stops the execution of all the threads. Unlike the debugging of a forked process when one thread in a program hits a breakpoint, all the threads halt their execution.

Another point to note in the process inspector window is the information listed with each thread. For example, thread 8 was running in the `sub_f()` routine when it was halted. Also note the `b` and the `1@5` next to the thread ID. They inform us that the thread is bound on LWP 5. The letter `a` next to some of the other threads indicates that those threads are active.

The process inspector can also be used to switch the debugger between the threads. This can be done by clicking on the thread in the process inspector window. We selected thread 8 (see Figure 8-15).

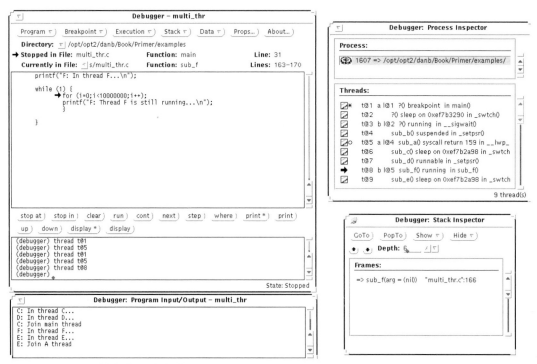

Figure 8-15   SPARCworks Debugger (Switching Between Threads)

Notice that when a thread is selected, the debugger changes the source displayed in the main debugger window. The code displayed is the code that the selected thread was executing when it was halted. Also notice that the stack inspector changed its display to match the selected threads stack.

The ability to switch the context of the debugger between the threads in a program can be of great help when you are debugging multithreaded programs. We have shown only some of the capabilities of SPARCworks Debugger, but enough, we hope, to show you that a thread-aware debugger is crucial in the development of multithreaded programs.

For More Information

You can find out more about Solaris threads and related issues on the World Wide Web (see Appendix C, *Threads on the Net*).

Also, the following manuals may be of interest:

SPARCworks Debugging a Program p/n 801-7105-12

LockLint User's Guide p/n 801-6692-10

LoopTool User's Guide p/n 801-6693-10

Thread Analyzer User's Guide p/n 801-6691-10

8

Threads Primer

Programming With Threads 9

In which some pointers on programming with threads are given.
Differences between single-threaded thinking and multithreaded
thinking are emphasized.

Historically, most code has been designed for single-threaded programs. This is
especially true for most of the library routines called from C programs. The
following implicit assumptions were made for single-threaded code:

- When you write into a global variable and then, a moment later, read from
  it, what you read is exactly what you just wrote.

- This is also true for nonglobal, static storage.

- You do not need synchronization because there is nothing to synchronize
  with.

The next few examples discuss some of the problems that arise in multithreaded
programs because of these assumptions, and how you can deal with them.

Global Variables (`errno`)

Traditional, single-threaded C and UNIX have a convention for handling errors
detected in system calls. System calls can return anything as a functional value
(for example, `write()` returns the number of bytes that were transferred).
However, the value -1 is reserved to indicate that something went wrong. So,
when a system call returns -1, you know that it failed.

Rather than return the actual error code (which could be confused with normal
return values), the error code is placed into the global variable `errno`. When the
system call fails, you can look in `errno` to find what went wrong.

Now consider what happens in a multithreaded environment when two threads
fail at about the same time, but with different errors. Both expect to find their
error codes in `errno`, but one copy of `errno` cannot hold both values. This global
variable approach simply does not work for multithreaded programs.

137

Both the Solaris threads package and POSIX solve this problem through a conceptually new storage class—thread-specific data. This storage is similar to global storage in that it can be accessed from any procedure in which a thread might be running. However, it is private to the thread—when two threads refer to the thread-specific data location of the same name, they are referring to two different areas of storage.

So, when threads are used, each reference to `errno` is thread specific because each thread has a private copy of `errno`.

Static Local Variables

Another problem, similar to the `errno` problem, is with static variables. This is a common problem with the getXbyY calls in Solaris. For example, the `gethostbyname()` call uses a static data structure to store the results of the call.

Returning a pointer to an automatic local variable is generally not a good idea, although it works in this case because the variable is static. However, when two threads call `gethostbyname()` at once with different computer names, the use of static storage conflicts. Since the data is static in the library call, one thread could store some information in the static structure while another thread is reading the data that it should have written to the data structure. This is why libraries need to be made thread safe.

The following example shows how a problem can arise if static data is not protected properly in threaded programs. Try running this program versus a similar program that does not use threads. Also, see if you can fix the static variable problem by using synchronization variables.

Code Example 9-1   Using Static Data (static.c)

```
#include <stdio.h>
#include <thread.h>

/* thread prototype */
void *thread();

/* global variable */
int num=2;

main()
{
int i;
```

Code Example 9-1   Using Static Data (static.c) (Continued)

```
/* set the level of concurrency we want */
thr_setconcurrency(5);

/* create 20 threads that execute the thread() routine */
for (i=0;i<20;i++) {
    thr_create(NULL, 0, thread, NULL, 0, NULL);
    }

/* wait for all the threads to finish */
for (i=0;i<20;i++) {
    thr_join(0,0,0);
    }
}

void *thread()
{
    /* call the add_to_num routine with a global variable */
    num = add_to_num(num);
    printf("The number is = %d\n", num);
}

/* this routine is called from the threads */
int add_to_num(int in)
{
/* note that the value variable is static */
static int value;

/* add in to the current value  */
value += in;

/* return the new value */
return(value);
}
```

The example uses the add_to_num() function, which just as well could have been a library function. The add_to_num() function uses local static data. The threads in the example do not know that the data in the function is static, so the programmer must ensure that the function is safe from calls from multiple threads.

Thread-specific data could be used on a replacement for static storage, as in the errno problem, but this involves dynamic allocation of storage and adds to the expense of the call. A better way to handle this kind of problem is to make the caller of gethostbyname() supply the storage for the result of the call. This is done by having the caller supply an additional argument, an output argument, to the routine. This requires a new interface to gethostbyname().

This technique is used in Solaris threads to fix many of these problems. In most cases, the name of the new interface is the old name with _r appended, as in gethostbyname_r(3N). The _r in this case represents the reentrant function.

Synchronizing Threads

The threads in an application must cooperate and synchronize when sharing the data and the resources of the process. A problem can arise when multiple threads call a function that manipulate a common object. Care must be taken to be sure that the threads don't affect each other in an adverse way.

Single-Lock Strategy

One strategy is to have a single, application-wide mutex lock that is acquired whenever any thread in the application is running and that is released before it must block. Since only one thread can be accessing shared data at any one time, each thread has a consistent view of memory.

Because this is effectively a single-threaded program, very little is gained by this strategy.

Reentrance

A better approach is to take advantage of the principles of modularity and data encapsulation. A reentrant function is one that behaves correctly if it is called simultaneously by several threads. Writing a reentrant function is a matter of understanding just what "behaves correctly" means for this particular function.

Functions that are callable by several threads must be made reentrant. This might require changes to the function interface or to the implementation.

Functions that access global state, like memory or files, have reentrance problems. These functions need to protect their use of global state with the appropriate synchronization mechanisms provided by threads library.

The two basic strategies for making functions in modules reentrant are code locking and data locking.

Code Locking

Code locking is done at the function call level and guarantees that a function executes entirely under the protection of a lock. The assumption is that all access to data is done through functions. Functions that share data should execute under the same lock.

Functions that are under the protection of the same mutex lock are guaranteed to execute atomically with respect to each other.

Data Locking

Data locking guarantees that access to a *collection* of data is maintained consistently. For data locking, the concept of locking code is still there, but code locking is around references only to shared (global) data. For a mutual-exclusion locking protocol, only one thread can be in the critical section for each collection of data.

Alternatively, in a multiple-readers, single-writer protocol, several readers can be allowed for each collection of data or one writer. Multiple threads can execute in a single module when they operate on different data collections and do not conflict on a single collection for the multiple-readers, single-writer protocol. So, data locking typically allows more concurrency than does code locking.

What strategy should you use when using locks (whether implemented with mutexes, condition variables, or semaphores) in a program? Should you try to achieve maximum parallelism by locking only when necessary and unlocking as soon as possible (*fine-grained locking*)? Or should you hold locks for long periods to minimize the overhead of taking and releasing them (*coarse-grained locking*)?

The granularity of the lock depends on the amount of data it protects. A very coarse-grained lock might be a single lock to protect all data. Dividing how the data is protected by the appropriate number of locks is very important. Too fine a granularity of locking can degrade performance. The small cost associated with acquiring and releasing locks can add up when there are too many locks.

The common wisdom is to start with a coarse-grained approach, identify bottlenecks, and add finer-grained locking where necessary to alleviate the bottlenecks. This is reasonably sound advice, but use your own judgment about taking it to the extreme.

Avoiding Deadlock

Deadlock is a permanent blocking of a set of threads that are competing for a set of resources. Just because some thread can make progress does not mean that there is not a deadlock somewhere else.

The most common error causing deadlock is *self-deadlock* or *recursive deadlock*: A thread tries to acquire a lock it is already holding. Recursive deadlock is very easy to program by mistake.

For example, if a function locks a mutex variable at the start of the function and then calls some code outside the function which, through some circuitous path, calls back into the function protected by the same mutex lock, then that function will deadlock.

The solution for this kind of deadlock is to avoid calling functions outside the module when you don't know whether they will call back into the module without reestablishing invariants and dropping all module locks before making the call. Of course, after the call completes and the locks are reacquired, the state must be verified to be sure the intended operation is still valid.

An example of another kind of deadlock is shown in Figure 9-1, in which two threads, thread 1 and thread 2, each acquire a mutex lock, A and B, respectively. Suppose that thread 1 tries to acquire mutex lock B and thread 2 tries to acquire mutex lock A. Thread 1 cannot proceed and it is blocked, waiting for mutex lock B. Thread 2 cannot proceed and it is blocked, waiting for mutex lock A. Nothing can change, so this is a permanent blocking of the threads, and a deadlock.

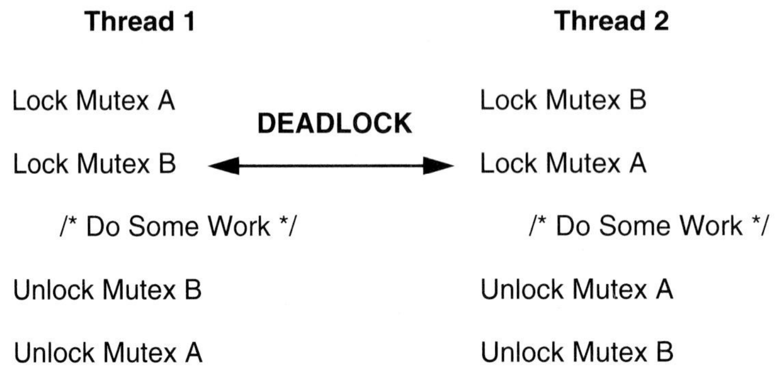

Thread 1		**Thread 2**
Lock Mutex A	**DEADLOCK**	Lock Mutex B
Lock Mutex B	◄————————►	Lock Mutex A
/* Do Some Work */		/* Do Some Work */
Unlock Mutex B		Unlock Mutex A
Unlock Mutex A		Unlock Mutex B

Figure 9-1   Out-of-Order Mutex Deadlock

This kind of deadlock is avoided by establishing an order in which locks are acquired (a *lock hierarchy*). When all threads always acquire locks in the specified order, this deadlock is avoided. LockLint can be used to aid in finding these type of locking problems. For more information about LockLint, see Chapter 8, *Programming Tools*.

Adhering to a strict order of lock acquisition is not always optimal. For example, thread 2 has many assumptions about the state of the module while holding mutex lock B; giving up mutex lock B to acquire mutex lock A and then reacquiring mutex lock B in order would cause it to discard its assumptions and reevaluate the state of the module.

The blocking synchronization primitives all have variants that attempt to get a lock and fail if they cannot, such as `mutex_trylock()`. This allows threads to violate the lock hierarchy when there is no contention. When there is contention, the held locks must usually be discarded and the locks reacquired in order.

Scheduling Problems

Because there is no guaranteed order in which locks are acquired, a common problem in threaded programs is that a particular thread never acquires a lock, even though it seems it should. This usually happens when the thread that holds the lock releases it, lets a small amount of time pass, and then reacquires it. Because the lock was released, it might seem that the other thread should acquire the lock. But, because nothing blocks the thread holding the lock, it continues to run from the time it releases the lock until it reacquires the lock, and so no other thread is run.

The threads library does not provide any time-slice mechanism for scheduling threads. If a single thread is running on a LWP and does not block or use any libthread calls, the thread can run indefinitely. You can usually solve this type of problem by calling `thr_yield(3T)` just before the call to reacquire the lock. This solution allows other threads to run and to acquire the lock.

Locking Guidelines

Here are some simple guidelines for locking.

- Try not to hold locks across long operations like I/O where performance can be adversely affected.

- Don't hold locks when calling a function that is outside the module and that might reenter the module.

- Don't try for excessive processor concurrency. Without intervening system calls or I/O operation, locks are usually held for short amounts of time and contention is rare. Fix only those locks that have measured contention.

- When using multiple locks, avoid deadlocks by making sure that all threads acquire the locks in the same order.

☰ 9

Following Some Basic Guidelines

- Know what you are importing and whether it is safe. A threaded program cannot arbitrarily enter nonthreaded code.

- Threaded code can safely refer to unsafe code only from the initial thread. This practice ensures that the static storage associated with the initial thread is used only by that thread.

- Sun-supplied libraries are defined to be *safe* unless explicitly documented as unsafe. If a reference manual entry does not say whether a function is MT safe, it is safe. All MT-unsafe functions are identified explicitly in the manual page.

- Use compilation flags to manage reentrant source changes. Either specify `-D_REENTRANT` when compiling or be sure that `_REENTRANT` is defined before any header file is included.

- When making a library safe for multithreaded use, do not thread global process operations.

  Do not change global operations (or actions with global side effects) to behave in a threaded manner. For example, if file I/O is controlled at a global level, then threads in the process should not try to manipulate file I/O because the order of the file operations is not guaranteed.

  For thread-specific behavior or *thread-aware* behavior, use thread facilities. For example, when the termination of `main()` should terminate only the thread that is exiting `main()`, the end of `main()` should be:
  ```
  thr_exit();
  /*NOTREACHED*/
  ```

Creating Threads

The Solaris threads package caches the threads data structure, stacks, and LWPs so that the repetitive creation of unbound threads can be inexpensive. Unbound thread creation is very inexpensive when compared to process creation or even to bound thread creation. In fact, the cost is similar to unbound thread synchronization when you include the context switches to stop one thread and start another.

So, creating and destroying threads as they are required is usually better than attempting to manage a pool of threads that wait for independent work. A good example is an RPC server that creates a thread for each request and destroys it when the reply is delivered, instead of trying to maintain a pool of threads to service requests.

While thread creation is relatively inexpensive when compared to process creation, it is not inexpensive when compared to the cost of a few instructions. Create threads for processing that lasts long enough to minimize the overhead of the thread creation.

Thread Concurrency

By default, Solaris threads attempts to adjust the system execution resources (LWPs) used to run unbound threads to match the real number of active threads. While the Solaris threads package cannot make perfect decisions, it at least ensures that the process continues to make progress.

When you have some idea of the number of unbound threads that should be simultaneously active (executing code or system calls), tell the library through `thr_setconcurrency(3T)`.

For example:

- A database server that has a thread for each user should tell Solaris threads the expected number of simultaneously active users.

- A window server that has one thread for each client should tell Solaris threads the expected number of simultaneously active clients.

- A file copy program that has one reader thread and one writer thread should tell Solaris threads that the desired concurrency level is 2.

Alternatively, the concurrency level can be incremented by 1 through the `THR_NEW_LWP` flag as each thread is created.

Include unbound threads blocked on interprocess (`USYNC_PROCESS`) synchronization variables as active when you compute thread concurrency. Exclude bound threads—they do not require concurrency support from Solaris threads because they are equivalent to LWPs.

Bound Threads

Bound threads are more expensive to create and schedule than unbound threads. Because bound threads are attached to their own LWP, the operating system provides a new LWP when a bound thread is created and destroys it when the bound thread exits.

Use bound threads only when a thread needs resources that are available only through the underlying LWP, such as when the thread must be visible to the kernel to be scheduled with respect to all other active threads in the system, as in real-time scheduling.

9

Threads Primer

Examples

> In which several example programs are presented, and their details and issues surrounding the way they use threads are discussed.

This chapter contains several examples that use the Solaris threads library and, in some cases, the POSIX threads library. Each example uses threads to demonstrate different concepts from previous chapters. Some of the examples may seem trivial, but keep in mind that these examples were created for demonstrating the basic concepts of threaded programming. All the example code has been compiled and run on the Solaris 2.4 operating system. Some of the examples may seem to have quite a bit of source code; this is intentional, because we believe that you should be able to run examples, not just look at them.

Please use this code in whatever manner you choose; many of the concepts demonstrated in the examples can be reworked to be used in your applications. All the source code used in this book is available on the SunSoft Press WWW server. (See *Threads on the World Wide Web* on page 205.)

Using `thr_create()` and `thr_join()`

This example exercises the `thr_create()` and `thr_join()` calls. There is not a parent/child relationship between threads as there is for processes. This can easily be seen in this example, because threads are created and joined by many different threads in the process. The example also shows how threads behave when created with different attributes and options.

Figure 10-1 illustrates the flow of execution for this example. Use the diagram in conjunction with the code sections to see how this example comes together. As you can see from diagram, threads can be created by any thread and joined by any other.

147

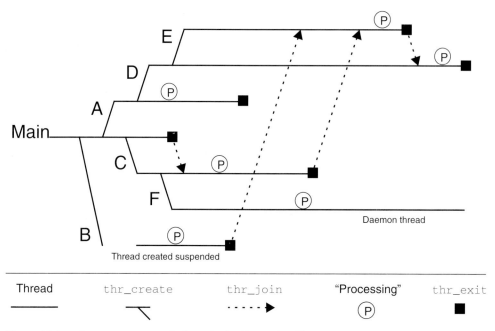

Figure 10-1 `thr_create` *and* `thr_join` *Execution Flow*

The main thread: In this example the main thread's sole purpose is to create new threads. Threads A, B, and C are created by the main thread. Notice that thread B is created suspended. After creating the new threads, the main thread exits. Also notice that the main thread exited by calling `thr_exit()`. If the main thread had used the `exit()` call, the whole process would have exited. The main thread's exit status and resources are held until it is joined by thread C.

Code Example 10-1   Thread Create/Join Example [main thread]

```
#define _REENTRANT
#include <stdio.h>
#include <thread.h>

/* Function prototypes for thread routines */
void *sub_a(void *);
void *sub_b(void *);
void *sub_c(void *);
void *sub_d(void *);
void *sub_e(void *);
void *sub_f(void *);
```

Code Example 10-1   Thread Create/Join Example [main thread] (Continued)

```
thread_t thr_a, thr_b, thr_c;

void main()
{
thread_t main_thr;

main_thr = thr_self();
printf("Main thread = %d\n", main_thr);

if (thr_create(NULL, 0, sub_b, NULL, THR_SUSPENDED|THR_NEW_LWP,
&thr_b))
    fprintf(stderr,"Can't create thr_b\n"), exit(1);

if (thr_create(NULL, 0, sub_a, (void *)thr_b, THR_NEW_LWP, &thr_a))
    fprintf(stderr,"Can't create thr_a\n"), exit(1);

if (thr_create(NULL, 0, sub_c, (void *)main_thr, THR_NEW_LWP,
&thr_c))
    fprintf(stderr,"Can't create thr_c\n"), exit(1);


printf("Main Created threads A:%d B:%d C:%d\n", thr_a, thr_b,
thr_c);
printf("Main Thread exiting...\n");
thr_exit((void *)main_thr);
}
```

Thread A: The first thing thread A does after it is created is to create thread D. Thread A then simulates some processing and then exits, using `thr_exit()`. Notice that thread A was created with the `THR_DETACHED` flag, so thread A's resources will be immediately reclaimed upon its exit. There is no way for thread A's exit status to be collected by a `thr_join()` call.

Code Example 10-2   Thread Create/Join Example [thread A]

```
void *sub_a(void *arg)
{
thread_t thr_b = (thread_t) arg;
thread_t thr_d;
int i;

printf("A: In thread A...\n");
if (thr_create(NULL, 0, sub_d, (void *)thr_b, THR_NEW_LWP, &thr_d))
    fprintf(stderr, "Can't create thr_d\n"), exit(1);
```

Code Example 10-2   Thread Create/Join Example [thread A] (Continued)

```
printf("A: Created thread D:%d\n", thr_d);

/* process
*/
for (i=0;i<1000000*(int)thr_self();i++);

printf("A: Thread exiting...\n");
thr_exit((void *)77);
}
```

Thread B: Thread B was created in a suspended state, so it is not able to run until thread D continues it by making the `thr_continue()` call. After thread B is continued, it simulates some processing and then exits. Thread B's exit status and thread resources are held until joined by thread E.

Code Example 10-3   Thread Create/Join Example [thread B]

```
void * sub_b(void *arg)
{
int i;
printf("B: In thread B...\n");

/* process
*/
for (i=0;i<1000000*(int)thr_self();i++);
printf("B: Thread exiting...\n");
thr_exit((void *)66);
}
```

Thread C: The first thing that thread C does is to create thread F. Thread C then joins the main thread. This action will collect the main thread's exit status and allow the main thread's resources to be reused by another thread. Thread C will block, waiting for the main thread to exit, if the main thread has not yet called `thr_exit()`. After joining the main thread, thread C will simulate some processing and then exit. Again, the exit status and thread resources are held until joined by thread E.

Code Example 10-4   Thread Create/Join Example [thread C]

```
void * sub_c(void *arg)
{
void *status;
int i;
```

Code Example 10-4   Thread Create/Join Example [thread C] (Continued)

```
thread_t main_thr, ret_thr;

main_thr = (thread_t)arg;

printf("C: In thread C...\n");

if (thr_create(NULL, 0, sub_f, (void *)0, THR_BOUND|THR_DAEMON,
NULL))
    fprintf(stderr, "Can't create thr_f\n"), exit(1);

printf("C: Join main thread\n");
if (thr_join(main_thr,(thread_t *)&ret_thr, &status))
    fprintf(stderr, "thr_join Error\n"), exit(1);

printf("C: Main thread (%d) returned thread (%d) w/status %d\n",
main_thr, ret_thr, (int) status);

/* process
*/
for (i=0;i<1000000*(int)thr_self();i++);

printf("C: Thread exiting...\n");
thr_exit((void *)88);
}
```

Thread D: Thread D immediately creates thread E. After creating thread E, thread D continues thread B by making the `thr_continue()` call. This call will allow thread B to start its execution. Thread D then tries to join thread E, blocking until thread E has exited. Thread D then simulates some processing and exits. If all went well, thread D should be the last nondaemon thread running. When thread D exits, it should do two things: Stop the execution of any daemon threads and stop the execution of the process.

Code Example 10-5   Thread Create/Join Example [thread D]

```
void * sub_d(void *arg)
{
thread_t thr_b = (thread_t) arg;
int i;
thread_t thr_e, ret_thr;
void *status;

printf("D: In thread D...\n");
if (thr_create(NULL, 0, sub_e, NULL, THR_NEW_LWP, &thr_e))
```

Code Example 10-5   Thread Create/Join Example [thread D] (Continued)

```
        fprintf(stderr,"Can't create thr_e\n"), exit(1);

    printf("D: Created thread E:%d\n", thr_e);


    printf("D: Continue B thread = %d\n", thr_b);
    thr_continue(thr_b);

    printf("D: Join E thread\n");
    if(thr_join(thr_e,(thread_t *)&ret_thr, &status))
        fprintf(stderr,"thr_join Error\n"), exit(1);
    printf("D: E thread(%d) returned thread(%d) w/status %d\n", thr_e,
    ret_thr, (int) status);

    /* process
    */
    for (i=0;i<1000000*(int)thr_self();i++);
    printf("D: Thread exiting...\n");
    thr_exit((void *)55);
    }
```

Thread E: Thread E starts by joining two threads, threads B and C. Thread E will block, waiting for each of these thread to exit. Thread E will then simulate some processing and will exit. Thread E's exit status and thread resources are held by the operating system until joined by thread D.

Code Example 10-6   Thread Create/Join Example [thread E]

```
void * sub_e(void *arg)
{
int i;
thread_t ret_thr;
void *status;

printf("E: In thread E...\n");

printf("E: Join A thread\n");
if(thr_join(thr_a,(thread_t *)&ret_thr, &status))
    fprintf(stderr,"thr_join Error\n"), exit(1);
printf("E:A thread(%d) returned thread(%d) w/status %d\n", ret_thr,
ret_thr, (int) status);

printf("E: Join B thread\n");
if(thr_join(thr_b,(thread_t *)&ret_thr, &status))
```

Code Example 10-6   Thread Create/Join Example [thread E] (Continued)

```
     fprintf(stderr,"thr_join Error\n"), exit(1);
printf("E: B thread (%d) returned thread (%d) w/status %d\n", thr_b,
ret_thr, (int) status);

printf("E: Join C thread\n");
if(thr_join(thr_c,(thread_t *)&ret_thr, &status))
     fprintf(stderr,"thr_join Error\n"), exit(1);
printf("E: C thread (%d) returned thread (%d) w/status %d\n", thr_c,
ret_thr, (int) status);

/*
*/
for (i=0;i<1000000*(int)thr_self();i++);
printf("E: Thread exiting...\n");
thr_exit((void *)44);
}
```

Thread F: Thread F was created as a bound, daemon thread by using the
`THR_BOUND` and `THR_DAEMON` flags in the `thr_create()` call. This means that it
will run on its own LWP until all the nondaemon threads have exited the process.
This type of thread can be used when you want some type of "background"
processing to always be running, except when all the "regular" threads have
exited the process. If thread F was created as a nondaemon thread, then it would
continue to run forever, because a process will continue while there is at least one
thread still running. Thread F will exit when all the nondaemon threads have
exited. In this case, thread D should be the last nondaemon thread running, so
when thread D exits, it will also cause thread F to exit.

Code Example 10-7   Thread Create/Join Example [thread F]

```
void *sub_f(void *arg)
{
int i;

printf("F: In thread F...\n");

while (1) {
    for (i=0;i<10000000;i++);
    printf("F: Thread F is still running...\n");
    }
}
```

This example, however trivial, shows how threads behave differently, based on their creation options. It also shows what happens on the exit of a thread, again based on how it was created. If you understand this example and how it flows, you should have a good understanding of how to use `thr_create()` and `thr_join()` in your own programs. Hopefully, you can also see how easy it is to create and join threads.

Producer / Consumer

This example will show how condition variables can be used to control access of reads and writes to a buffer. This example can also be thought as a producer/consumer problem, where the producer adds items to the buffer and the consumer removes items from the buffer.

Two condition variables control access to the buffer. One condition variable is used to tell if the buffer is full, and the other is used to tell if the buffer is empty. When the producer wants to add an item to the buffer, it checks to see if the buffer is full; if it is full, then the producer blocks on the `cond_wait()` call, waiting for an item to be removed from the buffer. When the consumer removes an item from the buffer, the buffer is no longer full, so the producer is awakened from the `cond_wait()` call. The producer is then allowed to add another item to the buffer.

The consumer works, in many ways, the same as the producer. The consumer uses the other condition variable to determine if the buffer is empty. When the consumer wants to remove an item from the buffer, it checks to see if it is empty. If the buffer is empty, the consumer then blocks on the `cond_wait()` call, waiting for an item to be added to the buffer. When the producer adds an item to the buffer, the consumer's condition is satisfied, so it can then remove an item from the buffer.

The example copies a file by reading data into a shared buffer (producer) and then writing data out to the new file (consumer). The `Buf` data structure is used to hold both the buffered data and the condition variables that control the flow of the data.

The main thread opens both files, initializes the `Buf` data structure, creates the consumer thread, and then assumes the role of the producer. The producer reads data from the input file, then places the data into an open buffer position. If no buffer positions are available, then the producer waits via the `cond_wait()` call. After the producer has read all the data from the input file, it closes the file and waits for (joins) the consumer thread.

The consumer thread reads from a shared buffer and then writes the data to the output file. If no buffers positions are available, then the consumer waits for the producer to fill a buffer position. After the consumer has read all the data, it closes the output file and exits.

If the input file and the output file were residing on different physical disks, then this example could execute the reads and writes in parallel. This parallelism would significantly increase the throughput of the example through the use of threads.

Code Example 10-8   Producer/Consumer Example

```
#define _REEENTRANT
#include <stdio.h>
#include <thread.h>
#include <fcntl.h>
#include <unistd.h>
#include <sys/stat.h>
#include <sys/types.h>
#include <sys/uio.h>

#define BUFSIZE 512
#define BUFCNT   4

/* this is the data structure that is used between the producer
   and consumer threads */
struct {
    char buffer[BUFCNT][BUFSIZE];
    int byteinbuf[BUFCNT];
    mutex_t buflock;
    mutex_t donelock;
    cond_t adddata;
    cond_t remdata;
    int nextadd, nextrem, occ, done;
} Buf;


/* function prototype */
void *consumer(void *);

main(int argc, char **argv)
{

int ifd, ofd;
thread_t cons_thr;
```

Code Example 10-8   Producer/Consumer Example (Continued)

```
/* check the command line arguments */
if (argc != 3)
    printf("Usage: %s <infile> <outfile>\n", argv[0]), exit(0);

/* open the input file for the producer to use */
if ((ifd = open(argv[1], O_RDONLY)) == -1)
    {
    fprintf(stderr, "Can't open file %s\n", argv[1]);
    exit(1);
    }

/* open the output file for the consumer to use */
if ((ofd = open(argv[2], O_WRONLY|O_CREAT, 0666)) == -1)
    {
    fprintf(stderr, "Can't open file %s\n", argv[2]);
    exit(1);
    }

/* zero the counters */
Buf.nextadd = Buf.nextrem = Buf.occ = Buf.done = 0;

/* set the thread concurrency to 2 so the producer and consumer can
   run concurrently */

thr_setconcurrency(2);

/* create the consumer thread */
thr_create(NULL, 0, consumer, (void *)ofd, NULL, &cons_thr);

/* the producer ! */
while (1) {

    /* lock the mutex */
    mutex_lock(&Buf.buflock);

    /* check to see if any buffers are empty */
    /* If not then wait for that condition to become true */
    while (Buf.occ == BUFCNT)
        cond_wait(&Buf.remdata, &Buf.buflock);

    /* read from the file and put data into a buffer */
    Buf.byteinbuf[Buf.nextadd] =
read(ifd,Buf.buffer[Buf.nextadd],BUFSIZE);
```

Code Example 10-8 Producer/Consumer Example (Continued)

```
    /* check to see if done reading */
    if (Buf.byteinbuf[Buf.nextadd] == 0) {
        /* lock the done lock */
        mutex_lock(&Buf.donelock);

        /* set the done flag and release the mutex lock */
        Buf.done = 1;
        mutex_unlock(&Buf.donelock);

        /* signal the consumer to start consuming */
        cond_signal(&Buf.adddata);

        /* release the buffer mutex */
        mutex_unlock(&Buf.buflock);

        /* leave the while loop */
        break;
        }

    /* set the next buffer to fill */
    Buf.nextadd = ++Buf.nextadd % BUFCNT;

    /* increment the number of buffers that are filled */
    Buf.occ++;

    /* signal the consumer to start consuming */
    cond_signal(&Buf.adddata);

    /* release the mutex */
    mutex_unlock(&Buf.buflock);
    }

close(ifd);

/* wait for the consumer to finish */
thr_join(cons_thr, 0, NULL);

/* exit the program */
return(0);
}


/* The consumer thread */
void *consumer(void *arg)
```

Code Example 10-8   Producer/Consumer Example (Continued)

```
{
int fd = (int) arg;

/* check to see if any buffers are filled or if the done flag is set */
while (1) {

    /* lock the mutex */
    mutex_lock(&Buf.buflock);

    if (!Buf.occ && Buf.done) {
        mutex_unlock(&Buf.buflock);
        break;
        }

    /* check to see if any buffers are filled */
    /* if not then wait for the condition to become true */
    while (Buf.occ == 0 && !Buf.done)
        cond_wait(&Buf.adddata, &Buf.buflock);

    /* write the data from the buffer to the file */
    write(fd, Buf.buffer[Buf.nextrem], Buf.byteinbuf[Buf.nextrem]);

    /* set the next buffer to write from */
    Buf.nextrem = ++Buf.nextrem % BUFCNT;

    /* decrement the number of buffers that are full */
    Buf.occ--;

    /* signal the producer that a buffer is empty */
    cond_signal(&Buf.remdata);

    /* release the mutex */
    mutex_unlock(&Buf.buflock);
    }

/* exit the thread */
thr_exit((void *)0);
}
```

Matrix Multiplication

The matrix multiplication example was written in C++ to show how an object-oriented program might be written to use threads. The concepts and ideas discussed thus far also apply to the C++ language. All the examples in this book could have just as well been written in C++ as in C.

This example simply performs a matrix multiplication, the multiplication of two simple N x N matrices. Essentially, the matrix multiplication performs many mathematical calculations that can be executed independently. This example executes the multiplication of the matrices in parallel by using multiple threads in the processes. The user is allowed to change the size of the matrix objects and the number of threads on which to execute the multiplication.

The example also places all the threaded code into a shared library. This way, all the threaded routines are hidden from the main program. Using this library concept also shows how programs can be changed to use threads without affecting all of the code. In this case, the main program could use a nonthreaded library as well as a threaded one.

This example is rather long, but it demonstrates many of the concepts that have been covered in previous chapters. The program falls into two main parts. The first part is the main thread, which creates the matrix objects and starts the matrix multiplication. The second part is the library code, which performs the multiplication on the matrix objects.

The main thread creates the matrix objects, based on user-supplied arguments. The main thread then calls the `MatMult()` routine, which starts the multiplication. A global data structure (thread control block) is used in the library by all the threads in the program. The data structure contains the synchronization variables and other data needed to control the worker threads. This data structure is filled before any threads are created, because the threads use this data during their execution.

The worker threads are created as bound daemon threads. They are bound threads because of the compute nature of the work they do. For all the worker threads to execute in parallel, the level of concurrency would have to be increased, or the threads could be created as bound threads. The threads are also daemon threads because the worker threads should die when the main thread has finished executing. Because this example is compute intensive, the worker threads are created only once; there is no need to recreate the threads for each matrix multiply. The worker threads will always wait for more work to do. If there is no work to be done, then they go to sleep, waiting on a condition variable.

Once there is work to be done, signaled from the main thread, the worker threads wake up and perform the matrix operations on the data specified in the control data structure. At the same time, the main thread waits for all the worker threads to signal that they have finished the work. When the worker threads have finished and have signaled the main thread, they start over again, waiting for more work to do.

This example may look complicated at first, but spend some time here and make sure you understand how this program works. Also, you may want to try running this program with different size matrices and a different number of threads. Here is an example of some test runs, run on a SPARCstation 10 with four 50 MHz SuperSPARC CPUs.

```
> Matrix 400 1
Matrix size: [400x400]
Number of worker threads: 1
Matrix multiplication time = 44.3368 seconds = 44336817000
                                                nanoseconds

(This defines the baseline for efficiency.)


> Matrix 400 2
Matrix size: [400x400]
Number of worker threads: 2
Matrix multiplication time = 22.1987 seconds = 22198718000
                                                nanoseconds

(99.9% efficiency)


> Matrix 400 3
Matrix size: [400x400]
Number of worker threads: 3
Matrix multiplication time = 14.8932 seconds = 14893245000
                                                nanoseconds

(99% efficiency)


> Matrix 400 4
Matrix size: [400x400]
Number of worker threads: 4
Matrix multiplication time = 11.6228 seconds = 11622836000
                                                nanoseconds

(99% efficiency)


> Matrix 400 6
Matrix size: [400x400]
Number of worker threads: 6
Matrix multiplication time = 13.1921 seconds = 13192145000
                                                nanoseconds

(75% efficiency)
```

Going from one thread to four threads reduced the time needed to perform the matrix multiplication. Also note that running with six threads did not cut the runtime down any more than four threads did, because the workstation had only four CPUs and the extra threads created a scheduling overhead.

Because the multiply routine uses a single global structure, it is not reentrant itself. For CPU-intensive problems such as this, that is not a major problem. Doing one multiply will completely saturate the machine, so there is nothing to be gained from running multiple versions of the multiply routine concurrently.

Code Example 10-9   Matrix Multiplication Example

```
// #define _REENTRANT
#include <iostream.h>
#include <iomanip.h>
#include <stdlib.h>
#include <thread.h>
#include "Matrix.h"


// Main program
main(int argc, char **argv)
{
int size;
int num_threads;
hrtime_t start, stop;

if (argc != 3) {
    cout << "Usage: " << argv[0] << " Matrix-size Threads" << endl;
    exit(0);
    }

// set the size of the matrix and total threads for this run
size = atoi(argv[1]);
num_threads = atoi(argv[2]);

SetMaxThreads(num_threads);

if (size < num_threads) {
    cerr << "The size of the matrix MUST be greater then number of
threads." << endl;
    exit(1);
    }

cout << "Matrix size: [" << size << "x" << size << "]" << endl;
cout << "Number of worker threads: " << num_threads << endl;
```

Code Example 10-9 Matrix Multiplication Example (Continued)

```
// Create the Matrix
Matrix a('A', size), b('B', size), c('C', size);

// fill A & B with data and clear C
a.fill(); b.fill(); c.clear();

// Start the timer
start = gethrtime();

// Do the matrix multiply
MatMult(a, b, c);

// Stop the timer
stop = gethrtime();

// Print the results -- Only if matrix size is small enough
cout << a << b << c;

// Print the run time
cout << "Matrix multiplication time = "
     << (double)(stop-start)/(double)1000000000
     << " seconds = " << stop-start << " nanoseconds" << endl;

}
```

Code Example 10-10 Matrix Multiplication Library

```
#define _REENTRANT
#include <iostream.h>
#include <iomanip.h>
#include <stdlib.h>
#include <thread.h>
#include "Matrix.h"


const true = 1;
const false = 0;

// Thread control block - used by all threads as global data
struct thr_cntl_block {
  mutex_t start_mutex;
  cond_t  start_cond;
  mutex_t stop_mutex;
```

Code Example 10-10 Matrix Multiplication Library (Continued)

```
   cond_t   stop_cond;

   Matrix *a, *b, *c;
   int work2do;
   int thrs_running;
   int total_threads;
   int queue;
} TCB;


//////////////////////////////////////////////////////////////////
//   Matrix Class Member Functions
//////////////////////////////////////////////////////////////////

// Matrix constructor
Matrix::Matrix(char id, int size)
{
matid = id;
matsize = size;
data = new double[matsize*matsize];
}

// Matrix destructor
Matrix::~Matrix()
{
matsize = 0;
matid = 0;
delete[] data;
}

// Fills a matrix object with random data
void Matrix::fill()
{
int i;

for (i=0;i<matsize*matsize;i++)
   data[i] = double(rand()/1000);
srand(rand());
}

// Sets all elements of the matrix to 0.0
void Matrix::clear()
{
int i;
```

Code Example 10-10 Matrix Multiplication Library (Continued)

```
for (i=0;i<matsize*matsize;i++)
    data[i] = .0;
}

// Prints a Matrix object (if it is small enough)
void Matrix::print(ostream &s) const
{
int i;

if (matsize < 9) {

    s << "Matrix: " << matid << endl;
    for (i=0;i<matsize*matsize;i++)
    {
        s << setiosflags(ios::fixed) << setprecision(1)
            << setw(8) << data[i] << " ";
    if ((i%matsize) == matsize-1) s << endl;
    }
    s << endl << endl;
    }
}

// Overloaded << operator - for ease of printing
ostream &operator<<(ostream &s, const Matrix &mat)
{
    mat.print(s);
    return(s);
}


// Sets the maximum number of threads to use
void SetMaxThreads(int num)
{
TCB.total_threads = num;
}



// The matrix multiply subroutine
MatMult(Matrix &a, Matrix &b, Matrix &c)
{
int static running = false;
int i;
```

Code Example 10-10 Matrix Multiplication Library (Continued)

```
// Only run this code once, if MatMult is called multiple times
// then there is no need to recreate the threads
if (!running)
    {
    // Initialize the synch stuff.
    mutex_init(&TCB.start_mutex, USYNC_THREAD, 0);
    mutex_init(&TCB.stop_mutex, USYNC_THREAD, 0);
    cond_init(&TCB.start_cond, USYNC_THREAD, 0);
    cond_init(&TCB.stop_cond, USYNC_THREAD, 0);

    // set global variables
    TCB.work2do = 0;
    TCB.thrs_running = 0;
    TCB.queue = 0;
    if (!TCB.total_threads) TCB.total_threads = 1;


    // Create the threads - Bound daemon threads
    for (i = 0; i < TCB.total_threads; i++)
    thr_create(NULL,0, MultWorker, NULL, THR_BOUND|THR_DAEMON,
NULL);

    // set the running flag to true so we don't execute this again
    running = true;
    }


// Assign global pointers to the Matrix objects
TCB.a = &a;
TCB.b = &b;
TCB.c = &c;

mutex_lock(&TCB.start_mutex);
  // Assign the number of threads and the amount of work to do
  TCB.work2do = TCB.total_threads;
  TCB.thrs_running = TCB.total_threads;
  TCB.queue = 0;
  // tell all the threads to wake up!
  cond_broadcast(&TCB.start_cond);
mutex_unlock(&TCB.start_mutex);

// yield this LWP
thr_yield();
```

Code Example 10-10 Matrix Multiplication Library (Continued)

```
// Wait for all the threads to finish
mutex_lock(&TCB.stop_mutex);
while (TCB.thrs_running)
    cond_wait(&TCB.stop_cond, &TCB.stop_mutex);
mutex_unlock(&TCB.stop_mutex);

return(0);
}



// Thread routine called from thr_create() as a Bound Daemon Thread
void *MultWorker(void *arg)
{
  int row, col, j, start, stop, id, size;

  // Do this loop forever - or until all the Non-Daemon threads have
exited
  while(true)
    {
      // Wait for some work to do
      mutex_lock(&TCB.start_mutex);
      while (!TCB.work2do)
    cond_wait(&TCB.start_cond, &TCB.start_mutex);
      // decrement the work to be done
      TCB.work2do--;
      // get a unique id for work to be done
      id = TCB.queue++;
      mutex_unlock(&TCB.start_mutex);

      // set up the boundary for matrix operation - based on the
unique id
      size = TCB.a->getsize();
      start = id * (int)(size/TCB.total_threads);
      stop = start + (int)(size/TCB.total_threads) - 1;
      if (id == TCB.total_threads - 1) stop = size - 1;

      // print what this thread will work on
      //cout << "Thread " << thr_self() << ": Start Row = " << start
      //      << ", Stop Row = " << stop << endl << flush;

      // Do the matrix multiply - within the bounds set above
      for (row=start; row<=stop; row++)
```

Code Example 10-10 Matrix Multiplication Library (Continued)

```
            for (col = 0; col < size; col++)
                for (j = 0; j < size; j++)
                TCB.c->getdata()[row*size+col] +=
                    TCB.a->getdata()[row*size+j] *
                    TCB.b->getdata()[j*size+col];

        // signal the main thread that this thread is done with the work
        mutex_lock(&TCB.stop_mutex);
        TCB.thrs_running--;
        cond_signal(&TCB.stop_cond);
        mutex_unlock(&TCB.stop_mutex);
    }

    return 0;
}
```

Code Example 10-11 Matrix Multiplication Header

```
#ifndef _matrix_h_
#define _matrix_h_



class Matrix
{
int matsize;
char matid;
double *data;

public:
Matrix(char id, int size);
virtual ~Matrix();

int getsize() {return(matsize);}
double *getdata() {return(data);}



void fill();
void clear();
void print(ostream &s) const;
};

// Function Prototypes
MatMult(Matrix &a, Matrix &b, Matrix &c);// Matrix Multiply
```

```
void *MultWorker(void *arg);// Matrix Thread Function
ostream &operator<<(ostream &s, const Matrix &mat);  // Overloaded
output
void SetMaxThreads(int num); // Sets the number of threads to use

#endif _matrix_h_
```

Threads and Windows

This example uses threads in conjunction with X11 and Motif®. Threads lend themselves quite well to window-based programs, because each widget or each window client in a program can be tied to a thread. Since threads are lightweight, many threads can be created to manage or execute the windows needs.

For example, in a "normal" windowing application, when a button is pressed, some task is executed and then control in the program is returned to the window. This is fine if the time required to execute the task is minimal. If the time required for the task is not minimal, then the window *freezes* or the clock icon is displayed while the task is executing. This behavior, in most cases, is not desirable, because the graphical interface should always be active for the user to select other actions.

This example demonstrates how we can get around the *freezing* problem. In the example a simple window is created and filled with push-button widgets. When a button is pushed, the program simulates some processing that would normally cause the interface to freeze. However, threads used in this example execute the work requested by each button press. That way, when a button is pressed, a thread is created to do the work, and the window can return to its event processing for the user.

When you run this example, you will see that when a button is pressed, it changes colors and is deactivated while the work is executed in the thread. However, you can press as many buttons as you like, one right after the other without waiting for the work to be completed.

This example uses a command-line argument that can enable or disable the threads in the process, so you can see how the program behaves with and without threads (see Figure 10-2).

```
> ThreadWin 100 MT
```

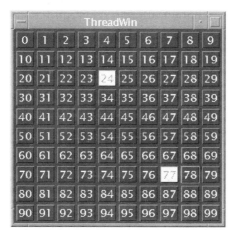

Figure 10-2   ThreadWin Example Execution

The X11 programming libraries will not be thread safe until release 6 (R6). This example was originally written for use on X11R6; however, it may run just fine on nonsafe X11 libraries. If you run this program and it fails, most likely you are not running a thread-safe X11 library. In that case, this example shows what you will be able to do with thread-safe window libraries.

Code Example 10-12 Example Using Threads and X11

```
#define _REENTRANT
#include <X11/Intrinsic.h>
#include <Xm/Xm.h>
#include <X11/X.h>
#include <X11/StringDefs.h>
#include <Xm/RowColumn.h>
#include <Xm/PushB.h>
#include <unistd.h>
#include <stdlib.h>
#include <math.h>
#include <thread.h>

/* function prototypes */
int ThrCB();
void *thr_sub(void *);

main(int argc, char **argv)
{
Widget toplevel, base, button[200];
Arg wargs[10];
```

Code Example 10-12 Example Using Threads and X11 (Continued)

```
int i, MT=0;
char but_label[5];

/* check arguments */
if (argc > 3 || argc < 2)
    printf("Usage: %s <number of buttons> [MT]\n", argv[0]), exit(0);

/* check multithreaded mode */
if (argc == 3 && strcmp(argv[2], "MT") == 0) MT = 1;

if (atoi(argv[1]) > 200)
    printf("Too many buttons...\n"), exit(1);


/* set up our main window */
toplevel = XtInitialize(argv[0], "ThreadWin", NULL, 0, &argc, argv);

/* set some arguments for our Row/Column Widget */
XtSetArg(wargs[0], XmNorientation, XmHORIZONTAL);
XtSetArg(wargs[1], XmNentryAlignment, XmALIGNMENT_CENTER);
XtSetArg(wargs[2], XmNisAligned, True);
XtSetArg(wargs[3], XmNnumColumns,
(int)floor(sqrt((double)atoi(argv[1]))));
XtSetArg(wargs[4], XmNpacking, XmPACK_COLUMN);

/* create the Row/Column Widget */
base=XtCreateManagedWidget("base", xmRowColumnWidgetClass,
toplevel, wargs, 5);


/* create the button widgets with the button number as its label */
for (i=0;i<atoi(argv[1]);i++) {
    sprintf(but_label, "%d", i);
    XtSetArg(wargs[0], XmNlabelString, XmStringCreate(but_label,
XmSTRING_DEFAULT_CHARSET));
    button[i] = XmCreatePushButton(base, "button", wargs, 1);

    /* tell the button to call the ThrCB() routine when pushed */
    XtAddCallback(button[i], XmNactivateCallback, ThrCB, MT);
    }

/* set the level of concurrency to the number of processors on-line */
thr_setconcurrency(sysconf(_SC_NPROCESSORS_ONLN)+1);
```

Code Example 10-12 Example Using Threads and X11 (Continued)

```
/* manage the buttons and go into the X event loop */
XtManageChildren(button, atoi(argv[1]));
XtRealizeWidget(toplevel);
XtMainLoop();

return(0);
}


/*
   Button callback routine -- Called when a button is pushed
*/

ThrCB(Widget w, int MT)
{

/* check to see if we should run multithreaded
   if so, create a thread that runs the thr_sub() routine
   if not, just call the thr_sub() routine   */

if (MT) thr_create(NULL, 0, thr_sub, (void *)w, THR_DETACHED,
NULL);
else thr_sub((void *)w);

return(0);
}


/*
   thr_sub() -- called from ThrCB() routine.  This is the
   routine that changes the button and simulates some work
*/

void *thr_sub(void *arg)
{

Widget w = (Widget) arg;
Pixel fg, bg;
XEvent event;
Arg warg[2];
int j;
Display *disp;
Window win;
```

Code Example 10-12 Example Using Threads and X11 (Continued)

```
/* grey out the button */
XtSetSensitive(w, False);

/* get the button's foreground and background colors */
XtSetArg(warg[0], XmNforeground, &fg);
XtSetArg(warg[1], XmNbackground, &bg);
XtGetValues(w, warg, 2);

/* swap the button's foreground and background colors */
XtSetArg(warg[0], XmNforeground, bg);
XtSetArg(warg[1], XmNbackground, fg);
XtSetValues(w, warg, 2);


/* force a pointer movement event to make the button changes
   visible */

disp = XtDisplay(w);
win = XtWindow(w);
event.xmotion.display = disp;
event.xmotion.window = win;
XSendEvent(disp, win, TRUE, PointerMotionMask, &event);
XFlush(disp);


/* simulate some processing */
for (j=0;j<40000000;j++);


/* swap the button colors back */
XtSetArg(warg[0], XmNforeground, fg);
XtSetArg(warg[1], XmNbackground, bg);
XtSetValues(w, warg, 2);

/* make the button active again */
XtSetSensitive(w, True);

/* force another X event so that the window will redisplay */
XSendEvent(disp, win, TRUE, PointerMotionMask, &event);
XFlush(disp);

return((void *)0);
}
```

Socket Server

The socket server example uses threads to implement a "standard" socket port server. The example shows how easy it is to use `thr_create()` calls in the place of `fork()` calls in existing programs.

A standard socket server should listen on a socket port and, when a message arrives, fork a process to service the request. Since a `fork()` system call would be used in a nonthreaded program, any communication between the parent and child would have to be done through some sort of interprocess communication.

We can replace the `fork()` call with a `thr_create()` call. Doing so offers a few advantages: `thr_create()` can create a thread much faster than a `fork()` could create a new process, and any communication between the "server" and the new thread can be done with common variables. This technique makes the implementation of the socket server much easier to understand and should also make it respond much faster to incoming requests.

The server program first sets up all the needed socket information. This is the basic setup for most socket servers. The server then enters an endless loop, waiting to service a socket port. When a message is sent to the socket port, the server wakes up and creates a new thread to handle the request. Notice that the server creates the new thread as a detached thread and also passes the socket descriptor as an argument to the new thread.

The newly created thread can then read or write, in any fashion it wants, to the socket descriptor that was passed to it. At this point, the server could be creating a new thread or waiting for the next message to arrive. The key is that the server thread does not care what happens to the new thread after it creates it.

In our example, the created thread reads from the socket descriptor and then increments a global variable. This global variable keeps track of the number of requests that were made to the server. Notice that a mutex lock is used to protect access to the shared global variable. The lock is needed because many threads might try to increment the same variable at the same time. The mutex lock provides serial access to the shared variable. See how easy it is to share information among the new threads! If each thread were a process, then a significant effort would have to be made to share this information among the processes.

The client piece of the example sends a given number of messages to the server. This client code could also be run from different machines by multiple users, thus increasing the need for concurrency in the server process.

Code Example 10-13 Threaded Socket Example

```c
#define _REENTRANT
#include <stdio.h>
#include <sys/types.h>
#include <sys/socket.h>
#include <netinet/in.h>
#include <string.h>
#include <sys/uio.h>
#include <unistd.h>
#include <thread.h>

/* the TCP port that is used for this example */
#define TCP_PORT    6500

/* function prototypes and global variables */
void *do_chld(void *);
mutex_t lock;
int service_count;

main()
{
    int sockfd, newsockfd, clilen;
    struct sockaddr_in cli_addr, serv_addr;
    thread_t chld_thr;

    if((sockfd = socket(AF_INET, SOCK_STREAM, 0)) < 0)
        fprintf(stderr,"server: can't open stream socket\n"),
exit(0);

    memset((char *) &serv_addr, 0, sizeof(serv_addr));
    serv_addr.sin_family = AF_INET;
    serv_addr.sin_addr.s_addr = htonl(INADDR_ANY);
    serv_addr.sin_port = htons(TCP_PORT);

    if(bind(sockfd, (struct sockaddr *) &serv_addr,
sizeof(serv_addr)) < 0)
        fprintf(stderr,"server: can't bind local address\n"),
exit(0);

    /* set the level of thread concurrency we desire */
    thr_setconcurrency(5);

    listen(sockfd, 5);

    for(;;){
```

Code Example 10-13 Threaded Socket Example (Continued)

```
        clilen = sizeof(cli_addr);
        newsockfd = accept(sockfd, (struct sockaddr *) &cli_addr,
&clilen);

        if(newsockfd < 0)
            fprintf(stderr,"server: accept error\n"), exit(0);

        /* create a new thread to process the incomming request */
        thr_create(NULL, 0, do_chld, (void *) newsockfd,
THR_DETACHED, &chld_thr);

        /* the server is now free to accept another socket request */
        }

    return(0);
}


/*
    This is the routine that is executed from a new thread
*/

void *do_chld(void *arg)
{
int mysocfd = (int) arg;
char data[100];
int i;

    printf("Child thread [%d]: Socket number = %d\n", thr_self(),
mysocfd);

    /* read from the given socket */
    read(mysocfd, data, 40);
    printf("Child thread [%d]: My data = %s\n", thr_self(), data);

    /* simulate some processing */
    for (i=0;i<1000000*thr_self();i++);

    printf("Child [%d]: Done Processing...\n", thr_self());

    /* use a mutex to update the global service counter */
    mutex_lock(&lock);
    service_count++;
    mutex_unlock(&lock);
```

Code Example 10-13 Threaded Socket Example (Continued)

```
    printf("Child thread [%d]: The total sockets served = %d\n",
thr_self(), service_count);

    /* close the socket and exit this thread */
    close(mysocfd);
    thr_exit((void *)0);
}
```

Code Example 10-14 Socket Client Example

```
#include <stdio.h>
#include <sys/types.h>
#include <sys/socket.h>
#include <netinet/in.h>
#include <arpa/inet.h>
#include <string.h>
#include <unistd.h>
#include <stdlib.h>

/* you many want to change the following information for your network */
#define TCP_PORT    6500
#define SERV_HOST_ADDR    "11.22.33.44"

main(int argc, char **argv)
{
    int i, sockfd, ntimes = 1;
    struct sockaddr_in serv_addr;
    char buf[40];

    memset((char *) &serv_addr, 0, sizeof(serv_addr));
    serv_addr.sin_family = AF_INET;
    serv_addr.sin_addr.s_addr = inet_addr(SERV_HOST_ADDR);
    serv_addr.sin_port = htons(TCP_PORT);

    if (argc == 2) ntimes = atoi(argv[2]);

    for (i=0; i < ntimes; i++) {
        if ((sockfd = socket(AF_INET, SOCK_STREAM, 0)) < 0)
            perror("clientsoc: can't open stream socket"), exit(0);

        if (connect(sockfd, (struct sockaddr *) &serv_addr,
sizeof(serv_addr)) < 0)
            perror("clientsoc: can't connect to server"), exit(0);
```

```
        printf("sending segment %d\n", i);
        sprintf(buf, "DATA SEGMENT %d", i);
        write(sockfd, buf, strlen(buf));

        close(sockfd);
        }

    return(0);
}
```

Using Many Threads

Here is an example that shows how easy it is to create many threads of execution in Solaris. Because of the lightweight nature of threads, it is possible to create literally thousands of threads. Most applications may not need a very large number of threads, but this example shows just how lightweight the threads can be.

We have said before that anything you can do with threads, you can do without them. This may be a case where it would be very hard to do without threads. If you have some spare time (and lots of memory), try implementing this program by using processes, instead of threads. If you try this, you will see why threads can have an advantage over processes.

This program takes as an argument the number of threads to create. Notice that all the threads are created with a user-defined stack size, which limits the amount of memory that the threads will need for execution. The stack size for a given thread can be hard to calculate, so some testing usually needs to be done to see if the chosen stack size will work. You may want to change the stack size in this program and see how much you can lower it before things stop working. The Solaris threads library provides the thr_min_stack() call, which returns the minimum allowed stack size. Take care when adjusting the size of a threads stack—a stack overflow can happen quite easily to a thread with a small stack.

After each thread is created, it blocks, waiting on a mutex variable. This mutex variable was locked before any of the threads were created, which prevents the threads from proceeding in their execution. When all of the threads have been created and the user presses Return, the mutex variable is unlocked, allowing all the threads to proceed.

After the main thread has created all the threads, it waits for user input and then tries to join all the threads. Notice that the thr_join() call does not care what thread it joins; it is just counting the number of joins it makes.

This example is rather trivial and does not serve any real purpose except to show that it is possible to create a lot of threads in one process. However, there are situations when many threads are needed in an application. An example might be a network port server, where a thread is created each time an incoming or outgoing request is made.

Code Example 10-15 Using Many Threads Example

```
#define _REENTRANT
#include <stdio.h>
#include <stdlib.h>
#include <thread.h>

/* function prototypes and global variables */
void *thr_sub(void *);
mutex_t lock;

main(int argc, char **argv)
{
int i, thr_count = 100;
char buf;

/* check to see if user passed an argument
   -- if so, set the number of threads to the value
      passed to the program */

if (argc == 2) thr_count = atoi(argv[1]);

printf("Creating %d threads...\n", thr_count);

/* lock the mutex variable -- this mutex is being used to
   keep all the other threads created from proceeding   */
mutex_lock(&lock);

/* create all the threads -- Note that a specific stack size is
   given.  Since the created threads will not use all of the
   default stack size, we can save memory by reducing the threads'
   stack size */

for (i=0;i<thr_count;i++) {
    thr_create(NULL,2048,thr_sub,0,0,NULL);
    }

printf("%d threads have been created and are running!\n", i);

printf("Press <return> to join all the threads...\n", i);
```

Code Example 10-15 Using Many Threads Example (Continued)

```
/* wait till user presses return, then join all the threads */
gets(&buf);

printf("Joining %d threads...\n", thr_count);
/* now unlock the mutex variable, to let all the threads proceed */
mutex_unlock(&lock);

/* join the threads */
for (i=0;i<thr_count;i++)
    thr_join(0,0,0);

printf("All %d threads have been joined, exiting...\n", thr_count);

return(0);
}


/*
    The routine that is executed by the created threads */

void *thr_sub(void *arg)
{

/* try to lock the mutex variable -- since the main thread has
    locked the mutex before the threads were created, this thread
    will block until the main thread unlock the mutex */

mutex_lock(&lock);

printf("Thread %d is exiting...\n", thr_self());

/* unlock the mutex to allow another thread to proceed */
mutex_unlock(&lock);

/* exit the thread */
return((void *)0);
}
```

≡ 10

Real-time Thread

This example uses the Solaris real-time extensions to make a single bound thread within a process run in the real-time scheduling class. Using a thread in the real-time class is more desirable than running a whole process in the real-time class because of the many problems that can arise with a process in a real-time state. For example, it would not be desirable for a process to perform any I/O or large memory operations while in real time, because a real-time process has priority over system-related processes; if a real-time process requests a page fault, it can starve, waiting for the system to fault in a new page. We can limit this exposure by using threads to execute only the instructions that need to run in real time.

Since this book does not cover the concerns that arise with real-time programming, we have included this code only as an example of how to promote a thread into the real-time class. *You must be very careful when you use real-time threads in your applications.* For more information on real-time programming, see the Solaris documentation.

This example should be safe from the pitfalls of real-time programs because of its simplicity. However, changing this code in any way could have adverse affects on your system.

The example creates a new thread from the main thread. This new thread is then promoted to the real-time class by looking up the real-time class ID and then setting a real-time priority for the thread. After the thread is running in real time, it simulates some processing. Since a thread in the real-time class can have an infinite time quantum, the process is allowed to stay on a CPU as long as it likes. The time quantum is the amount of time a thread is allowed to stay running on a CPU. For the timesharing class, the time quantum (time-slice) is 1/100th of a second by default.

In this example, we set the time quantum for the real-time thread to infinity. That is, it can stay running as long as it likes; it will not be preempted or scheduled off the CPU. If you run this example on a UP machine, it will have the effect of stopping your system for a few seconds while the thread simulates its processing. The system does not actually stop, it is just working in the real-time thread. When the real-time thread finishes its processing, it exits and the system returns to normal.

Using real-time threads can be quite useful when you need an extremely high priority and response time but can also cause big problems if not used properly. Also note that this example must be run as root or have root execute permissions.

Code Example 10-16 Real-time Thread Example

```
#define _REENTRANT
#include <stdio.h>
#include <thread.h>
#include <string.h>
#include <sys/priocntl.h>
#include <sys/rtpriocntl.h>

/* thread prototype */
void *rt_thread(void *);

main()
{

/* create the thread that will run in real time */
thr_create(NULL, 0, rt_thread, 0, THR_DETACHED, 0);

/* loop here forever, this thread is the TS scheduling class */
while (1) {
    printf("MAIN: In time share class... running\n");
    sleep(1);
    }

return(0);
}

/*
    This is the routine that is called by the created thread
*/

void *rt_thread(void *arg)
{
pcinfo_t pcinfo;
pcparms_t pcparms;
int i;

/* let the main thread run for a bit */
sleep(4);

/* get the class ID for the real-time class */
strcpy(pcinfo.pc_clname, "RT");
if (priocntl(0, 0, PC_GETCID, (caddr_t)&pcinfo) == -1)
    fprintf(stderr, "getting RT class id\n"), exit(1);
```

Code Example 10-16 Real-time Thread Example (Continued)

```
/* set up the real-time parameters */
pcparms.pc_cid = pcinfo.pc_cid;
((rtparms_t *)pcparms.pc_clparms)->rt_pri = 10;
((rtparms_t *)pcparms.pc_clparms)->rt_tqnsecs = 0;

/* set an infinite time quantum */
((rtparms_t *)pcparms.pc_clparms)->rt_tqsecs = RT_TQINF;

/* move this thread to the real-time scheduling class */
if (priocntl(P_LWPID, P_MYID, PC_SETPARMS, (caddr_t)&pcparms) == -1)
    fprintf(stderr, "Setting RT mode\n"), exit(1);

/* simulate some processing */
for (i=0;i<100000000;i++);

printf("RT_THREAD: NOW EXITING...\n");
thr_exit((void *)0);
}
```

POSIX Cancellation

This example uses the POSIX thread cancellation capability to kill a thread that is no longer needed. Random termination of a thread can cause problems in threaded applications because a thread may be holding a critical lock when it is terminated. Since the lock was held before the thread was terminated, another thread may deadlock, waiting for that same lock. The thread cancellation capability enables you to control when a thread can be terminated. (For more information about thread cancellation, see *Cancellation* on page 112). The example also demonstrates the capabilities of the POSIX thread library in implementing a program that performs a multithreaded search.

The example simulates a multithreaded search for a given number by taking random guesses at a target number. The intent here is to simulate the same type of search that a database might execute. For example, a database might create threads to start searching for a data item; after some amount of time, one or more threads might return with the target data item.

If a thread guesses the number correctly, there is no need for the other threads to continue their search. This is where thread cancellation can help. The thread that finds the number first should cancel the other threads that are still searching for the item and then return the results of the search.

The threads involved in the search can call a cleanup function that can clean up the thread's resources before it exits. In this case, the cleanup function prints the progress of the thread when it was cancelled.

Code Example 10-17 POSIX Cancellation Example

```c
#define _REENTRANT
#include <stdio.h>
#include <unistd.h>
#include <stdlib.h>
#include <sys/types.h>
#include <pthread.h>

/* defines the number of searching threads */
#define NUM_THREADS 25

/* function prototypes */
void *search(void *);
void print_it(void *);

/* global variables */
pthread_t  threads[NUM_THREADS];
pthread_mutex_t lock;
int tries;

main()
{
int i;
int pid;

/* create a number to search for */
pid = getpid();

/* initialize the mutex lock */
pthread_mutex_init(&lock, NULL);

printf("Searching for the number = %d...\n", pid);

/* create the searching threads */
for (i=0;i<NUM_THREADS;i++)
   pthread_create(&threads[i], NULL, search, (void *)pid);

/* wait for (join) all the searching threads */
for (i=0;i<NUM_THREADS;i++)
   pthread_join(threads[i], NULL);
```

Code Example 10-17 POSIX Cancellation Example (Continued)

```
printf("It took %d tries to find the number.\n", tries);

/* exit this thread */
pthread_exit((void *)0);
}

/*
   This is the cleanup function that is called when
   the threads are cancelled
*/

void print_it(void *arg)
{
int *try = (int *) arg;
pthread_t tid;

/* get the calling thread's ID */
tid = pthread_self();

/* print where the thread was in its search when it was cancelled */
printf("Thread %d was canceled on its %d try.\n", tid, *try);
}


/*
   This is the search routine that is executed in each thread
*/

void *search(void *arg)
{
int num = (int) arg;
int i=0, j;
pthread_t tid;

/* get the calling thread ID */
tid = pthread_self();

/*use the thread ID to set the seed for the random number generator */
srand(tid);

/* set the cancellation parameters --
   - Enable thread cancellation
   - Defer the action of the cancellation
*/
```

Code Example 10-17 POSIX Cancellation Example (Continued)

```
pthread_setcancelstate(PTHREAD_CANCEL_ENABLE, NULL);
pthread_setcanceltype(PTHREAD_CANCEL_DEFERRED, NULL);

/* push the cleanup routine (print_it) onto the thread
   cleanup stack.  This routine will be called when the
   thread is cancelled.  Also note that the pthread_cleanup_push
   call must have a matching pthread_cleanup_pop call.  The
   push and pop calls MUST be at the same lexical level
   within the code */

/* pass address of 'i' since the current value of 'i' is not
   the one we want to use in the cleanup function */
pthread_cleanup_push(print_it, (void *)&i);

/* loop forever */
while (1) {
    i++;

    /* does the random number match the target number? */
    if (num == rand()) {

        /* try to lock the mutex lock --
             if locked, check to see if the thread has been cancelled
             if not locked then continue */

        while (pthread_mutex_trylock(&lock) == EBUSY)
                pthread_testcancel();

        /* set the global variable for the number of tries */
        tries = i;
        printf("thread %d found the number!\n", tid);

        /* cancel all the other threads */
        for (j=0;j<NUM_THREADS;j++)
            if (threads[j] != tid) pthread_cancel(threads[j]);

        /* break out of the while loop */
        break;
        }

    /* every 100 tries check to see if the thread has been cancelled
         if the thread has not been cancelled then yield the thread's
         LWP to another thread that may be able to run */
```

Code Example 10-17 POSIX Cancellation Example (Continued)

```
    if (i%100 == 0) {
        pthread_testcancel();
        sched_yield();
        }
    }

/* The only way we can get here is when the thread breaks out
    of the while loop.  In this case the thread that makes it here
    has found the number we are looking for and does not need to run
    the thread cleanup function.  This is why the pthread_cleanup_pop
    function is called with a 0 argument; this will pop the cleanup
    function off the stack without executing it */

pthread_cleanup_pop(0);
return((void *)0);
}
```

Deadlock

This example demonstrates how a deadlock can occur in multithreaded programs that use synchronization variables. In this example, a thread is created that continually adds a value to a global variable. The thread uses a mutex lock to protect the global data.

The main thread creates the counter thread and then loops, waiting for user input. When the user presses the Return key, the main thread suspends the counter thread and then prints the value of the global variable. The main thread prints the value of the global variable under the protection of a mutex lock.

The problem arises in this example when the main thread suspends the counter thread while the counter thread is holding the mutex lock. After the main thread suspends the counter thread, it tries to lock the mutex variable. Since the mutex variable is already held by the counter thread, which is suspended, the main thread deadlocks.

This example may run fine for a while, as long as the counter thread just happens to be suspended when it is not holding the mutex lock. The example demonstrates how tricky some programming issues can be when you deal with threads.

Code Example 10-18 Deadlock Example

```
#define _REENTRANT
#include <stdio.h>
#include <thread.h>
```

Code Example 10-18 Deadlock Example (Continued)

```
/* Prototype for thread subroutine */
void *counter(void *);

int count;
mutex_t count_lock;

main()
{
char str[80];
thread_t ctid;

/* create the thread counter subroutine */
thr_create(NULL, 0, counter, 0, THR_NEW_LWP|THR_DETACHED, &ctid);

while(1) {
    gets(str);
    thr_suspend(ctid);
    mutex_lock(&count_lock);
    printf("\n\nCOUNT = %d\n\n", count);
    mutex_unlock(&count_lock);
    thr_continue(ctid);
     }

return(0);
}


void *counter(void *arg)
{
int i;

while (1) {
    printf("."); fflush(stdout);
    mutex_lock(&count_lock);
    count++;
    for (i=0;i<50000;i++);
    mutex_unlock(&count_lock);
    for (i=0;i<50000;i++);
    }

return((void *)0);
}
```

☰ 10

Software Race Condition

This example shows a trivial software race condition. A software race condition occurs when the execution of a program is affected by the order and timing of a threads execution. Most software race conditions can be alleviated by using synchronization variables to control the threads' timing and access of shared resources. If a program depends on order of execution, then threading that program may not be a good solution, because the order in which threads execute is nondeterministic.

In the example, thr_continue() and thr_suspend() calls continue and suspend a given thread, respectively. Although both of these calls are valid, use caution when implementing them. It is very hard to determine where a thread is in its execution. Because of this, you may not be able to tell where the thread will suspend when the call to thr_suspend() is made. This behavior can cause problems in threaded code if not used properly.

The following example uses thr_continue() and thr_suspend() to try to control when a thread starts and stops. The example looks trivial but, as you will see, can cause a big problem.

Code Example 10-19 Software Race Condition Example

```
#define _REENTRANT
#include <stdio.h>
#include <thread.h>

/* Prototype for thread subroutine */
void *thread_sub(void *);

main()
{
thread_t thread_id, main_id;

/* get the thread id for the main thread */
main_id = thr_self();

/* give library a hint about the concurrency we want */
thr_setconcurrency(2);

/* create the thread subroutine - suspended */
thr_create(NULL, 0, thread_sub, (void *)main_id, THR_SUSPENDED,
&thread_id);

while(1) {
    /* Continue the thread subroutine */
```

Code Example 10-19 Software Race Condition Example (Continued)

```
            printf("MAIN: continuing subroutine thread\n");
fflush(stdout);
            thr_continue(thread_id);

    /* Suspend ourself */
            printf("MAIN: suspending self\n"); fflush(stdout);
            thr_suspend(thr_self());
    }

return(0);
}



void *thread_sub(void *arg)
{
thread_t main_thr = (thread_t) arg;

while(1) {
    /* Continue the main thread */
    printf("THREAD: continuing main thread\n"); fflush(stdout);
    thr_continue(main_thr);

    /* Suspend ourself */
    printf("THREAD: suspending self\n"); fflush(stdout);
    thr_suspend(thr_self());
    }

return((void *)0);
}
```

Do you see the problem? If you guessed that the program would eventually suspend itself, you were correct! The example attempts to flip-flop between the main thread and a subroutine thread. Each thread continues the other thread and then suspends itself.

Thread A continues thread B and then suspends thread A; now the continued thread B can continue thread A and then suspend itself. This should continue back and forth all day long, right? Wrong! We can't guarantee that each thread will continue the other thread and then suspend itself in one atomic action, so a software race condition could be created. Calling thr_continue() on a running thread and calling thr_suspend() on a suspended thread has no effect, so we don't know if a thread is already running or suspended.

If thread A continues thread B and if between the time thread A suspends itself, thread B continues thread A, then both of the threads will call `thr_suspend()`. This is the race condition in this program that will cause the whole process to become suspended.

It is very hard to use these calls, because you never really know the state of a thread. If you don't know exactly where a thread is in its execution, then you don't know what locks it holds and where it will stop when you suspend it.

Signal Handler

This example shows how easy it is to handle signals in multithreaded programs. In most programs, a different signal handler would be needed to service each type of signal that you wanted to catch. Writing each of the signal handlers can be time consuming and can be a real pain to debug.

This example shows how you can implement a signal handler thread that will service all asynchronous signals that are sent to your process. This is an easy way to deal with signals, because only one thread is needed to handle all the signals. It also makes it easy when you create new threads within the process, because you need not worry about signals in any of the threads.

First, in the main thread, mask out all signals and then create a signal handling thread. Since threads inherit the signal mask from their creator, any new threads created after the new signal mask will also mask all signals. This idea is key, because the only thread that will receive signals is the one thread that does not block all the signals.

The signal handler thread waits for all incoming signals with the `sigwait()` call. This call unmasks the signals given to it and then blocks until a signal arrives. When a signal arrives, `sigwait()` masks the signals again and then returns with the signal ID of the incoming signal.

You can extend this example for use in your application code to handle all your signals. Notice also that this signal concept could be added in your existing nonthreaded code as a simpler way to deal with signals.

Code Example 10-20 Signal Handler Thread Example

```
#define _REENTRANT
#include <stdio.h>
#include <thread.h>
#include <signal.h>
#include <sys/types.h>

void *signal_hand(void *);
```

Code Example 10-20 Signal Handler Thread Example (Continued)

```
main()
{
sigset_t set;

/* block all signals in main thread.  Any other threads that are
   created after this will also block all signals */

sigfillset(&set);
thr_sigsetmask(SIG_SETMASK, &set, NULL);

/* create a signal handler thread.  This thread will catch all
   signals and decide what to do with them.  This will only
   catch nondirected signals.  (I.e., if a thread causes a SIGFPE
   then that thread will get that signal. */

thr_create(NULL, 0, signal_hand, 0,
THR_NEW_LWP|THR_DAEMON|THR_DETACHED, NULL);

while (1) {
/*

Do your normal processing here....

*/
    }   /* end of while */

return(0);
}


void *signal_hand(void *arg)
{
sigset_t set;
int sig;

sigfillset(&set); /* catch all signals */

while (1) {
    /* wait for a signal to arrive */
    switch (sig=sigwait(&set)) {

      /* here you would add whatever signal you needed to catch */

      case SIGINT : {
```

Code Example 10-20 Signal Handler Thread Example (Continued)

```
            printf("Interrupted with signal %d, exiting...\n", sig);
            exit(0);
            }

    default : printf("GOT A SIGNAL = %d\n", sig);

    } /* end of switch */
    } /* end of while */
return((void *)0);
} /* end of signal_hand */
```

Interprocess Synchronization

This example uses some of the synchronization variables available in the threads library to synchronize access to a resource shared between two processes. The synchronization variables used in the threads library are an advantage over standard IPC synchronization mechanisms because of their speed. The synchronization variables in the threads libraries have been tuned to be very lightweight and very fast. This speed can be an advantage when your application is spending time synchronizing between processes.

This example shows how semaphores from the threads library can be used between processes. Note that this program does not use threads; it is just using the lightweight semaphores available from the threads library.

When using synchronization variables between processes, it is important to make sure that only one process initializes the variable. If both processes try to initialize the synchronization variable, then one of the processes will overwrite the state of the variable set by the other process.

Code Example 10-21 Interprocess Synchronization Example

```
#include <stdio.h>
#include <fcntl.h>
#include <sys/mman.h>
#include <synch.h>
#include <sys/types.h>
#include <unistd.h>

/* a structure that will be used between processes */
typedef struct {
    sema_t mysema;
    int num;
} buf_t;
```

Code Example 10-21 Interprocess Synchronization Example (Continued)

```
main()
{
int i, j, fd;
buf_t *buf;

/* open a file to use in a memory mapping */
fd = open("/dev/zero", O_RDWR);

/* create a shared memory map with the open file for the data
   structure that will be shared between processes */

buf=(buf_t *)mmap(NULL, sizeof(buf_t), PROT_READ|PROT_WRITE,
MAP_SHARED, fd, 0);

/* initialize the semaphore -- note the USYNC_PROCESS flag; this
   makes the semaphore visible from a process level */

sema_init(&buf->mysema, 0, USYNC_PROCESS, 0);

/* fork a new process */
if (fork() == 0) {
    /* The child will run this section of code */

    for (j=0;j<5;j++)
        {
        /* have the child "wait" for the semaphore */
        printf("Child PID(%d): waiting...\n", getpid());
        sema_wait(&buf->mysema);

        /* the child decremented the semaphore */
        printf("Child PID(%d): decrement semaphore.\n", getpid());
        }

    /* exit the child process */
    printf("Child PID(%d): exiting...\n", getpid());
    exit(0);
    }

/* The parent will run this section of code */

/* give the child a chance to start running */
sleep(2);
for (i=0;i<5;i++)
    {
```

Code Example 10-21 Interprocess Synchronization Example (Continued)

```
    /* increment (post) the semaphore */
    printf("Parent PID(%d): posting semaphore.\n", getpid());
    sema_post(&buf->mysema);

    /* wait a second */
    sleep(1);
    }

/* exit the parent process */
printf("Parent PID(%d): exiting...\n", getpid());

return(0);
}
```

Arrays

This example uses a data structure that contains multiple arrays of data. Multiple threads will concurrently vie for access to the arrays. To control this access, a mutex variable is used within the data structure to lock the entire array and serialize the access to the data.

The main thread first initializes the data structure and the mutex variable. It then sets a level of concurrency and creates the worker threads. The main thread then blocks by joining all the threads. When all the threads have exited, the main thread prints the results.

The worker threads modify the shared data structure from within a loop. Each time the threads need to modify the shared data, they lock the mutex variable associated with the shared data. After modifying the data, the threads unlock the mutex, allowing another thread access to the data.

This example may look quite simple, but it shows how important it is to control access to a simple, shared data structure. The results can be quite different if the mutex variable is not used, as shown in Table 10-1.

Table 10-1   Array Example Results

Array Run With Mutex Locks		Array Run Without Mutex Locks	
integer value[0]	40000	integer value[0]	36054
float value[0]	60000	float value[0]	54045
integer value[1]	40000	integer value[1]	36036
float value[1]	60000	float value[1]	53979

Table 10-1   Array Example Results (Continued)

Array Run With Mutex Locks		Array Run Without Mutex Locks	
integer value[2]	40000	integer value[2]	36040
float value[2]	60000	float value[2]	54024
integer value[3]	40000	integer value[3]	36030
float value[3]	60000	float value[3]	54042
integer value[4]	40000	integer value[4]	36046
float value[4]	60000	float value[4]	53982

Code Example 10-22 Array Example

```
#define _REENTRANT
#include <stdio.h>
#include <thread.h>


/* sample array data structure */
struct {
    mutex_t data_lock[5];
    int int_val[5];
    floatfloat_val[5];
    } Data;


/* thread function */
void *Add_to_Value();

main()
{
int i;

/* initialize the mutexes and data */
for (i=0; i<5; i++) {
    mutex_init(&Data.data_lock[i], USYNC_THREAD, 0);
    Data.int_val[i] = 0;
    Data.float_val[i] = 0;
    }

/* set concurrency and create the threads */
thr_setconcurrency(4);
for (i=0; i<5; i++)
    thr_create(NULL, 0, Add_to_Value, (void *)(2*i), 0, NULL);
```

Code Example 10-22 Array Example (Continued)

```
/* wait till all threads have finished */
for (i=0; i<5; i++)
    thr_join(0,0,0);

/* print the results */
printf("Final Values.....\n");
for (i=0; i<5; i++) {
    printf("integer value[%d] =\t%d\n", i, Data.int_val[i]);
    printf("float value[%d] =\t%.0f\n\n", i, Data.float_val[i]);
    }

return(0);
}


/* Threaded routine */
void *Add_to_Value(void *arg)
{
int inval = (int) arg;
int i;

for (i=0;i<10000;i++){
    mutex_lock(&Data.data_lock[i%5]);
        Data.int_val[i%5] += inval;
        Data.float_val[i%5] += (float) 1.5 * inval;
    mutex_unlock(&Data.data_lock[i%5]);
    }

return((void *)0);
}
```

Answers

Question 0 -, "How many Californians does it take to change a light bulb?"

One, but the light bulb must want to change.

Chapter 4, Question 1 -, "Explain why this model can make MT programs run faster than their single-threaded counterparts on uniprocessor machines."

The issue here is that a machine spends a considerable amount of its waking hours waiting for I/O to complete. In an MT program, one LWP can make the blocking system call, while the other LWPs can continue to run. On uniprocessors, a process that would otherwise have to block for all these calls can continue to run its other threads.

Chapter 4, Question 2 -, "There cannot be a thread of higher priority on the runnable queue. Prove it."

Every call that can possibly change the priority of a thread or make a higher priority thread runnable will also call the scheduler, and it in turn will preempt the lower priority active thread. So there will never be a runnable, higher-priority thread.

Chapter 4, Question 3 -, "Someone always asks something like: 'If the process exits and there are still threads running, will they continue to run?' What's the answer?"

When a process exits, it takes everything with it—the LWPs, the process structure, the memory space, everything, including the threads.

Chapter 4, Question 4 -, "Could you create cancellation in Solaris threads? If so, how?"

Most of it's easy. As a matter of fact, the previous paragraph describes it! To effect a cancellation, you send the thread a signal. If the thread does not want to be cancelled just then, it sets its signal mask to ignore the signal. Any time it is ready to exit, it just needs to reset the signal mask to see if there's a signal pending. Cancellation is really just putting all of that into the API.

The bigger point is that cancellation is still not obvious. You still have to carefully analyze your code to allow cancellation to occur only at safe points.

Chapter 5, Question 5 –, "Clearly, if some data were in use by CPU 2 when CPU 1 flushed that data from its store buffer, it would be a formula for disaster. This never happens. Why?"

Because that data is known to be shared data. A good programmer would *never* allow shared data to be used without a lock around.

Chapter 5, Question 6 –, "When a thread tries to obtain a lock and fails, it is put on the mutex's sleep queue. The mutex is a shared data item, of course, as is its sleep queue. How do we ensure the integrity of that sleep queue? What happens when two threads both decide to sleep on a mutex at exactly the same time?"

The sleep queue for the mutex has its own mutex, which the soon-to-be-blocked thread must obtain before it can put itself onto the queue. If there's contention for this mutex too, the contender will make a system call and block there. And if there's contention in the kernel, then ultimately the poor thread will be forced to spin. The probability of this last occurring is somewhere in the vicinity of once every million years.

Chapter 5, Question 7 –, "The decision of when to use a reader/writer lock is tricky to calculate. Produce a first-order estimate and defend it."

Assume reading dominates, so forget writing completely. Assume that you have two threads using some global data. Assume that for each time duration, D, each thread obtains a read lock once. Let S be the amount of time spent inside of that protected section. Assume locking/unlocking time to be much less than S. Let T be the total runtime of the program. Let M be the cost of mutex lock/unlock, and (3 * M) is the cost of a reader lock/unlock (empirically determined). Assume even distribution of locking. Assume a uniprocessor and two LWPs.

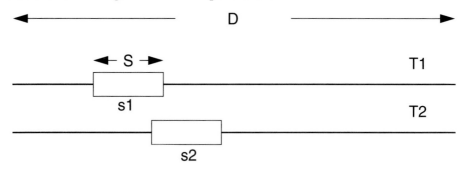

Figure A-1   Determining When to Use RW Locks

From Figure A-1, you can see that contention for the section exists whenever s1 and s2 overlap. The probability of contention for this section is then $2S/D$. The total number of times the section will be locked is $(T/D) = L$. The expected number of contentions is therefore $(2S/D) * L = C$, while the expected number of noncontention locks is $L - C = N$. The cost of blocking and then unblocking for a mutex is 30M (empirically determined). The expected cost of running the protected sections of the program is:

with mutexes: $Tm = (N * (M + S)) + (C * (30 * M + S))$
(The first term is the cost of the noncontention locks, the second is the cost of the contention locks.)

with RW locks: $Tr = (N + C) * (3 * M + S)$

The question now becomes "When is $Tr < Tm$?"

A bit of algebra gives us the answer: "When $S/D > 4\%$."

So, a general rule of thumb is to use RW locks only when the critical section is large (> 10,000 instructions) and reading dominates.

As you notice, there were a lot of simplifying assumptions! We'll leave it to you to figure out the general answer.

Chapter 5, Question 8 –, "Why must a spin lock critical section be short, have contention, and be on a multiprocessor machine?"

First, if the protected section is large, say it takes 1000 µs, then expending great effort trying to save 46 µs is sort of silly. Plus the fact that the chances of obtaining the lock in a small number of spins is very low. Second, if there is low contention for the lock, then the chance of ever making use of the spin lock is very low. Lots of work for little gain. Finally, if you only have one CPU, there is no chance of a spin lock ever saving you any time, because the spinner thread must give up the CPU before the owner thread can run and release the mutex.

Figure A-2 illustrates the interaction charts for spin locks versus regular locks. Wo is the work the program does outside the critical section, Wi is the work it does inside the critical section, and M is the cost of a mutex function call, including wake-up time. The whole point of these charts is for you to look at the wake-up time. That is what a spin lock saves you.

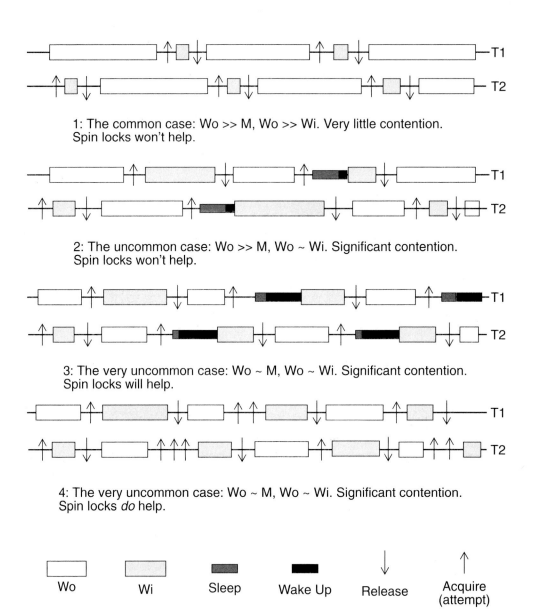

1: The common case: Wo >> M, Wo >> Wi. Very little contention.
Spin locks won't help.

2: The uncommon case: Wo >> M, Wo ~ Wi. Significant contention.
Spin locks won't help.

3: The very uncommon case: Wo ~ M, Wo ~ Wi. Significant contention.
Spin locks will help.

4: The very uncommon case: Wo ~ M, Wo ~ Wi. Significant contention.
Spin locks *do* help.

Figure A-2   Timing Charts for Spin Locks

Chapter 5, Question 9 –, "We have just explained the functionality of TSD by showing you an implementation. There is nothing that says TSD has to be implemented by using offsets to arrays hanging off the thread structure. Give some different possible implementations."

It could be implemented by having one big array that is shared by all threads. When a new thread is created, you would just copy the entire array into a slightly bigger one. You could build a linked list of values for each thread. This would mean that added new elements would be very fast, but looking up old ones would be slower. You could build a global hash table. Lots of possibilities.

Chapter 5, Question 10 –, "As it is possible to add new keys dynamically, what happens when the array fills up?"

This is an implementation detail. Solaris does "lazy" TSD creation. At `thr_create()` time, an array that is large enough to contain all the current TSD key/value pairs is allocated for the thread. In the thread structure, it records the current high value for TSD keys. Should your program subsequently create another key, *then nothing happens (yet)*. When this thread attempts to use the newly created key, it looks at its recorded high value. It discovers that this new key is higher than that! So, it makes room for this new key at that point and continues.

"Making room" can mean either the currently allocated array had some extra space in it, so that space is used, or the currently allocated array didn't have any room. So, a new array is malloc'd, all the data from the current array will be copied into the new array, and the old array will be freed.

Chapter 6, Question 11 –, "Actually, there are a few parallelism-only issues that you can choose to address. Some are mentioned in this book. What are they?"

Spin locks are the one real parallelism issue that you see at user level. Some of the details about why locks are required and how they work are also parallelism issues, but you never deal with those directly.

A

Threads Primer

Solaris Signal Implementation   B ▤

As we have said previously, we wish to keep implementation aspects separate from the specifications and talk about implementation only when necessary for clarity's sake. In the body of the text, we have told you everything you need in order to use signals correctly, and there is no need to say anything more. We include this section only because we know that bugs happen, and you are likely to run into this aspect of the implementation when debugging your program.

Once again, this is a peek under the covers. Do not base any of your programming upon what you read here!

The threads library has a distinguished bound thread of its own that handles all signal delivery issues (see Figure B-1). This thread is created at startup time and promptly calls `sigwait()` (see `sigwait(3T)` on page 230), waiting for any and all signals. It is hence assured that every signal will be delivered to it.

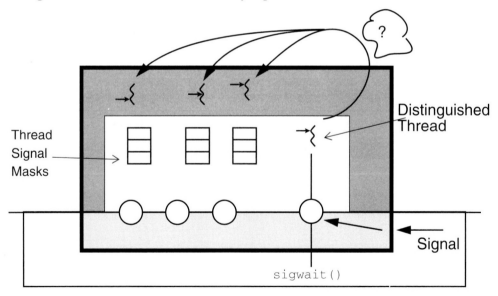

Figure B-1   Solaris 2.4 Signal Handler Implementation

When a signal is delivered to the process, that thread then looks around at all the user threads, comparing thread signal masks and considering run-state (active, runnable, sleeping, etc.). It decides which thread is to run the signal handler. The chosen thread is interrupted, it runs the signal handler, then returns to whatever it was doing before (which could be sleeping!).

Should one of your threads call sigwait() itself, the threads library will interpose its own definition of sigwait(). This interposed function will be called instead of the real one. When a signal comes in that your thread should receive its sigwait() call, the distinguished thread will figure this out and cause the interposed function to return as if the actual signal had been delivered to sigwait() as specified.

By the way, this is the implementation that is being used in Solaris 2.4 and 2.5. A completely different implementation was used in Solaris 2.3 that did not rely on the use of sigwait() at all (it also didn't work very well). If somebody comes up with a better idea for Solaris 2.6, it could all change again. But no matter what kind of implementation is used, the specification will remain constant, so your programs will continue to work properly.

Threads on the Net   C ☰

Threads on the World Wide Web

You can access the Sun WWW server by connecting to Sun's main home page:
http://www.sun.com. There is also a page specifically oriented to MT issues. It can
be accessed via a long chain of pages from the main home page or directly via the
URL below. The threads home page includes all the white papers and case studies
that we've written on threads, along with pointers to other papers and relevant
pages. It also includes an FAQ that is updated regularly, performance data,
demonstration programs, and all the code for the examples in this book.

http://www.sun.com/sunsoft/Products/Developer-products/sig/threads/index.html.

The SPILT Package for Solaris/POSIX Compatibility

In order to make it easier to move Solaris threads code over to POSIX, Sun has
written a package that maps the missing parts into POSIX. Reader/writer locks,
for example, are included in the SPILT package. You can write a program in
Solaris threads today, then use this package to run the exact same program on a
POSIX threads library. This package can be obtained from the WWW threads
page.

Threads Newsgroup

For discussion, questions and answers, and just general debate about threading
issues, there is to be a new newsgroup on the Internet. The issues discussed are
not confined to any one vendor, implementation, standard, or specification. (As of
this writing, 20 July 1995, the creation of this group was in the Internet
newsgroup creation queue for consideration, right behind rec.alt.emu-interest.)
We expect the name to be comp.programming.threads, but who knows!
Notification will appear on the WWW page.

≡ C

Code Examples

All the code examples in this book are available via the WWW. From the threads page listed above, you will be able to find all the code we used in writing this book, along with the programs we used to verify timing considerations.

The Authors on the Net

If you have questions about threads, you can send mail to Threads_Hotline@Sun.COM. This is a mail alias that is read by many knowledgeable people at Sun. If you would like to contact the authors directly, you can send mail to Daniel.Berg@Sun.COM and Bil.Lewis@Sun.COM. We would like to hear from you about what you liked or disliked about the book.

Timings   D ≡

The choice of which synchronization variable to use depends slightly on the
speed at which it executes. In particular, the choice between using a mutex lock
and reader/writer lock is partially based on how long each takes to execute.
Table D-1 lists performance numbers for various functions on a 40 MHz
SPARCstation 10/41[1].

Because of the dependence of these test upon several unusual instructions
(`ldstub` and `stbar` on SPARC), machines with different cache or bus designs
will exhibit nonuniform scaling (meaning that a context switch may be twice as
fast on a 20 MHz processor as it is on a 10 MHz processor, but locking a mutex
might take the same amount of time). The programs we ran to get these numbers
are available on the WWW.

Table D-1   Timings of Various Thread-related Functions

Function	Microseconds	Ratio
No Contention Mutex Lock	1.6	1
Local Mutex Lock with Contention	48	30
Cross-Process Mutex Lock with Contention	105	65
Mutex Trylock	0.7	0.5
No Contention Reader Lock	4.3	3
No Contention Writer Lock	2.9	3
Reader Trylock	2.1	1
Writer Trylock	1.2	1
No Contention Semaphore	6.9	4
Semaphore Trywait	3.3	2
Reference a Global Variable	0.02	1
Get Thread-specific Data	0.79	40

1. The SPARCstation 10, model 41 is a high-performance workstation based on a 40 MHz SuperSPARC chip with a
   one-megabyte external cache. It was launched in May 1992.

D

The tests are respectively:

No Contention Mutex Lock

Acquire, then release, a mutex with no contention. (It's the same operation, whether in the same process or across processes.)

Local Mutex Lock with Contention

On a mutex-initialized `USYNC_THREAD`, block on a mutex acquire, context switch off the LWP, sleep, have the other thread release the mutex, wake up the first thread, get context switched back on to the LWP, complete the acquire, then release it.

Cross-Process Mutex Lock with Contention

On a mutex-initialized `USYNC_PROCESS`, do the same as above.

Mutex Trylock

Call `mutex_trylock()` on a held lock.

No Contention Reader Lock

Acquire, then release, a reader/writer lock as a reader with no contention.

No Contention Writer Lock

Acquire, then release, a reader/writer lock as a writer with no contention.

Reader Trylock

Call `rw_tryrdlock()` on a held lock.

Writer Trylock

Call `rw_trywrlock()` on a held lock.

No Contention Semaphore

Decrement a semaphore that is greater than zero, then increment it.

Semaphore Trywait

Call `sema_trywait()` on a held lock.

Reference a Global Variable

Load a single word into a register.

Get Thread-specific Data

Call `thr_getspecific()`. (A call to `thr_setspecific()` takes the same amount of time.)

Threads Primer

Common Bugs   E ≡

This is a list of the most common bugs that we see people making.

Failure to Check Return Values for Errors

Many of the thread library functions can legitimately return error codes instead of succeeding. Most system calls can also return error codes.

The most pervasively ignored return code is EINTR, which can be returned by many different functions. It doesn't mean the call failed, it just means that it was interrupted. The usual thing to do is to write a loop that checks for this return code and reissues the call. Watch out for sema_wait() in particular. (See *Semaphores* on page 69.)

Using errno Without Checking the Return Value

This isn't a threads programming bug per se, but it's very common anyway. It is legal for errno to contain any old crazy value until a system call returns an error code.

Not Joining on Nondetached Threads

If you are not going to join a thread, you must create it with the THR_DETACHED flag. (See *That's Not a Bug, That's a Feature!* on page 58.)

Failure to Verify that Library Calls Are MT Safe

lint really ought to do this for you. Until it does, you have to do it yourself. Third-party libraries are a common problem.

≡ *E*

Insufficient Swap Space

Because thread stacks are mapped in without any required backing store, it is possible to create a large number of threads, have your program run perfectly for weeks, and then suddenly crash for no apparent reason with a SIGSEGV or SIGBUS in some random location. What happened is that you ran out of swap space. When your program tried to push one more word onto the stack, the system discovered that it needed to map in a new page, but there were no pages left!

The existence of this feature is a very good thing and saves a great deal of time for programs and programmers; however, when it goes wrong... It can be a rather obscure bug and very difficult to find unless you're aware of its existence. (See the man pages for mmap().)

Creating Excessive LWPs

One favorite mistake is to create a bound thread and also pass the flag THR_NEW_LWP. The effect of this is to create one LWP for the thread to be bound to and a second LWP for the unbound threads pool. Creating more LWPs than you need will not improve your program's performance. Think about what you need first, then test it. (See *How Many LWPs?* on page 52.)

Forgetting to Include the –D_REENTRANT Flag

This negligence is sort of nasty, as you won't notice a thing until you try to check errno or get weird synchronization errors from getc(). Compile *all* libraries with the flag. You'll be much happier two years from now when you suddenly decide that you need that library in an MT program.

As an option, you can also include the line #define _REENTRANT in your files. To the SunSoft compiler, you can put the -mt flag on the compile line, and it will do both -D_REENTRANT -lthread.

Using Spin Locks

You practically never need these things! If you really want to use 'em, prove that they are working for you first. (See *Spin Locks* on page 71.)

Depending upon Scheduling Order

Write your MT programs to depend upon synchronization. It is very rare to care about scheduling or scheduling priorities.

Using `errno` for Threads Library Functions

All of the functions in the Solaris threads library return error codes directly and do not set `errno`. You cannot use `errno`, nor `perror()`, unless the manual page for the function in question specifically states that it will be set (this goes for all library calls, not just threads). The error codes returned from threads functions are listed in `errno.h`, so `strerror()` will return an appropriate error string. In POSIX, semaphores are not part of the threads library, and they do use `errno`.

One particularly bewildering aspect of this situation is that it may appear that `errno` is being set in some cases. This has fooled more than one programmer (e.g., the authors). A call to `thr_create()` may legally fail, returning the error value EAGAIN—not enough resources. To find out that there weren't enough resources, `thr_create()` had to make a system call. That system call returned an error and set `errno` to EAGAIN. It was the system call that `thr_create()` happened to call that set `errno`, not `thr_create()` itself.

This is a bit of serendipity that must not be relied upon. It could change.

Not Recognizing Shared Data

It is not unusual for a programmer to fail to protect some piece of data because it wasn't obvious that it needed protection. This is especially true for complex structures such as lists, where you might protect part of the data without realizing that you've left another part unprotected. Consider this structure, where the programmer has carefully provided a lock for each element of a list.

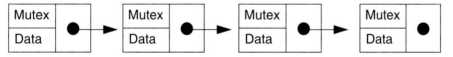

What does the mutex protect? The programmer intended it to protect the entire node, which is perfectly acceptable. However, he also expected one thread to be able to do a search down the list at the same time that another thread was changing the order of the nodes. ("As long as I hold the mutex for node 1, I can reposition it in the list without disturbing the rest of the list. And the other threads can do searches, just as long as they don't try to change node 1.")

Nope. To be able to change the order of the list, the programmer would have to obtain both the lock for the current node and the lock for the previous node. To be able to search the list at the same time, the programmer would have to obtain, then release, each lock as the thread moved down the list. This would work, but it would probably be very expensive.

E

Threads Primer

Compile and Debug Specifics   F ≡

Here are some miscellaneous tips to help you when you compile and debug your multithreaded programs.

Compiling a Multithreaded Application

When compiling multithreaded programs, you must include the _REENTRANT flag. This flag is used to include the reentrant definitions of all the library functions used in your program. If the flag is not used, then the standard interface definitions will be used. For example, the errno.h include file has a reentrant version and a standard definition of the errno variable.

The _REENTRANT flag can be specified on the compile line—

```
cc -c -D_REENTRANT program.c
```

—or placed in the source module before any other include files.

```
#define _REENTRANT
#include <stdio.h>
#include < ... >
```

The _REENTRANT flag must be used in every module of a new application. If the _REENTRANT flag is not used on every module of a threaded application, then the compiler will include some reentrant definitions and some non-reentrant definitions in the same application. This can cause some problems if the threads are calling into functions that are not using reentrant definitions.

Using libthread

To use libthread, either specify -lthread before -lc on the ld command line or specify it last on the cc command line.

The -mt flag can also be specified on the compile line in place of -lthread and -D_REENTRANT flag for the Sun compiler.

```
cc -o thr_program thr_program.c -mt
```

All calls to `libthread` functions are no-ops if the application does not link `libthread`. `libc` has defined stubs that are null procedures for all `libthread` functions. True procedures are interposed by `libthread` when the application links both `libc` and `libthread`. Thus, `libthread` must come after `libc`.

The behavior of the C library is undefined if a program is constructed with an `ld` command line that includes the fragment:

```
.o's ... -lc -lthread ...
```

Do not link a single-threaded program with `-lthread` unless you need it. Doing so establishes multithreading mechanisms at link time that are initiated at runtime. These waste resources and produce misleading results when you debug your code.

Debugging Multithreaded Programs

The following list points out some of the more frequent oversights that can cause bugs in multithreaded programming.

- Accessing global memory (shared changeable state) without the protection of a synchronization mechanism.

- Creating deadlocks caused by two threads trying to acquire rights to the same pair of global resources in alternate order (so that one thread controls the first resource, the other controls the second resource, and neither can proceed until the other gives up).

- Creating a hidden gap in synchronization protection. The gap is caused when a code segment protected by a synchronization mechanism contains a call to a function that frees and then reacquires the synchronization mechanism before it returns to the caller. The result is that it appears to the caller that the global data has been protected when it actually has not.

- Making deeply nested, recursive calls and using large automatic arrays. This practice can cause problems because multithreaded programs have a more limited stack size than do single-threaded programs.

- Specifying an inadequate stack size.

- Providing a user-defined stack and stack management.

And, note that multithreaded programs (especially buggy ones) often behave differently in two successive runs given identical inputs because of differences in the thread-scheduling order.

In general, multithreading bugs are statistical instead of deterministic in character. Tracing is usually more effective in finding problems in the order of execution than is breakpoint-based debugging. Using breakpoints can change the order of execution and timing of your program, making it difficult to figure out where such a bug exists.

Using adb

When you bind all threads in a multithreaded program, a thread and an LWP are synonymous. Then, you can access each thread with the adb commands, listed in Table F-1, that support multithreaded programming.

Table F-1   MT adb Commands

Command	Action
pid:A	Attaches to process # *pid*. This stops the process and all its LWPs.
:R	Detaches from process. This resumes the process and all its LWPs.
$L	Lists all active LWPs in the (stopped) process.
n:l	Switches focus to LWP # *n*.
$l	Shows the LWP currently focused.
num:i	Ignores signal number *num*.

Using dbx

With the dbx utility, you can debug and execute source programs written in C++, ANSI C, FORTRAN, and Pascal. dbx accepts the same commands as the SPARCworks Debugger but uses a standard terminal (tty) interface. Both dbx and the SPARCworks Debugger now support debugging of multithreaded programs.

For a full overview of dbx(1), see the manual page; for more information on the SPARCworks Debugger, consult the user's guide, *Debugging a Program*.

Table F-2 lists dbx options that support multithreaded programs.

Table F-2   dbx Options for MT Programs

Option	Action
cont at *line* [*signo*] [*id*]	Continues execution at line *line* with signal *signo*. See continue for dbx command language loop control. The *id*, if present, specifies which thread or LWP to continue. Default value is *all*.
lwp [*lwpid*]	Displays current LWP. Switches to given LWP [*lwpid*].

Table F-2   dbx Options for MT Programs   (Continued)

`lwps`	Lists all LWPs in the current process.
`next` *tid*	Steps the given thread. When a function call is skipped, all LWPs are implicitly resumed for the duration of that function call. Nonactive threads cannot be stepped.
`next` *lid*	Steps the given LWP. Does not implicitly resume all LWPs when skipping a function.
`step` *tid*	Steps the given thread. When a function call is skipped, all LWPs are implicitly resumed for the duration of that function call. Nonactive threads cannot be stepped.
`step` *lid*	Steps the given LWP. Does not implicitly resume all LWPs when skipping a function.
`thread` *tid*	Displays current thread. Switches to thread *tid*. In all the following variations, an optional *tid* implies the current thread.
`thread -info` [*tid*]	Prints everything known about the given thread.
`thread -locks` [*tid*]	Prints all locks held by the given thread.
`thread -suspend` [*tid*]	Puts the given thread into suspended state.
`thread -continue` [*tid*]	Unsuspends the given thread.
`thread -hide` [*tid*]	Hides the given (or current) thread. It will not show up in the generic `threads` listing.
`thread -unhide` [*tid*]	Unhides the given (or current) thread.
`allthread-unhide`	Unhides all threads.
`threads`	Prints the list of all known threads.
`threads-all`	Prints threads that are not usually printed (zombies).

Application Program Interface G ☰

This appendix contains all the functions that are available to you in the Solaris threads library. Each function shown in the table below is listed with a call synopsis, a short description of its action and return codes. This is only a brief listing; refer to the Sun documentation *Solaris Multithreaded Programming Guide* for more complete information. The POSIX-related function is also listed with each Solaris function. For more information on the POSIX functions, see Appendix H, *Pthreads API (POSIX 1003.1c)*.

Function Type	Function	Page
CONDITION FUNCTIONS	cond_broadcast	219
	cond_destroy	219
	cond_init	220
	cond_signal	220
	cond_timedwait	221
	cond_wait	221
MUTEX FUNCTIONS	mutex_destroy	222
	mutex_init	222
	mutex_lock	223
	mutex_trylock	223
	mutex_unlock	224
READER/WRITER LOCK FUNCTIONS	rw_rdlock	224
	rw_tryrdlock	225
	rw_trywrlock	225
	rw_unlock	226
	rw_wrlock	226
	rwlock_destroy	227
	rwlock_init	227
SEMAPHORE FUNCTIONS	sema_destroy	228
	sema_init	228
	sema_post	229
	sema_trywait	229
	sema_wait	230

≡ G

Function Type	Function	Page
	`sigwait`	230
	`thr_continue`	231
	`thr_create`	231
	`thr_exit`	232
	`thr_getconcurrency`	232
	`thr_getprio`	232
	`thr_getspecific`	233
THREAD FUNCTIONS	`thr_join`	233
	`thr_keycreate`	234
	`thr_kill`	234
	`thr_self`	235
	`thr_setconcurrency`	235
	`thr_setprio`	235
	`thr_setspecific`	236
	`thr_sigsetmask`	236
	`thr_suspend`	237
	`thr_yield`	237

Threads Primer

Condition Functions

`cond_broadcast(3T)`   Broadcasts that a condition is true.

```
#include <thread.h>

int cond_broadcast(cond_t *cvp);

POSIX: pthread_cond_broadcast();
```

`cond_broadcast()` returns zero after completing successfully. When the following condition occurs the function fails and returns the corresponding value.

    EFAULT   *cvp* points to an illegal address.

`cond_destroy(3T)`   Destroys a condition variable.

```
#include <thread.h>

int cond_destroy(cond_t *cvp);

POSIX: pthread_cond_destroy();
```

`cond_destroy()` returns zero after completing successfully. When the following `condition` occurs, the function fails and returns the corresponding value.

    EFAULT   *cvp* points to an illegal address.

≡ G

cond_init(3T)   Initializes a condition variable.

```
#include <thread.h>

int cond_init(cond_t *cvp, int type, int arg);

POSIX: pthread_cond_init();
```

cond_init() returns zero after completing successfully. When any of the following conditions occur, the function fails and returns the corresponding value.

EINVAL   *type* is not a recognized type.

EFAULT   *cvp* or *arg* points to an illegal address.

cond_signal(3T)   Signals that a condition is true.

```
#include <thread.h>

int cond_signal(cond_t *cvp);

POSIX: pthread_cond_signal();
```

cond_signal() returns zero after completing successfully. When the following condition occurs, the function fails and returns the corresponding value.

EFAULT   *cvp* points to an illegal address.

cond_timedwait(3T)   Waits a given time for a condition to become true.

```
#include <thread.h>

int cond_timedwait(cond_t *cvp, mutex_t *mp,
    timestruc_t *abstime);

POSIX: pthread_cond_timedwait();
```

cond_timedwait() returns zero after completing successfully. When any of the following conditions occur, the function fails and returns the corresponding value.

EINVAL	The specified number of seconds in *abstime* is greater than the start time of the application plus 50,000,000, or the number of nanoseconds is greater than or equal to 1,000,000,000.
EFAULT	*cvp* or *abstime* points to an illegal address.
EINTR	The wait was interrupted by a signal or a fork().
ETIME	The time specified by *abstime* has passed.

cond_wait(3T)   Waits for a condition to become true.

```
#include <thread.h>

int cond_wait(cond_t *cvp, mutex_t *mp);

POSIX: pthread_cond_wait();
```

cond_wait() returns zero after completing successfully. When any of the following conditions occur, the function fails and returns the corresponding value.

EFAULT	*cvp* points to an illegal address.
EINTR	The wait was interrupted by a signal or a fork().

≡ G

Mutex Functions

`mutex_destroy(3T)`   Destroys a mutex variable.

```
#include <thread.h>

int mutex_destroy(mutex_t *mp);

POSIX: pthread_mutex_destroy();
```

`mutex_destroy()` returns zero after completing successfully. When any of the following conditions occur, the function fails and returns the corresponding value.

    EINVAL   Invalid argument.

    EFAULT   *mp* points to an illegal address.

`mutex_init(3T)`   Initializes a mutex variable.

```
#include <thread.h>

int mutex_init(mutex_t *mp, int type, void * arg);

POSIX: pthread_mutex_init();
```

`mutex_init()` returns zero after completing successfully. When any of the following conditions occur, the function fails and returns the corresponding value.

    EINVAL   Invalid argument.

    EFAULT   *mp* or *arg* points to an illegal address.

`mutex_lock(3T)`   Locks a mutex variable.

```
#include <thread.h>

int mutex_lock(mutex_t *mp);

POSIX: pthread_mutex_lock();
```

`mutex_lock()` returns zero after completing successfully. When any of the following conditions occur, the function fails and returns the corresponding value.

    EINVAL   Invalid argument.

    EFAULT   *mp* points to an illegal address.

`mutex_trylock(3T)`   Tries to lock a mutex variable.

```
#include <thread.h>

int mutex_trylock(mutex_t *mp);

POSIX: pthread_mutex_trylock();
```

`mutex_trylock()` returns zero after completing successfully. When any of the following conditions occur, the function fails and returns the corresponding value.

    EINVAL   Invalid argument.

    EFAULT   *mp* points to an illegal address.

    EBUSY   The mutex pointed to by *mp* was already locked.

mutex_unlock(3T)   Unlocks a mutex variable.

```
#include <thread.h>

int mutex_unlock(mutex_t *mp);

POSIX: pthread_mutex_unlock();
```

mutex_unlock() returns zero after completing successfully. When any of the following conditions occur, the function fails and returns the corresponding value.

EINVAL   Invalid argument.

EFAULT   *mp* points to an illegal address.

Reader/Writer Lock Functions

rw_rdlock(3T)   Locks a reader/writer variable for a reader.

```
#include <thread.h>

int rw_rdlock(rwlock_t *rwlp);

POSIX: NONE
```

rw_rdlock() returns zero after completing successfully. When any of the following conditions occur, the function fails and returns the corresponding value.

EINVAL   Invalid argument.

EFAULT   *rwlp* points to an illegal address.

rw_tryrdlock(3T)   Tries to lock a reader/writer variable for a reader.

```
#include <thread.h>

int rw_tryrdlock(rwlock_t *rwlp);

POSIX: NONE
```

rw_tryrdlock() returns zero after completing successfully. When any of the following conditions occur, the function fails and returns the corresponding value.

    EINVAL   Invalid argument.

    EFAULT   *rwlp* points to an illegal address.

    EBUSY   The reader/writer lock pointed to by *rwlp* was already locked.

rw_trywrlock(3T)   Tries to lock a reader/writer variable for a writer.

```
#include <thread.h>

int rw_trywrlock(rwlock_t *rwlp);

POSIX: NONE
```

rw_trywrlock() returns zero after completing successfully. When any of the following conditions occur, the function fails and returns the corresponding value.

    EINVAL   Invalid argument.

    EFAULT   *rwlp* points to an illegal address.

    EBUSY   The reader/writer lock pointed to by *rwlp* was already locked.

rw_unlock(3T)   Unlocks a reader/writer variable.

```
#include <thread.h>

int rwlock_tryrdlock(rwlock_t *rwlp);

POSIX: NONE
```

rw_unlock() returns zero after completing successfully. When any of the following conditions occur, the function fails and returns the corresponding value.

EINVAL   Invalid argument.

EFAULT   *rwlp* points to an illegal address.

rw_wrlock(3T)   Locks a reader/writer variable for a writer.

```
#include <thread.h>

int rw_wrlock(rwlock_t *rwlp);

POSIX: NONE
```

rw_wrlock() returns zero after completing successfully. When any of the following conditions occur, the function fails and returns the corresponding value.

EINVAL   Invalid argument.

EFAULT   *rwlp* points to an illegal address.

rwlock_destroy(3T)   Destroys a reader/writer variable.

```
#include <thread.h>

int rwlock_destroy(rwlock_t *rwlp);

POSIX: NONE
```

rwlock_destroy() returns zero after completing successfully. When any of the following conditions occur, the function fails and returns the corresponding value.

    EINVAL   Invalid argument.

    EFAULT   *rwlp* points to an illegal address.

rwlock_init(3T)   Initializes a reader/writer variable.

```
#include <thread.h>

int rwlock_init(rwlock_t *rwlp, int type, void * arg);

POSIX: NONE
```

rwlock_init() returns zero after completing successfully. When any of the following conditions occur, the function fails and returns the corresponding value.

    EINVAL   Invalid argument.

    EFAULT   *rwlp* or *arg* points to an illegal address.

≡ *G*

Semaphore Functions

`sema_destroy(3T)`   Destroys a semaphore variable.

```
#include <thread.h>

int sema_destroy(sema_t *sp);

POSIX: sem_destroy();
```

`sema_destroy()` returns zero after completing successfully. When any of the following conditions occur, the function fails and returns the corresponding value.

    `EINVAL`   Invalid argument.

    `EFAULT`   *sp* points to an illegal address.

`sema_init(3T)`   Initializes a semaphore variable.

```
#include <thread.h>

int sema_init(sema_t *sp, unsigned int count, int type, void * arg);

POSIX: sem_init();
```

`sema_init()` returns zero after completing successfully. When any of the following conditions occur, the function fails and returns the corresponding value.

    `EINVAL`   Invalid argument.

    `EFAULT`   *sp* or *arg* points to an illegal address.

sema_post(3T)   Increments a semaphore variable.

```
#include <thread.h>

int sema_post(sema_t *sp);

POSIX: sem_post();
```

sema_post() returns zero after completing successfully. When any of the
following conditions occur, the function fails and returns the corresponding
value.

    EINVAL   Invalid argument.

    EFAULT   *sp* points to an illegal address.

sema_trywait(3T)   Tries to decrement, but never waits.

```
#include <thread.h>

int sema_trywait(sema_t *sp);

POSIX: sem_trywait();
```

sema_trywait() returns zero after completing successfully. When any of the
following conditions occur, the function fails and returns the corresponding
value.

    EINVAL   Invalid argument.

    EFAULT   *sp* points to an illegal address.

    EBUSY   The semaphore pointed to by *sp* has a zero count.

`sema_wait(3T)` Waits for and then decrements a semaphore variable.

```
#include <thread.h>

int sema_wait(sema_t *sp);

POSIX: sem_wait();
```

`sema_wait()` returns zero after completing successfully. When any of the following conditions occur, the function fails and returns the corresponding value.

EINVAL   Invalid argument.

EFAULT   *sp* points to an illegal address.

EINTR   The wait was interrupted by a signal or a `fork()`.

Thread Functions

`sigwait(3T)` Waits until a signal is posted.

```
#include <signal.h>

int sigwait(sigset_t *set);

POSIX: NONE;
```

`sigwait()` returns a signal number after completing successfully. When any of the following conditions occur, `sigwait()` fails and returns the corresponding value.

EINVAL   The set contains an unsupported signal number.

EFAULT   The set points to an invalid address.

thr_continue(3T)   Continues the current thread's execution.

```
#include <thread.h>

int thr_continue(thread_t target_thread);

POSIX: NONE
```

thr_continue() returns zero after completing successfully. When the following condition occurs, thr_continue() fails and returns the corresponding value.

    ESRCH   target_thread cannot be found in the current process.

thr_create(3T)   Adds a new thread of execution to the current process.

```
#include <thread.h>

int thr_create(void *stack_base, size_t stack_size,
    void *(*start_routine) (void *), void *arg, long flags,
    thread_t *new_thread);

POSIX: pthread_create();
```

thr_create() returns zero when it completes successfully. When any of the following conditions are detected, thr_create() fails and returns the corresponding value.

    EAGAIN   A system limit is exceeded, for example, when too many LWPs
                have been created.

    ENOMEM   Not enough memory was available to create the new thread.

    EINVAL   stack_base is not NULL and stack_size is less than the value
                returned by thr_minstack().

≡ G

thr_exit(3T)   Terminates a thread.

```
#include <thread.h>

void thr_exit(void *status);

POSIX: pthread_exit();
```

thr_getconcurrency(3T)   Returns the current level of concurrency.

```
#include <thread.h>

int thr_getconcurrency(void);

POSIX: NONE
```

thr_getprio(3T)   Gets the current thread's priority.

```
#include <thread.h>

int thr_getprio(thread_t target_thread, int *pri);

POSIX: pthread_setschedparam();
```

thr_getprio() returns zero after completing successfully. When the following condition occurs, thr_getprio() fails and returns the corresponding value.

ESRCH   *target_thread* cannot be found in the current process.

thr_getspecific(3T) Gets a data value from thread-specific data.

```
#include <thread.h>

int thr_getspecific(thread_key_t key, void **valuep);

POSIX: pthread_getspecific();
```

thr_getspecific() returns zero after completing successfully. When the following condition occurs, thr_getspecific() fails and returns the corresponding value.

EINVAL *key* is invalid.

thr_join(3T) Waits for a thread to terminate.

```
#include <thread.h>

int thr_join(thread_t wait_for, thread_t *departed,
   void **status);

POSIX: pthread_join();
```

thr_join() returns zero when it completes successfully. When any of the following conditions are detected, thr_join() fails and returns the corresponding value.

ESRCH *wait_for* is not a valid, undetached thread in the current process.

EDEADLK *wait_for* specifies the calli g thread.

thr_keycreate(3T)   Allocates a key for thread-specific data.

```
#include <thread.h>

int thr_keycreate(thread_key_t *keyp,
 void (*destructor) (void *value);

POSIX: pthread_key_create();
```

thr_keycreate() returns zero after completing successfully. When any of the following conditions occur, thr_keycreate() fails and returns the corresponding value.

EAGAIN   The key name space is exhausted.

ENOMEM   Not enough memory is available.

thr_kill(3T)   Sends a signal to a given thread.

```
#include <thread.h>
#include <signal.h>

int thr_kill(thread_t target_thread, int sig);

POSIX: pthread_kill();
```

thr_kill() returns zero after completing successfully. When any of the following conditions occur, thr_kill() fails and returns the corresponding value.

EINVAL   *sig* is not a valid signal number.

ESRCH   *target_thread* cannot be found in the current process.

thr_self(3T)   Returns the thread ID for the calling thread.

```
#include <thread.h>

thread_t thr_self(void);

POSIX: pthread_self();
```

thr_setconcurrency(3T)   Sets the level of concurrency.

```
#include <thread.h>

int thr_setconcurrency(new_level);

POSIX: NONE
```

thr_setconcurrency() returns zero when it completes successfully. When any of the following conditions are detected, thr_setconcurrency() fails and returns the corresponding value.

 EAGAIN   The specified concurrency level would cause a system resource to be exceeded.

 EINVAL   The value for *new_level* is negative.

thr_setprio(3T)   Sets the priority of the current thread.

```
#include <thread.h>

int thr_setprio(thread_t target_thread, int pri);

POSIX: pthread_setschedparam();
```

thr_setprio() returns zero after completing successfully. When any of the following conditions occur, thr_setprio() fails and returns the corresponding value.

    ESRCH   *target_thread* cannot be found in the current process.

    EINVAL   The value of *pri* makes no sense for the scheduling class associated with the *target_thread*.

thr_setspecific(3T)   Sets a data value for a thread-specific data key.

```
#include <thread.h>

int thr_setspecific(thread_key_t key, void *value);

POSIX: pthread_setspecific();
```

thr_setspecific() returns zero after completing successfully. When any of the following conditions occur, thr_setspecific() fails and returns the corresponding value.

    ENOMEM   Not enough memory is available.

    EINVAL   *key* is invalid.

thr_sigsetmask(3T)   Changes or examines the current thread's signal mask.

```
#include <thread.h>
#include <signal.h>

int thr_sigsetmask(int how, const sigset_t *set, sigset_t *oset);

POSIX: pthread_sigmask();
```

`thr_sigsetmask()` returns zero when it completes successfully. When any of the following conditions are detected, `thr_sigsetmask()` fails and returns the corresponding value.

EINVAL   The value of *set* is not NULL and the value of *how* is not defined.

EFAULT   Either *set* or *oset* is not a valid address.

thr_suspend(3T)   Suspends the current thread's execution.

```
#include <thread.h>

int thr_suspend(thread_t target_thread);

POSIX: NONE
```

`thr_suspend()` returns zero after completing successfully. When the following condition occurs, `thr_suspend()` fails and returns the corresponding value.

ESRCH   *target_thread* cannot be found in the current process.

thr_yield(3T)   Yields the current thread's LWP.

```
#include <thread.h>

void thr_yield(void);

POSIX: sched_yield();
```

G

Threads Primer

Pthreads API (POSIX 1003.1c) H≡

This appendix contains all the functions that are available to you in the POSIX threads library. Each function shown in the table below is listed with a call synopsis, a short description of its action, and return codes. Some of the POSIX library calls reference similar Solaris threads library calls. For more information on the Solaris thread functions, see Appendix G.

≡ H

Function Type	Function	Page
PTHREAD FUNCTIONS	pthread_cancel	261
	pthread_cleanup_pop	262
	pthread_cleanup_push	262
	pthread_create	263
	pthread_equal	264
	pthread_exit	264
	pthread_getschedparam	265
	pthread_getspecific	266
	pthread_join	266
	pthread_key_create	267
	pthread_key_delete	268
	pthread_kill	268
	pthread_once	269
	pthread_self	270
	pthread_setcancelstate	270
	pthread_setspecific	272
	pthread_sigmask	273
	pthread_testcancel	274
	sched_yield	274
PTHREAD ATTRIBUTE FUNCTIONS	pthread_attr_destroy	275
	pthread_attr_getdetachstate	275
	pthread_attr_getinheritsched	276
	pthread_attr_getschedparam	276
	pthread_attr_getschedpolicy	277
	pthread_attr_getscope	278
	pthread_attr_getstackaddr	278
	pthread_attr_getstacksize	279
	pthread_attr_init	279
	pthread_attr_setdetachstate	280
	pthread_attr_setinheritsched	281
	pthread_attr_setschedparam	282
	pthread_attr_setschedpolicy	283
	pthread_attr_setscope	283
	pthread_attr_setstackaddr	284
	pthread_attr_setstacksize	285
SEMAPHORE FUNCTIONS	sem_destroy	286
	sem_init	286
	sem_post	287
	sem_trywait	288
	sem_wait	289

Condition Functions

pthread_cond_broadcast(3T)   Broadcasts a condition signal.

```
#include <pthread.h>

int pthread_cond_broadcast(pthread_cond_t *cond);
```

The pthread_cond_broadcast() function unblocks threads blocked on a condition variable. The pthread_cond_broadcast() call unblocks all threads currently blocked on the specified condition variable *cond*.

If more than one thread is blocked on a condition variable, then the scheduling policy determines the order in which threads are unblocked. When each thread unblocked as a result of a pthread_cond_broadcast() returns from its call to pthread_cond_wait() or pthread_cond_timedwait(), the thread owns the mutex with which it called pthread_cond_wait() or pthread_cond_timedwait(). The thread(s) that are unblocked contend for the mutex according to the scheduling policy and as if each had called pthread_mutex_lock().

Currently, the only supported policy is SCHED_OTHER. In Solaris, under the SCHED_OTHER policy, there is no established order in which threads are unblocked.

The pthread_cond_broadcast() function may be called by a thread whether or not it currently owns the mutex that threads calling pthread_cond_wait() or pthread_cond_timedwait() have associated with the condition variable during their waits. However, if predictable scheduling behavior is required, then that mutex is locked by the thread calling pthread_cond_broadcast().

The pthread_cond_broadcast() function has no effect if no threads are currently blocked on *cond*.

If successful, pthread_cond_broadcast() returns zero; otherwise, an error number is returned to indicate the error.

If the following condition is detected, pthread_cond_broadcast() fails and returns the corresponding value.

EFAULT   *cond* points to an illegal address.

`pthread_cond_destroy(3T)`   Destroys a condition variable.

```
#include <pthread.h>

int pthread_cond_destroy(pthread_cond_t *cond);
```

The function `pthread_cond_destroy()` destroys the given condition variable specified by *cond*. The memory used by the condition variable is not freed.

If successful, `pthread_cond_destroy()` returns zero; otherwise, an error number is returned to indicate the error.

If the following condition is detected, `pthread_cond_destroy()` fails and returns the corresponding value.

    `EFAULT`   *cond* points to an illegal address.

`pthread_cond_init(3T)`   Initializes a condition variable.

```
#include <pthread.h>

pthread_cond_t cond = PTHREAD_COND_INITIALIZER;

int pthread_cond_init(pthread_cond_t *cond, const
pthread_condattr_t *attr);
```

The function `pthread_cond_init()` initializes the condition variable referenced by *cond* with attributes referenced by *attr*. If *attr* is `NULL`, then the default condition variable attributes are used; the effect is the same as passing the address of a default condition variable attributes object. Upon successful initialization, the state of the condition variable becomes initialized. In the default case, the initialized condition variable can be operated on only by threads created within the same process. The `pthread_cond_init()` call is similar to the `cond_init()` call in the Solaris threads API.

In cases where default condition variable attributes are appropriate, the macro PTHREAD_COND_INITIALIZER can be used to initialize condition variables that are statically allocated. The effect is equivalent to dynamic initialization by a call to pthread_cond_init() with parameter *attr* specified as NULL, except that no error checks are performed.

If successful, pthread_cond_init() returns zero; otherwise, an error number is returned to indicate the error.

If any of the following conditions are detected, pthread_cond_init() fails and returns the corresponding value.

EINVAL   The value specified for *attr* is invalid.

EFAULT   *cond* or *attr* points to an illegal address.

pthread_cond_signal(3T)   Signals a condition.

```
#include <pthread.h>

int pthread_cond_signal(pthread_cond_t *cond);
```

The pthread_cond_signal() function unblocks threads blocked on a condition variable. The pthread_cond_signal() call unblocks at least one of the threads that are blocked on the specified condition variable *cond* (if any threads are blocked on *cond*). The pthread_cond_signal() call is identical to the cond_signal() call in the Solaris threads API.

If more than one thread is blocked on a condition variable, the scheduling policy determines the order in which threads are unblocked. When each thread unblocked as a result of a pthread_cond_signal() returns from its call to pthread_cond_wait() or pthread_cond_timedwait(), the thread owns the mutex with which it called pthread_cond_wait() or pthread_cond_timedwait(). The thread(s) that are unblocked contend for the mutex according to the scheduling policy and as if each had called pthread_mutex_lock().

Currently, the only supported policy in Solaris pthreads is SCHED_OTHER. In Solaris, under the SCHED_OTHER policy, there is no established order in which threads are unblocked.

The pthread_cond_signal() function may be called by a thread whether or not it currently owns the mutex that threads calling pthread_cond_wait() or `pthread_cond_timedwait()` have associated with the condition variable during their waits. However, if predictable scheduling behavior is required, then that mutex is locked by the thread calling `pthread_cond_signal()`.

The `pthread_cond_signal()` function has no effect if no threads are currently blocked on *cond*.

If successful, `pthread_cond_signal()` returns zero; otherwise, an error number is returned to indicate the error.

If the following condition is detected, `pthread_cond_signal()` fails and returns the corresponding value.

> EFAULT   *cond* points to an illegal address.

pthread_cond_timedwait(3T)   Waits a specified time for a condition.

```
#include <pthread.h>

int pthread_cond_timedwait(pthread_cond_t *cond, pthread_mutex_t
*mutex, const struct timespec *abstime);
```

The `pthread_cond_timedwait()` function is the same as `pthread_cond_wait()`, except that an error is returned if the absolute time specified by *abstime* passes (that is, system time equals or exceeds *abstime*) before the condition *cond* is signaled or broadcast, or if the absolute time specified by *abstime* has already been passed at the time of the call. When such time-outs occur, `pthread_cond_timedwait()` nonetheless releases and reacquires the mutex referenced by *mutex*. The function `pthread_cond_timedwait()` is also a cancellation point. The `pthread_cond_timedwait()` call is similar to the `cond_timedwait()` call in the Solaris threads API.

For more information, see the `pthread_cond_wait()` call.

If successful, `pthread_cond_timedwait()` returns zero; otherwise, it returns ETIME.

If any of the following conditions are detected, `pthread_cond_timedwait()` fails and returns the corresponding value.

> EFAULT   *cond*, *abstime*, or *mutex* points to an illegal address.
>
> ETIME   The time specified by *abstime* has passed.

pthread_cond_wait(3T)   Waits for a condition to become true.

```
#include <pthread.h>

int pthread_cond_wait(pthread_cond_t *cond, pthread_mutex_t
*mutex);
```

The pthread_cond_wait() function blocks on a condition variable. The function must be called with *mutex* locked by the calling thread, or undefined behavior will result. The pthread_cond_wait() call is identical to the cond_wait() call in the Solaris threads API.

pthread_cond_wait() atomically releases *mutex* and causes the calling thread to block on the condition variable *cond*. Atomically here means atomically with respect to access by another thread to the mutex and then the condition variable. That is, if another thread is able to acquire the mutex after the about-to-block thread has released it, then a subsequent call to pthread_cond_signal() or pthread_cond_broadcast() in that thread behaves as if it were issued after the about-to-block thread has blocked.

Upon successful return, the *mutex* has been locked and is owned by the calling thread.

When condition variables are used, there is always a boolean predicate, involving shared variables associated with each condition wait, that is true if the thread should proceed. Spurious wakeups from the pthread_cond_wait() function may occur. Since the return from pthread_cond_wait() does not imply anything about the value of this predicate, the predicate should be reevaluated upon such return. This can best be done by using pthread_cond_wait() from within a while loop.

The effect of using more than one mutex for concurrent pthread_cond_wait() operations on the same condition variable is undefined; that is, a condition variable becomes bound to a unique mutex when a thread waits on the condition variable, and this (dynamic) binding ends when the wait returns.

The pthread_cond_wait() call is a cancellation point. When the cancellability enable state of a thread is set to PTHREAD_CANCEL_DEFERRED, a side effect of acting on a cancellation request while in a condition wait is that the mutex is reacquired before calling the first cancellation cleanup handler. The effect is as if the thread were unblocked and allowed to execute up to the point of returning from the call to pthread_cond_wait(). At this point, the thread notices the cancellation request and, instead of returning to the caller of pthread_cond_wait(), starts the thread cancellation activities, which include calling cancellation cleanup handlers.

A thread that has been unblocked because it has been cancelled while blocked in a call to pthread_cond_wait() does not consume any condition signal that may be directed concurrently at the condition variable, if there are other threads blocked on the condition variable.

If a signal is delivered to a thread waiting for a condition variable, upon return from the signal handler, the thread resumes waiting for the condition variable as if it were not interrupted, or it returns zero due to spurious wakeup.

If successful, pthread_cond_wait() returns zero; otherwise, an error number is returned to indicate the error.

If the following condition is detected, pthread_cond_wait() fails and returns the corresponding value.

    EFAULT   *cond* or *mutex* points to an illegal address.

Condition Attribute Functions

pthread_condattr_destroy(3T)   Destroys an attribute object.

```
#include <pthread.h>

int pthread_condattr_destroy(pthread_condattr_t *attr);
```

The pthread_condattr_destroy() function destroys a condition variable attributes object; the object becomes, in effect, uninitialized. A destroyed condition variable attributes object can be reinitialized by pthread_condattr_init(); the results of otherwise referencing the object after it has been destroyed are undefined.

If successful, pthread_condattr_destroy() returns zero; otherwise, an error number is returned to indicate the error.

If the following condition is detected, pthread_condattr_destroy() returns the corresponding error number.

    EINVAL   The value specified by *attr* is invalid.

pthread_condattr_getpshared(3T)   Retrieves attribute information.

```
#include <pthread.h>

int pthread_condattr_getpshared (const pthread_condattr_t *attr,
int *pshared);
```

The pthread_condattr_getpshared() function obtains the value of the
process-shared attribute from the attributes object referenced by *attr*.

If the symbol _POSIX_THREAD_PROCESS_SHARED is defined, the
implementation provides the process-shared attribute and the associated function
pthread_condattr_getpshared(). If this symbol is not defined, then the
process-shared attribute and these functions are not supported. The process-
shared attribute is set to PTHREAD_PROCESS_SHARED to permit a condition
variable to be operated on by any thread that has access to the memory where the
condition variable is allocated, even if the condition variable is allocated in
memory that is shared by multiple processes. If the process-shared attribute is
PTHREAD_PROCESS_PRIVATE, then the condition variable can only be operated
on by threads created within the same process as the thread that initialized the
condition variable; if threads of differing processes attempt to operate on such a
condition variable, the behavior is undefined. The default value of the attribute is
PTHREAD_PROCESS_PRIVATE.

Currently, only the attribute *pshared* has been defined.

If successful, pthread_condattr_getpshared() returns zero and stores the
value of the process-shared attribute of *attr* into the object referenced by the
pshared parameter; otherwise, an error number is returned to indicate the error.

If the following condition is detected, pthread_condattr_getpshared()
returns the corresponding error number.

  EINVAL The value specified by *attr* is invalid.

H

`pthread_condattr_init(3T)`   Initializes an attribute object.

```
#include <pthread.h>

int pthread_condattr_init(pthread_condattr_t *attr);
```

The function `pthread_condattr_init()` initializes a condition variable attributes object *attr* with the default value for all the attributes.

Attempting to initialize an already initialized condition variable attributes object leaves the storage allocated by the previous initialization unallocated.

After a condition variable attributes object has been used to initialize one or more condition variables, any function affecting the attributes object (including destruction) does not affect any previously initialized condition variables.

If successful, `pthread_condattr_init()` returns zero; otherwise, an error number is returned to indicate the error.

If the following condition occurs, `pthread_condattr_init()` returns the corresponding error number.

ENOMEM   Insufficient memory exists to initialize the condition variable attributes object.

`pthread_condattr_setpshared(3T)`
                                Sets condition variable attribute information.

```
#include <pthread.h>

int pthread_condattr_setpshared(pthread_condattr_t *attr, int
pshared);
```

The `pthread_condattr_setpshared()` function sets the process-shared attribute in an initialized attributes object referenced by *attr*.

If the symbol `_POSIX_THREAD_PROCESS_SHARED` is defined, the implementation provides the process-shared attribute and the associated function `pthread_condattr_setpshared()`. If this symbol is not defined, then the process-shared attribute and these functions are not supported. The process-shared attribute is set to `PTHREAD_PROCESS_SHARED` to permit a condition variable to be operated on by any thread that has access to the memory where the condition variable is allocated, even if the condition variable is allocated in memory that is shared by multiple processes. If the process-shared attribute is `PTHREAD_PROCESS_PRIVATE`, the condition variable can only be operated on by threads created within the same process as the thread that initialized the condition variable; if threads of differing processes attempt to operate on such a condition variable, the behavior is undefined. The default value of the attribute is `PTHREAD_PROCESS_PRIVATE`.

Currently, only the attribute *pshared* has been defined.

If successful, `pthread_condattr_setpshared()` returns zero; otherwise, an error number is returned to indicate the error.

For each of the following conditions, if the condition is detected, `pthread_condattr_setpshared()` returns the corresponding error number.

> EINVAL   The value specified by *attr* is invalid.
>
> EINVAL   The new value specified for the attribute is outside the range of legal values for that attribute.

Mutex Functions

`pthread_mutex_destroy(3T)`   Destroys a mutex variable.

```
#include <pthread.h>

int pthread_mutex_destroy(pthread_mutex_t *mutex);
```

The `pthread_mutex_destroy()` function destroys the mutex object referenced by *mutex*; the mutex object becomes, in effect, uninitialized. The memory used by the mutex variable is not freed.

If successful, `pthread_mutex_destroy()` returns zero; otherwise, an error number is returned to indicate the error.

If the following condition is detected, `pthread_mutex_destroy()` fails and returns the corresponding value.

> EFAULT   *mutex* points to an illegal address.

H

`pthread_mutex_getprioceiling(3T)`

Retrieves the priority ceiling of a mutex.

```
#include <pthread.h>

int pthread_mutex_getprioceiling (const pthread_mutex_t *mutex,
int *prioceiling);
```

The `pthread_mutex_getprioceiling()` function returns the current priority ceiling of the *mutex* in *prioceiling*.

If successful, `pthread_mutex_getprioceiling()` returns zero; otherwise, an error number is returned to indicate the error.

If any of the following conditions occur, `pthread_mutex_getprioceiling()` returns the corresponding error number.

ENOTSUP   The option `_POSIX_THREAD_PRIO_PROTECT` is not defined, and the implementation does not support the `pthread_mutex_getprioceiling()` function.

EINVAL   The priority requested by *prioceiling* is out of range.

In the current implementation, `_POSIX_THREAD_PRIO_PROTECT` is not defined and the function `pthread_mutex_getprioceiling()` returns ENOTSUP.

`pthread_mutex_init(3T)`

Initializes a mutex variable.

```
#include <pthread.h>

pthread_mutex_t mutex = PTHREAD_MUTEX_INITIALIZER;

int pthread_mutex_init(pthread_mutex_t *mutex, const
pthread_mutexattr_t *attr);
```

The `pthread_mutex_init()` function initializes the mutex variable referenced by *mutex* with attributes specified by *attr*. If *attr* is NULL, the default mutex attributes are used; the effect is the same as passing the address of a default mutex attribute object. Upon successful initialization, the state of the mutex becomes initialized and unlocked. In the default case, the initialized mutex variable can be operated on only by threads created within the same process.

In cases where default mutex attributes are appropriate, the macro `PTHREAD_MUTEX_INITIALIZER` can be used to initialize mutexes that are statically allocated. The effect is equivalent to dynamic initialization by a call to `pthread_mutex_init()` with parameter *attr* specified as `NULL`, except that no error checks are performed.

If successful, `pthread_mutex_init()` returns zero; otherwise, an error number is returned to indicate the error.

If any of the following conditions are detected, `pthread_mutex_init()` fails and returns the corresponding value.

EINVAL   The value specified by *attr* is invalid.

EFAULT   *mutex* or *attr* points to an illegal address.

`pthread_mutex_lock(3T)`   Locks a mutex variable.

```
#include <pthread.h>

int pthread_mutex_lock(pthread_mutex_t *mutex);
```

`pthread_mutex_lock()` is identical to the `mutex_lock()` in the Solaris threads API. The mutex object referenced by *mutex* is locked by calling `pthread_mutex_lock()`. If the mutex is already locked, the calling thread blocks until the mutex becomes available. This operation returns with the mutex object referenced by *mutex* in the locked state with the calling thread as its owner. An attempt by the current owner of a mutex to relock the mutex results in undefined behavior.

If a signal is delivered to a thread waiting for a mutex, upon return from the signal handler the thread resumes waiting for the mutex as if it were not interrupted.

If successful, `pthread_mutex_lock()`, returns zero; otherwise, an error number is returned to indicate the error.

If the following condition is detected, `pthread_mutex_lock()` fails and returns the corresponding value.

EFAULT   *mutex* points to an illegal address.

pthread_mutex_setprioceiling(3T) Sets the priority ceiling of a mutex.

```
#include <pthread.h>

int pthread_mutex_setprioceiling(pthread_mutex_t *mutex, int
prioceiling, int *old_ceiling);
```

The pthread_mutex_setprioceiling() function either locks the *mutex* if it is unlocked or blocks until it can successfully lock the *mutex*; then, it changes the mutex's priority ceiling specified in *prioceiling* and releases the *mutex*. When the change is successful, the previous value of the priority ceiling is returned in *old_ceiling*.

If the pthread_mutex_setprioceiling() function fails, the mutex priority ceiling is not changed.

If successful, pthread_mutex_setprioceiling() returns zero; otherwise, an error number is returned to indicate the error.

If any of the following conditions occur, pthread_mutex_setprioceiling() returns the corresponding error number.

ENOTSUP The option _POSIX_THREAD_PRIO_PROTECT is not defined, and the implementation does not support the pthread_mutex_setprioceiling() function.

EINVAL The priority requested by *prioceiling* is out of range.

In the current implementation, _POSIX_THREAD_PRIO_PROTECT is not defined and the function pthread_mutex_setprioceiling() returns ENOTSUP.

pthread_mutex_trylock(3T) Tries to lock a mutex variable.

```
#include <pthread.h>

int pthread_mutex_trylock(pthread_mutex_t *mutex);
```

The function pthread_mutex_trylock() is identical to pthread_mutex_lock(), except that if the mutex object referenced by *mutex* is currently locked (by any thread, including the current thread), the call returns immediately with an error. The `pthread_mutex_trylock()` is identical to the `mutex_trylock()` call in the Solaris threads API.

If a signal is delivered to a thread waiting for a mutex, then, upon return from the signal handler, the thread resumes waiting for the mutex as if it were not interrupted.

`pthread_mutex_trylock()` returns zero if a lock on the mutex object referenced by mutex is acquired; otherwise, an error number is returned to indicate the error.

If any of the following conditions are detected, `pthread_mutex_trylock()` fails and returns the corresponding value.

> EFAULT   *mutex* points to an illegal address.
>
> EBUSY   The mutex pointed to by *mutex* is already locked.

`pthread_mutex_unlock(3T)`   Unlocks a mutex variable.

```
#include <pthread.h>

int pthread_mutex_unlock(pthread_mutex_t *mutex);
```

The function `pthread_mutex_unlock()` is called by the owner of the mutex object referenced by *mutex* to release it. A `pthread_mutex_unlock()` call by a thread that is not the owner of the mutex results in undefined behavior. Calling `pthread_mutex_unlock()` when the mutex object is unlocked also results in undefined behavior. If there are threads blocked on the mutex object referenced by *mutex* when `pthread_mutex_unlock()` is called, the mutex becomes available and the scheduling policy is used to determine which thread acquires the mutex. The `pthread_mutex_unlock()` call is identical to the `mutex_unlock()` call in the Solaris threads API.

Currently, the only supported policy is SCHED_OTHER. In Solaris, under the SCHED_OTHER policy, there is no established order in which threads are unblocked.

If successful, `pthread_mutex_unlock()` returns zero; otherwise, an error number is returned to indicate the error.

If the following condition is detected, `pthread_mutex_unlock()` fails and returns the corresponding value.

EFAULT   *mutex* points to an illegal address.

Mutex Attribute Functions

`pthread_mutexattr_destroy(3T)`   Destroys a mutex attribute object.

```
#include <pthread.h>

int pthread_mutexattr_destroy(pthread_mutexattr_t *attr);
```

The `pthread_mutexattr_destroy()` function destroys the mutex attributes object *attr*; the object becomes, in effect, uninitialized. A destroyed mutex attributes object can be reinitialized by `pthread_mutexattr_init()`; the results of otherwise referencing the object after it has been destroyed are undefined.

Upon successful completion, `pthread_mutexattr_destroy()` returns zero; otherwise, an error number is returned to indicate the error.

If the following condition is detected, `pthread_mutexattr_destroy()` returns the corresponding error number.

EINVAL   The value specified by *attr* is invalid.

`pthread_mutexattr_getprioceiling(3T)`
                              Retrieves a mutex attribute priority value.

```
#include <pthread.h>
int pthread_mutexattr_getprioceiling (const pthread_mutexattr_t
*attr, int *prioceiling);
```

The `pthread_mutexattr_getprioceiling()` function retrieves a mutex attribute object pointed to by *attr*, which has been previously created by the function `pthread_mutexattr_init()`.

Upon successful completion, `pthread_mutexattr_getprioceiling()` returns zero; otherwise, an error number is returned to indicate the error.

If any of the following conditions occur, `pthread_mutexattr_getprioceiling()` returns the corresponding error number.

EINVAL	The value specified by *attr* is invalid.
ENOTSUP	The options _POSIX_THREAD_PRIO_INHERIT and _POSIX_THREAD_PRIO_PROTECT are not defined, and the implementation does not support the `pthread_mutexattr_getprioceiling()` function.
EPERM	The caller does not have the privilege to perform the operation.

In the current implementation, _POSIX_THREAD_PRIO_INHERIT and _POSIX_THREAD_PRIO_PROTECT are not defined, and the function `pthread_mutexattr_getprioceiling()` returns ENOTSUP.

pthread_mutexattr_getprotocol(3T)
Retrieves a mutex attribute protocol value.

```
#include <pthread.h>

int pthread_mutexattr_getprotocol (const pthread_mutexattr_t
*attr, int *protocol);
```

The `pthread_mutexattr_getprotocol()` function retrieves a mutex attribute object pointed to by *attr*, which has been previously created by the function `pthread_mutexattr_init()`.

Upon successful completion, `pthread_mutexattr_getprotocol()` returns zero; otherwise, an error number is returned to indicate the error.

If any of the following conditions occur, `pthread_mutexattr_getprotocol()` returns the corresponding error number.

EINVAL	The value specified by *attr* is invalid.
ENOTSUP	The options _POSIX_THREAD_PRIO_INHERIT and _POSIX_THREAD_PRIO_PROTECT are not defined, and the

implementation does not support the
pthread_mutexattr_getprotocol() function.

EPERM   The caller does not have the privilege to perform the operation.

In the current implementation, _POSIX_THREAD_PRIO_INHERIT and
_POSIX_THREAD_PRIO_PROTECT are not defined, and the function
pthread_mutexattr_getprotocol() returns ENOTSUP.

pthread_mutexattr_getpshared(3T)

Retrieves the process-shared attribute value.

```
#include <pthread.h>

int pthread_mutexattr_getpshared (const pthread_mutexattr_t *attr,
int *pshared);
```

The pthread_mutexattr_getpshared() function obtains the value of the
process-shared attribute, *pshared*, from the attributes object referenced by *attr*.

If the symbol _POSIX_THREAD_PROCESS_SHARED is defined, the
implementation provides the process-shared attribute and the associated function
pthread_mutexattr_getpshared(). If this symbol is not defined, then the
process-shared attribute and this function are not supported. The process-shared
attribute is set to PTHREAD_PROCESS_SHARED to permit a mutex to be operated
on by any thread that has access to the memory where the mutex is allocated,
even if the mutex is allocated in memory that is shared by multiple processes. If
the process-shared attribute is PTHREAD_PROCESS_PRIVATE, the mutex can only
be operated on by threads created within the same process as the thread that
initialized the mutex; if threads of differing processes attempt to operate on such
a mutex, the behavior is undefined. The default value of the attribute is
PTHREAD_PROCESS_PRIVATE.

Currently, only the attribute *pshared* has been defined.

Upon successful completion, pthread_mutexattr_getpshared() returns zero
and stores the value of the process-shared attribute of *attr* into the object
referenced by the *pshared* parameter; otherwise, an error number is returned to
indicate the error.

If the following condition is detected, pthread_mutexattr_getpshared()
returns the corresponding error number.

EINVAL   The value specified by *attr* is invalid.

`pthread_mutexattr_init(3T)`   Initializes a mutex attribute object.

```
#include <pthread.h>

int pthread_mutexattr_init(pthread_mutexattr_t *attr);
```

The function `pthread_mutexattr_init()` initializes a mutex attributes object *attr* with the default value for all of the attributes.

Attempting to initialize an already initialized mutex variable attributes object leaves the storage allocated by the previous initialization unallocated.

After a mutex attributes object has been used to initialize one or more mutexes, any function affecting the attributes object (including destruction) does not affect any previously initialized mutexes.

Upon successful completion, `pthread_mutexattr_init()` returns zero; otherwise, an error number is returned to indicate the error.

If the following condition is detected, `pthread_mutexattr_init()` returns the corresponding error number.

> ENOMEM   Insufficient memory exists to initialize the mutex attributes object.

`pthread_mutexattr_setprioceiling(3T)`
                                    Sets mutex attribute priority ceiling value.

```
#include <pthread.h>

int pthread_mutexattr_setprioceiling (pthread_mutexattr_t *attr,
int prioceiling);
```

The `pthread_mutexattr_setprioceiling()` function manipulates a mutex attribute object pointed to by *attr*, which has been previously created by the function `pthread_mutexattr_init()`.

If the symbol `_POSIX_THREAD_PRIO_PROTECT` is defined, the `pthread_mutexattr_t` mutex attributes objects includes the *prioceiling* attribute.

≡ *H*

The *prioceiling* attribute contains the priority ceiling of initialized mutexes. The value of *prioceiling* is within the maximum range of priorities defined by SCHED_FIFO.

When a thread owns a mutex with the PTHREAD_PRIO_NONE protocol attribute, its priority and scheduling are not affected by its mutex ownership.

When a thread is blocking higher-priority threads because of owning one or more mutexes with the PTHREAD_PRIO_INHERIT protocol attribute, it executes at the higher of its priority or the priority of the highest-priority thread waiting on any of the mutexes owned by this thread and initialized with this protocol.

When a thread owns one or more mutexes initialized with the PTHREAD_PRIO_PROTECT protocol, it executes at the higher of its priority or the highest of the priority ceilings of all the mutexes owned by this thread and initialized with this attribute, regardless of whether other threads are blocked on any of these mutexes. The *prioceiling* attribute defines the priority ceiling of initialized mutexes, which is the minimum priority level at which the critical section guarded by the mutex is executed. In order to avoid priority inversion, the priority ceiling of the mutex is set to a priority higher than or equal to the highest priority of all the threads that may lock that mutex. The values of *prioceiling* are within the maximum range of priorities defined under the SCHED_FIFO scheduling policy.

If a thread simultaneously owns several mutexes initialized with different protocols, it will execute at the highest of the priorities that it would have obtained by each of these protocols.

When a thread makes a call to pthread_mutex_lock(), if the symbol _POSIX_THREAD_PRIO_INHERIT is defined and the mutex was initialized with the protocol attribute having the value PTHREAD_PRIO_INHERIT, then, when the calling thread is blocked because the mutex is owned by another thread, that owner thread inherits the priority level of the calling thread as long as it continues to own the mutex. The implementation updates its execution priority to the maximum of its assigned priority and all its inherited priorities. Furthermore, if this owner thread itself becomes blocked on another mutex, the same priority inheritance effect is propagated to this other owner thread, in a recursive manner.

Upon successful completion, pthread_mutexattr_setprioceiling() returns zero; otherwise, an error number is returned to indicate the error.

If any of the following conditions occur, pthread_mutexattr_setprioceiling() returns the corresponding error number.

EINVAL   The value specified by *attr* or *prioceiling* is invalid.

ENOTSUP   The options _POSIX_THREAD_PRIO_INHERIT and
           _POSIX_THREAD_PRIO_PROTECT are not defined, and the
           implementation does not support the
           pthread_mutexattr_setprioceiling() function.

EPERM   The caller does not have the privilege to perform the operation.

In the current implementation, _POSIX_THREAD_PRIO_INHERIT and
_POSIX_THREAD_PRIO_PROTECT are not defined, and the function
pthread_mutexattr_setprioceiling() returns ENOTSUP.

pthread_mutexattr_setprotocol(3T) Sets a mutex attribute protocol value.

```
#include <pthread.h>

int pthread_mutexattr_setprotocol(pthread_mutexattr_t *attr, int
protocol);
```

The pthread_mutexattr_setprotocol() function manipulates a mutex
attribute object pointed to by *attr*, which has been previously created by the
function pthread_mutexattr_init().

The *protocol* attribute defines the protocol to be followed in using mutexes. The
value of *protocol* may be one of PTHREAD_PRIO_NONE,
PTHREAD_PRIO_INHERIT, or PTHREAD_PRIO_PROTECT, which is defined by the
header pthread.h. The PTHREAD_PRIO_PROTECT value is valid if the symbol
_POSIX_THREAD_PRIO_PROTECT is defined, and the PTHREAD_PRIO_INHERIT
value is valid if the symbol _POSIX_THREAD_PRIO_INHERIT is defined.

When a thread owns a mutex with the PTHREAD_PRIO_NONE protocol attribute,
its priority and scheduling are not affected by its mutex ownership.

Upon successful completion, pthread_mutexattr_setprotocol() returns
zero; otherwise, an error number is returned to indicate the error.

If any of the following conditions occur, pthread_mutexattr_setprotocol()
returns the corresponding error number.

EINVAL   The value specified by *attr* or *protocol* is invalid.

ENOTSUP   The options _POSIX_THREAD_PRIO_INHERIT and
           _POSIX_THREAD_PRIO_PROTECT are not defined and the

implementation does not support the
pthread_mutexattr_setprotocol() function.

ENOTSUP   The value specified by *protocol* is an unsupported value.

EPERM   The caller does not have the privilege to perform the operation.

In the current implementation, _POSIX_THREAD_PRIO_INHERIT and
_POSIX_THREAD_PRIO_PROTECT are not defined, and the function
pthread_mutexattr_setprotocol() returns ENOTSUP.

pthread_mutexattr_setpshared(3T)

Sets the process-shared attribute for a mutex.

```
#include <pthread.h>

int pthread_mutexattr_setpshared(pthread_mutexattr_t *attr, int
pshared);
```

The pthread_mutexattr_setpshared() function sets the process-shared
attribute in an initialized mutex attributes object referenced by *attr*.

If the symbol _POSIX_THREAD_PROCESS_SHARED is defined, the
implementation provides the process-shared attribute and the associated function
pthread_mutexattr_setpshared(). If this symbol is not defined, then the
process-shared attribute and this function are not supported. The process-shared
attribute is set to PTHREAD_PROCESS_SHARED to permit a mutex to be operated
on by any thread that has access to the memory where the mutex is allocated,
even if the mutex is allocated in memory that is shared by multiple processes. If
the process-shared attribute is PTHREAD_PROCESS_PRIVATE, the mutex can only
be operated on by threads created within the same process as the thread that
initialized the mutex; if threads of differing processes attempt to operate on such
a mutex, the behavior is undefined. The default value of the attribute is
PTHREAD_PROCESS_PRIVATE.

Currently, only the attribute *pshared* has been defined.

Upon successful completion, pthread_mutexattr_setpshared() returns
zero; otherwise, an error number is returned to indicate the error.

For each of the following conditions, if the condition is detected,
pthread_mutexattr_setpshared() returns the corresponding error number.

EINVAL   The value specified by *attr* is invalid.

EINVAL   The new value specified for the attribute is outside the range of
           legal values for that attribute.

Pthread Functions

pthread_cancel(3T)   Sends a cancel request to a thread.

```
#include <pthread.h>

int pthread_cancel(pthread_t thread);
```

The pthread_cancel() function requests that *thread* be cancelled. The target
thread's cancellability state and type determines when the cancellation takes
effect. When the cancellation is acted on, the cancellation cleanup handlers for
thread are called. When the last cancellation cleanup handler returns, the thread-
specific data destructor functions are called for *thread*. When the last destructor
function returns, *thread* is terminated.

If successful, pthread_cancel() returns zero; otherwise, an error number is
returned to indicate the error.

If the following condition is detected, pthread_cancel() returns the
corresponding error number.

ESRCH   No thread could be found corresponding to that specified by
           the given *thread* ID.

H

pthread_cleanup_pop(3t)   Retrieves a function from the cleanup stack.

```
#include <pthread.h>

void pthread_cleanup_pop(int execute);
```

The pthread_cleanup_pop() function removes the routine at the top of the calling thread's cancellation cleanup stack and optionally invokes it (if *execute* is non-zero).

Anytime the pthread_clenaup_pop() call is used, a matching call to pthread_cleanup_push() is required.

The effect of calling longjmp(3C) or siglongjmp(3C) is undefined if any calls to pthread_cleanup_push() or pthread_cleanup_pop() were made without the matching call since the jump buffer was filled. The effect of calling longjmp() or siglongjmp() from inside a cancellation cleanup handler is also undefined, unless the jump buffer was also filled in the cancellation cleanup handler.

pthread_cleanup_push(3T)   Puts a function onto the cleanup stack.

```
#include <pthread.h>

void pthread_cleanup_push(void (*routine)(void *), void *arg);
```

The pthread_cleanup_push() function pushes the specified cancellation cleanup handler *routine* onto the calling thread's cancellation cleanup stack. Anytime the pthread_cleanup_push() call is used, a matching call to pthread_cleanup_pop() is required.

The effect of calling longjmp(3C) or siglongjmp(3C) is undefined if any calls to pthread_cleanup_push() were made without the matching call since the jump buffer was filled. The effect of calling longjmp() or siglongjmp() from inside a cancellation cleanup handler is also undefined, unless the jump buffer was also filled in the cancellation cleanup handler.

pthread_create(3T)   Creates a new thread of execution.

```
#include <pthread.h>

int pthread_create(pthread_t *thread, const pthread_attr_t *attr,
void * (*start_routine)(void *), void *arg);
```

The pthread_create() function creates a new thread, with attributes specified by *attr*, within a process. If *attr* is NULL, then the default thread attributes are used. If the attributes specified by *attr* are later modified, the thread's attributes are not affected. Upon successful completion, pthread_create() stores the ID of the created thread in the location referenced by *thread*.

The thread is created by executing *start_routine* with *arg* as its sole argument. If the *start_routine* returns, the effect is as if there were an implicit call to pthread_exit(), using the return value of *start_routine* as the exit status. Note that the thread in which main() was originally invoked differs from this. When it returns from main(), the effect is as if there were an implicit call to exit(), using the return value from main() as the exit status.

The signal state of the new thread is initialized as follows:

1. The signal mask is inherited from the creating thread.

2. The set of signals pending for the new thread is empty.

If pthread_create() fails, no new thread is created and the contents of the location referenced by *thread* are undefined.

If successful, pthread_create() returns zero; otherwise, an error number is returned to indicate the error. If any of the following conditions occur, pthread_create() returns the corresponding error number.

EAGAIN	The system lacked the necessary resources to create another thread, or the system-imposed limit on the total number of threads in a process PTHREAD_THREADS_MAX would be exceeded.
EINVAL	The value specified by *attr* is invalid.

H

pthread_equal(3T)   Compares two thread IDs.

```
#include <pthread.h>

int pthread_equal(pthread_t t1, pthread_t t2);
```

The pthread_equal() function compares the thread IDs *t1* and *t2*. You cannot rely on the test (t1 == t2).

pthread_equal() returns a non-zero value if *t1* and *t2* are equal; otherwise, zero is returned.

If either *t1* or *t2* is not a valid thread ID, the behavior is undefined.

pthread_exit(3T)   Terminates a thread's execution.

```
#include <pthread.h>

void pthread_exit(void *value_ptr);
```

The pthread_exit() function terminates the calling thread and makes the *value_ptr* available to any successful join with the terminating thread. Any cancellation cleanup handlers that have been pushed and not yet popped are popped in the reverse order in which they were pushed and then executed. After all cancellation cleanup handlers have been executed, if the thread has any thread-specific data, then appropriate destructor functions will be called in an unspecified order. Thread termination does not release any application-visible process resources, including, but not limited to, mutexes and file descriptors, nor does it perform any process level cleanup actions, including, but limited to, calling any atexit() routines that may exist.

An implicit call to pthread_exit() is made when a thread other than the thread in which main() was first invoked returns from the start routine that was used to create it. The function's return value serves as the thread's exit status.

The behavior of pthread_exit() is undefined if called from a cancellation cleanup handler or destructor function that was invoked as a result of either an implicit or explicit call to pthread_exit().

After a thread has terminated, the result of access to local (auto) variables of the thread is undefined. Thus, references to local variables of the exiting thread should not be used for the pthread_exit() *value_ptr* parameter value.

The process exits with an exit status of zero after the last thread has been terminated. The behavior is as if the implementation called `exit()` with a zero argument at thread termination time.

`pthread_exit()` cannot return to its caller.

pthread_getschedparam(3T)   Returns a thread's scheduling parameters.

```
#include <sched.h>
#include <pthread.h>

int pthread_getschedparam(pthread_t thread, int *policy, struct
sched_param *param);
```

The `pthread_getschedparam()` function allows the scheduling policy and scheduling parameters of individual threads within a multithreaded process to be retrieved. For `SCHED_FIFO` and `SCHED_RR`, the only required member of the sched_param structure is the priority sched_priority. For `SCHED_OTHER`, the affected scheduling parameter is also the priority sched_priority member of the sched_param structure.

The `pthread_getschedparam()` function retrieves the scheduling policy and scheduling parameters for the thread whose thread ID is given by *thread* and stores those values in *policy* and *param*, respectively. The priority value returned from `pthread_getschedparam()` is the value specified by the most recent `pthread_setschedparam()` or `pthread_create()` call affecting the target thread; the value does not reflect any temporary adjustments to its priority as a result of any priority inheritance or ceiling functions.

If successful, `pthread_getschedparam()` returns zero; otherwise, an error number is returned to indicate the error.

For each of the following conditions, if the condition is detected, `pthread_getschedparam()` returns the corresponding error number.

> ESRCH   The value specified by *thread* does not refer to a existing thread.
>
> EINVAL   The value specified by *policy* or one of the scheduling parameters associated with the scheduling policy is invalid, if *policy* or *param* is NULL.

`pthread_getspecific(3T)`   Retrieves a thread-specific data value.

```
#include <pthread.h>

void *pthread_getspecific(pthread_key_t key);
```

The `pthread_getspecific()` function returns the value currently bound to the specified *key* on behalf of the calling thread. The `pthread_getspecific()` call is similar to the `thr_getspecific()` call in the Solaris threads API.

The effect of calling `pthread_getspecific()` with a *key* value not obtained from `pthread_key_create()` or after *key* has been deleted with `pthread_key_delete()` is undefined.

`pthread_getspecific()` may be called either explicitly or implicitly from a thread-specific data destructor function.

`pthread_getspecific()` returns the thread-specific data value associated with the given *key*. If no thread-specific data value is associated with key, then NULL is returned.

No errors are returned from `pthread_getspecific()`.

`pthread_join(3T)`   Waits for a thread to terminate.

```
#include <pthread.h>

int pthread_join(pthread_t thread, void **value_ptr);
```

The `pthread_join()` function suspends execution of the calling thread until the target *thread* terminates, unless the target *thread* has already terminated. On return from a successful `pthread_join()` call, with a non-null *value_ptr* argument, the value passed to `pthread_exit()` by the terminating thread is placed in the location referenced by *value_ptr*. The results of multiple simultaneous calls to `pthread_join()` specifying the same target thread are undefined. If the thread calling `pthread_join()` is cancelled, then the target *thread* remains joinable by `pthread_join()`.

If successful, `pthread_join()` returns zero; otherwise, an error number is returned to indicate the error. If any of the following conditions occur, `pthread_join()` returns the corresponding error number.

ESRCH   No thread could be found corresponding to that specified by the given *thread* ID.

EDEADLK   A deadlock was detected or the value of *thread* specifies the calling thread.

Unlike Solaris threads, POSIX cannot join on "any" thread. If the target *thread* ID is zero, `pthread_join()` returns with the error code ESRCH.

`pthread_key_create(3T)`   Creates a thread-specific data key.

```
#include <pthread.h>

int pthread_key_create(pthread_key_t *key, void (*destructor(void
*))));
```

`pthread_key_create()` is identical to the `thr_keycreate()` call in the Solaris threads API. This function creates a thread-specific data key visible to all threads in the process. Upon key creation, the value NULL is associated with the new key in all active threads. Upon thread creation, the value NULL is associated with all defined keys in the new thread.

An optional *destructor* function may be associated with each *key* value. At thread exit, if a key value has a non-null *destructor* pointer and the thread has a non-null value associated with that *key*, the function pointed to is called with the current associated value as its sole argument. The order of destructor calls is unspecified if more than one *destructor* exists for a thread when it exits.

If successful, `pthread_key_create()` function stores the newly created key value at *key* and returns zero; otherwise, an error number is returned to indicate the error.

If any of the following conditions occur, `pthread_key_create()` returns the corresponding error number.

EAGAIN   The system lacked the necessary resources to create another thread-specific data *key*.

ENOMEM   Insufficient memory exists to create the *key*.

≡ H

pthread_key_delete(3T) Deletes a thread-specific data key.

```
#include <pthread.h>

int pthread_key_delete(pthread_key_t key);
```

The pthread_key_delete() function deletes a thread-specific data key previously returned by pthread_key_create(). The thread-specific data values associated with *key* need not be NULL at the time pthread_key_delete() is called. It is the responsibility of the application to free any storage or perform any cleanup actions for data structures related to the deleted *key* or associated thread-specific data in any threads; this cleanup can be done either before or after pthread_key_delete() is called. Any attempt to use *key* following the call to pthread_key_delete() results in undefined behavior. No destructor functions are invoked by pthread_key_delete().

If successful, pthread_key_delete() returns zero; otherwise, an error number is returned to indicate the error.

If the following condition is detected, then pthread_key_delete() returns the corresponding error number.

> EINVAL   The *key* value is invalid.

pthread_kill(3T) Sends a signal to a thread.

```
#include <signal.h>
#include <pthread.h>

int pthread_kill(pthread_t thread, int sig);
```

pthread_kill() is identical to the thr_kill() call in the Solaris threads API. pthread_kill() sends the signal, *sig*, to *thread*. The thread must be a thread within the same process as the calling thread. *sig* must be a valid signal specified in the list given in signal(5). If *sig* is zero, then error checking is performed but no signal is actually sent; this can be used to check if *thread* exists.

Upon successful completion, pthread_kill() returns zero; otherwise, it returns an error number listed below. If pthread_kill() fails, no signal is sent.

ESRCH   No thread could be found corresponding to that specified by
            the given *thread* ID.

EINVAL   The value of the *sig* argument is invalid or an unsupported
            signal number.

pthread_once(3T)   Provides initialization control.

```
#include <pthread.h>

pthread_once_t once_control = PTHREAD_ONCE_INIT;

int pthread_once(pthread_once_t *once_control, void
(*init_routine)(void));
```

The first call to pthread_once() by any thread in a process with a given
once_control will call the *init_routine()* with no arguments. Subsequent calls of
pthread_once() with the same *once_control* will not call the *init_routine()*. On
return from pthread_once(), it is guaranteed that *init_routine()* has completed.
The *once_control* parameter is used to determine whether the associated
initialization routine has been called.

The function pthread_once() is not a cancellation point. However, if
init_routine() is a cancellation point and is cancelled, the effect on *once_control* will
be as if pthread_once() were never called.

The constant PTHREAD_ONCE_INIT is defined in the header pthread.h.

The behavior of pthread_once() is undefined if *once_control* has automatic
storage duration or is not initialized by PTHREAD_ONCE_INIT.

Upon successful completion, pthread_once() returns zero; otherwise, an error
number is returned to indicate the error.

If the following condition is detected, then pthread_once() returns the
corresponding error number.

EINVAL   *once_control* or *init_routine* is NULL.

≡ H

pthread_self(3T)   Returns the thread ID of the calling thread.

```
#include <pthread.h>

pthread_t pthread_self(void);
```

pthread_self() is identical to the thr_self() call in the Solaris threads API. pthread_self() returns the thread ID of the calling thread.

pthread_setcancelstate(3T)   Sets a thread's cancel state.

```
#include <pthread.h>

int pthread_setcancelstate(int state, int *oldstate);
```

The pthread_setcancelstate() function atomically both sets the calling thread's cancellability *state* to the indicated state and returns the previous cancellability state at the location referenced by a non-null *oldstate*. Legal values for *state* are PTHREAD_CANCEL_ENABLE and PTHREAD_CANCEL_DISABLE.

The cancellability state of any newly created threads, including the thread in which main() was first invoked, is PTHREAD_CANCEL_ENABLE.

If successful, pthread_setcancelstate() returns zero; otherwise, an error number is returned to indicate the error.

If the following condition is detected, pthread_setcancelstate() returns the corresponding error.

EINVAL   The specified *state* is not PTHREAD_CANCEL_ENABLE or PTHREAD_CANCEL_DISABLE.

pthread_setcanceltype(3T)   Sets a thread's cancel type.

```
#include <pthread.h>

int pthread_setcanceltype(int type, int *oldtype);
```

The pthread_setcanceltype() function atomically both sets the calling thread's cancellability type to the indicated *type* and returns the previous cancellability type at the location referenced by a non-null *oldtype*. Legal values for *type* are PTHREAD_CANCEL_DEFERRED and PTHREAD_CANCEL_ASYNCHRONOUS.

The cancelability type of any newly created threads, including the thread in which main() was first invoked, is PTHREAD_CANCEL_DEFERRED.

If successful, pthread_setcanceltype() returns zero; otherwise, an error number is returned to indicate the error.

If the following condition is detected, pthread_setcanceltype() returns the corresponding error.

> EINVAL   The specified *type* is not PTHREAD_CANCEL_DEFERRED or PTHREAD_CANCEL_ASYNCHRONOUS.

pthread_setschedparam(3T)   Sets a thread's scheduling parameters.

```
#include <sched.h>
#include <pthread.h>

int pthread_setschedparam(pthread_t thread, int policy, const struct
sched_param *param);
```

The pthread_setschedparam() functions allow the scheduling policy and scheduling parameters of individual threads within a multithreaded process to be set. For SCHED_FIFO and SCHED_RR, the only required member of the sched_param structure is the priority sched_priority. For SCHED_OTHER, the affected scheduling parameter is also the priority sched_priority member of the sched_param structure.

H

The `pthread_setschedparam()` function sets the scheduling policy and associated scheduling parameters for *thread* to the policy and associated parameters provided in *policy* and *param*, respectively.

If `pthread_setschedparam()` fails, no scheduling parameters are changed for the target thread.

If successful, `pthread_setschedparam()` returns zero; otherwise, an error number is returned to indicate the error.

For each of the following conditions, if the condition is detected, `pthread_setschedparam()` returns the corresponding error number.

ESRCH	The value specified by *thread* does not refer to an existing thread.
EINVAL	The value specified by *policy* or one of the scheduling parameters associated with the scheduling policy is invalid, if *policy* or *param* are NULL.
ENOTSUP	An attempt was made to set the policy or scheduling parameters to an unsupported value.

Currently, the only policy supported by the Solaris pthreads library is SCHED_OTHER. Attempting to set policy as SCHED_FIFO or SCHED_RR will result in the error ENOTSUP.

pthread_setspecific(3T)   Sets a thread-specific data value.

```
#include <pthread.h>

int pthread_setspecific(pthread_key_t key, const void *value);
```

`pthread_setspecific()` is identical to the `thr_setspecific` call in the Solaris threads API. The `pthread_setspecific()` function associates a thread-specific *value* with a *key* obtained via a previous call to `pthread_key_create()`. Different threads may bind different values to the same *key*. These values are typically pointers to blocks of dynamically allocated memory that have been reserved for use by the calling thread.

The effect of calling `pthread_setspecific()` with a *key* value not obtained from `pthread_key_create()` or after *key* has been deleted with `pthread_key_delete()` is undefined.

pthread_setspecific() may be called either explicitly or implicitly from a thread- specific data destructor function. However, calling pthread_setspecific() from a destructor may result in lost storage or infinite loops.

If successful, pthread_setspecific() returns zero; otherwise, an error number is returned to indicate the error.

If any of the following conditions occur, pthread_setspecific() returns the corresponding error number.

ENOMEM   Insufficient memory exists to associate the *value* with the *key*.

EINVAL   The *key* value is invalid.

pthread_sigmask(3T)   Sets and/or examines a thread's signal mask.

```
#include <signal.h>
#include <pthread.h>

int pthread_sigmask(int how, const sigset_t *set, sigset_t *oset);
```

pthread_sigmask() is identical to the thr_sigsetmask() call in the Solaris threads API. pthread_sigmask() examines and/or changes the calling thread's signal mask. If the value of the argument *set* is not NULL, then it points to a set of signals to be used to change the currently blocked set. The value of the argument *how* determines the manner in which the set is changed. *how* may have one of the following values:

SIG_BLOCK   *set* represents a set of signals to block. They are added to the current signal mask.

SIG_UNBLOCK   *set* represents a set of signals to unblock. These signals are deleted from the current signal mask.

SIG_SETMASK   *set* represents the new signal mask. The current signal mask is replaced by *set*.

If the value of *oset* is not NULL, then it points to the space where the previous signal mask is stored. If the value of *set* is NULL, the value of *how* is not significant and the thread's signal mask is unchanged; thus, pthread_sigmask() can be used to enquire about the currently blocked signals.

Upon successful completion, `pthread_sigmask()` returns zero; otherwise, a non-zero value is returned indicating an error.

If any of the following conditions are detected, `pthread_sigmask()` fails and returns the corresponding value.

EINVAL   *set* is not NULL and the value of *how* is not defined.

EFAULT   *set* or *oset* is not a valid address.

pthread_testcancel(3T)   Tests for a thread's cancellation.

```
#include <pthread.h>

void pthread_testcancel(void);
```

The `pthread_testcancel()` function defines a cancellation point in the calling thread; it has no effect if cancellability is disabled. If `pthread_setcancelstate()` is called with PTHREAD_CANCEL_ENABLE, then when `pthread_testcancel()` is called, that thread can be cancelled. If there are no outstanding cancellation requests, then `pthread_testcancel()` will return. If a cancellation request is outstanding, then `pthread_testcancel()` will not return and the thread will be cancelled.

sched_yield(3T)   Yields a threads execution.

```
/* NOTE - This call is defined in POSIX.1b, not Pthreads */

void sched_yield(void);
```

`sched_yield()` is identical to the `thr_yield()` call in the Solaris threads API. `sched_yield()` causes the current thread to yield its execution in favor of another thread with the same or greater priority.

Pthread Attribute Functions

`pthread_attr_destroy(3T)`   Destroys a thread attribute object.

```
#include <pthread.h>

int pthread_attr_destroy(pthread_attr_t *attr);
```

The `pthread_attr_destroy()` function destroys a thread attributes object. The behavior of the attribute if it is used after it has been destroyed is undefined.

Upon successful completion, `pthread_attr_destroy()` returns zero; otherwise, an error number is returned to indicate the error.

If the following condition occurs, `pthread_attr_destroy()` returns the corresponding error number.

    `EINVAL`   The value of *attr* is not valid.

`pthread_attr_getdetachstate(3T)`
                      Retrieves the detach state attribute value.

```
#include <pthread.h>

int pthread_attr_getdetachstate(const pthread_attr_t *attr, int
*detachstate);
```

The *detachstate* attribute controls whether the thread is created in a detached state. If the thread is created detached, then use of the ID of the newly created thread to the `pthread_join()` function is undefined.

The `pthread_attr_getdetachstate()` call gets the *detachstate* attribute in the *attr* object. *detachstate* is set to either `PTHREAD_CREATE_DETACHED` or `PTHREAD_CREATE_JOINABLE`. A value of `PTHREAD_CREATE_DETACHED` causes all threads created with *attr* to be in the detached state, whereas a value of `PTHREAD_CREATE_JOINABLE` causes all threads created with *attr* to be in the joinable state. The default value of the *detachstate* attribute is `PTHREAD_CREATE_JOINABLE`.

Upon successful completion, pthread_attr_getdetachstate() returns zero; otherwise, an error number is returned to indicate the error.

If the following condition occurs, pthread_attr_getdetachstate() returns the corresponding error number.

    EINVAL   The value of *attr* or *detachstate* is not valid.

pthread_attr_getinheritsched(3T)

                              Retrieves the inherit schedule attribute value.

```
#include <pthread.h>

int pthread_attr_getinheritsched(const pthread_attr_t *attr, int
*inheritsched);
```

The function pthread_attr_getinheritsched() gets the *inheritsched* attribute in the *attr* argument.

If successful, pthread_attr_getinheritsched() returns zero; otherwise, an error number is returned to indicate the error.

If the following condition is detected, pthread_attr_getinheritsched() returns the corresponding error number.

    EINVAL   The value of *attr* is not valid or *inheritsched* is NULL.

pthread_attr_getschedparam(3T)

                              Retrieves the schedule parameter attribute values.

```
#include <pthread.h>

int pthread_attr_getschedparam(const pthread_attr_t *attr, struct
sched_param *param);
```

The function pthread_attr_getschedparam() gets the scheduling policy and the scheduling parameter attributes in the *attr* argument, depending on the scheduling policy set in the *attr* object. The policy attribute can be set with pthread_setschedpolicy(). If not set explicitly, the default policy, SCHED_OTHER, which is set during pthread_attr_init(), is assumed. For the SCHED_OTHER, SCHED_FIFO, and SCHED_RR policies, the only required member of the *param* structure is sched_priority. By default, priority is NULL, meaning that the newly created thread inherits the priority of its parent thread.

Upon successful completion, pthread_attr_getschedparam() returns zero; otherwise, an error number is returned to indicate the error.

If the following condition occurs, pthread_attr_getschedparam() returns the corresponding error number.

EINVAL   The value of *attr* or *param* is not valid.

pthread_attr_getschedpolicy(3T)
                         Retrieves the schedule policy attribute value.

```
#include <pthread.h>

int pthread_attr_getschedpolicy(const pthread_attr_t *attr, int
*policy);
```

The function pthread_attr_getschedpolicy() gets the *schedpolicy* attribute in the *attr* argument and places it in *policy*.

If successful, pthread_attr_getschedpolicy() returns zero; otherwise, an error number is returned to indicate the error.

If the following condition is detected, pthread_attr_getschedpolicy() returns the corresponding error number.

EINVAL   The value of the *attr* being set is not valid or *policy* is NULL.

pthread_attr_getscope(3T)   Retrieves the scope attribute value.

```
#include <pthread.h>

int pthread_attr_getscope(const pthread_attr_t *attr, int
*contentionscope);
```

The pthread_attr_getscope() function gets the *contentionscope* attribute in the *attr* object. The *contentionscope* attribute may have the values PTHREAD_SCOPE_SYSTEM, signifying system scheduling contention scope, or PTHREAD_SCOPE_PROCESS, signifying process scheduling contention scope. The symbols PTHREAD_SCOPE_SYSTEM and PTHREAD_SCOPE_PROCESS are defined by the header pthread.h. The default value of *contentionscope* is PTHREAD_SCOPE_PROCESS.

Upon successful completion, pthread_attr_getscope() returns zero; otherwise, an error number is returned to indicate the error.

If the following condition occurs, pthread_attr_getscope() returns the corresponding error number.

EINVAL   The value of *attr* or *contentionscope* is not valid.

pthread_attr_getstackaddr(3T)

                                Retrieves the stack address attribute value.

```
#include <pthread.h>

int pthread_attr_getstackaddr(const pthread_attr_t *attr, void
**stackaddr);
```

If the symbol _POSIX_THREAD_ATTR_STACKADDR is defined, then the implementation supports a stackaddr attribute that specifies the location of storage to be used for the created thread's stack. The size of the storage is at least PTHREAD_STACK_MIN. The function pthread_attr_getstackaddr() gets the thread creation stackaddr attribute in the *attr* object and places it in *stackaddr*. The default *stackaddr* is NULL.

Upon successful completion, pthread_attr_getstackaddr() returns zero; otherwise, an error number is returned to indicate the error.

If the following condition occurs, `pthread_attr_getstackaddr()` returns the corresponding error number.

EINVAL   The value of *attr* or *stackaddr* is not valid.

`pthread_attr_getstacksize(3T)`   Retrieves the stack size attribute value.

```
#include <pthread.h>

int pthread_attr_getstacksize(const pthread_attr_t *attr, size_t
*stacksize);
```

If the symbol `_POSIX_THREAD_ATTR_STACKSIZE` is defined, then the implementation supports a stacksize attribute for threads that defines the minimum stack size (in bytes). The function `pthread_attr_getstacksize()` gets the thread creation *stacksize* attribute in the *attr* object. The default stacksize is NULL.

Upon successful completion, `pthread_attr_getstacksize()` returns zero; otherwise, an error number is returned to indicate the error.

If the following condition occurs, `pthread_attr_getstacksize()` returns the corresponding error number.

EINVAL   The value of *attr* or *stacksize* is not valid.

`pthread_attr_init(3T)`   Initializes a thread attribute object.

```
#include <pthread.h>

int pthread_attr_init(pthread_attr_t *attr);
```

The function `pthread_attr_init()` initializes a thread attributes object *attr* with the default value for all of the individual attributes, as shown Table H-1.

Table H-1 Default Settings for Thread Attribute Objects

Attribute	Default Setting	Description
Scope	PTHREAD_SCOPE_PROCESS	Unbound thread
Detach State	PTHREAD_CREATE_JOINABLE	Nondetached thread
Stack Address	NULL	System-assigned base address
Stack Size	NULL	System default stack size
Priority	NULL	Inherit priority from creator

Attempting to initialize an already initialized condition variable attributes object leaves the storage allocated by the previous initialization unallocated.

The resulting attribute object (possibly modified by setting individual attribute values), when used by `pthread_create()`, defines the attributes of the thread created. A single attributes object can be used in multiple simultaneous calls to `pthread_create()`.

Upon successful completion, `pthread_attr_init()` returns zero; otherwise, an error number is returned to indicate the error.

If the following condition occurs, `pthread_attr_init()` returns the corresponding error number.

ENOMEM   Insufficient memory exists to create the thread attributes object.

pthread_attr_setdetachstate(3T)   Sets the detach state attribute value.

```
#include <pthread.h>

int pthread_attr_setdetachstate(pthread_attr_t *attr, int
detachstate);
```

The *detachstate* attribute controls whether the thread is created in a detached state. If the thread is created detached, then use of the ID of the newly created thread to the `pthread_join()` function is undefined.

The `pthread_attr_setdetachstate()` call sets the *detachstate* attribute in the *attr* object. *detachstate* is set to either PTHREAD_CREATE_DETACHED or PTHREAD_CREATE_JOINABLE. A value of PTHREAD_CREATE_DETACHED causes all threads created with *attr* to be in the detached state, whereas a value of PTHREAD_CREATE_JOINABLE causes all threads created with *attr* to be in the joinable state. The default value of the *detachstate* attribute is PTHREAD_CREATE_JOINABLE.

Upon successful completion, pthread_attr_setdetachstate() returns zero; otherwise, an error number is returned to indicate the error.

If the following condition occurs, pthread_attr_setdetachstate() returns the corresponding error number.

    EINVAL   The value of *attr* or *detachstate* is not valid.

pthread_attr_setinheritsched(3T)

                                  Sets the inherit schedule attribute value.

```
#include <pthread.h>

int pthread_attr_setinheritsched(pthread_attr_t *attr, int
inheritsched);
```

The function pthread_attr_setinheritsched() sets the *inheritsched* attribute in the *attr* argument. When the attribute objects are used by pthread_create(), the *inheritsched* attribute determines how the other scheduling attributes of the created thread are to be set.

PTHREAD_INHERIT_SCHED specifies that the scheduling policy and associated attributes are to be inherited from the creating thread and the scheduling attributes in this *attr* argument are to be ignored.

PTHREAD_EXPLICIT_SCHED specifies that the scheduling policy and associated attributes are to be set to the corresponding values from this attribute object.

The symbols PTHREAD_INHERIT_SCHED and PTHREAD_EXPLICIT_SCHED are defined in the header pthread.h. The default value of *inheritsched* is set to PTHREAD_EXPLICIT_SCHED.

The only *inheritsched* attribute supported is PTHREAD_EXPLICIT_SCHED. Attempting to set *inheritsched* as PTHREAD_INHERIT_SCHED will result in the error ENOTSUP.

If successful, `pthread_attr_setinheritsched()` returns zero; otherwise, an error number is returned to indicate the error.

For each of the following conditions, if the condition is detected, `pthread_attr_setinheritsched()` returns the corresponding error number.

EINVAL   The value of *attr* is not valid.

ENOTSUP   An attempt was made to set the attribute to an unsupported policy of *inheritsched*.

pthread_attr_setschedparam(3T)

Sets the schedule parameter attribute values.

```
#include <pthread.h>

int pthread_attr_setschedparam(pthread_attr_t *attr, const struct
sched_param *param);
```

The function `pthread_attr_setschedparam()` sets the scheduling policy and the scheduling parameter attributes in the *attr* argument, depending on the scheduling policy set in the *attr* object. The policy attribute can be set with `pthread_setschedpolicy()`. If not set explicitly, the default policy, SCHED_OTHER, which is set during `pthread_attr_init()`, is assumed. For the SCHED_OTHER, SCHED_FIFO, and SCHED_RR policies, the only required member of the *param* structure is sched_priority. By default, priority is NULL, meaning that the newly created thread inherits the priority of its parent thread.

Currently, the only policy supported is SCHED_OTHER. Attempting to set policy as SCHED_FIFO or SCHED_RR will result in the error ENOTSUP.

Upon successful completion, `pthread_attr_setschedparam()` returns zero; otherwise, an error number is returned to indicate the error.

If the following condition occurs, `pthread_attr_setschedparam()` returns the corresponding error number.

EINVAL   The value of *attr* or *param* is not valid.

pthread_attr_setschedpolicy(3T) Sets the schedule policy attribute value.

```
#include <pthread.h>

int pthread_attr_setschedpolicy(pthread_attr_t *attr, int policy);
```

The function pthread_attr_setschedpolicy() sets the scheduling policy attribute in the *attr* argument.

The supported values of *policy* include SCHED_FIFO, SCHED_RR, or SCHED_OTHER, which are defined by the header pthread.h. When threads executing with the scheduling policy SCHED_FIFO or SCHED_RR are waiting on a mutex, they will acquire the mutex in priority order when the mutex is unlocked. The default value of *policy* is set to SCHED_OTHER.

Currently, the only *policy* supported is SCHED_OTHER. Attempting to set *policy* as SCHED_FIFO or SCHED_RR will result in the error ENOTSUP.

If successful, pthread_attr_setschedpolicy() returns zero; otherwise, an error number is returned to indicate the error.

For each of the following conditions, if the condition is detected, pthread_attr_setschedpolicy() returns the corresponding error number.

    EINVAL   The value of *attr* is not valid.

    ENOTSUP   An attempt was made to set the attribute to an unsupported *policy*.

pthread_attr_setscope(3T)   Sets the scope attribute value.

```
#include <pthread.h>

int pthread_attr_setscope(pthread_attr_t *attr, int contentionscope);
```

The pthread_attr_setscope() function sets the *contentionscope* attribute in the *attr* object. The *contentionscope* attribute may have the values PTHREAD_SCOPE_SYSTEM, signifying system scheduling contention scope, or PTHREAD_SCOPE_PROCESS, signifying process scheduling contention scope. The symbols PTHREAD_SCOPE_SYSTEM and PTHREAD_SCOPE_PROCESS are defined by the header pthread.h. The default value of *contentionscope* is PTHREAD_SCOPE_PROCESS.

Upon successful completion, pthread_attr_setscope() returns zero; otherwise, an error number is returned to indicate the error.

If the following condition occurs, pthread_attr_setscope() returns the corresponding error number.

> EINVAL   The value of *attr* or *contentionscope* is not valid.

pthread_attr_setstackaddr(3T)   Sets the stack address attribute value.

```
#include <pthread.h>

int pthread_attr_setstackaddr(pthread_attr_t *attr, void
*stackaddr);
```

If the symbol _POSIX_THREAD_ATTR_STACKADDR is defined, then the implementation supports a stackaddr attribute that specifies the location of storage to be used for the created thread's stack. The size of the storage is at least PTHREAD_STACK_MIN. The function pthread_attr_setstackaddr() sets the thread creation stackaddr attribute in the *attr* object. The default stackaddr is NULL.

pthread_create() uses the stack starting at the address specified by *stackaddr* and continuing for stacksize bytes (see pthread_attr_setstacksize()). If *stackaddr* is NULL, then pthread_create() allocates a stack for the new thread with at least stacksize bytes.

Upon successful completion, pthread_attr_setstackaddr() returns zero; otherwise, an error number is returned to indicate the error.

If the following condition occurs, pthread_attr_setstackaddr() returns the corresponding error number.

> EINVAL   The value of *attr* is not valid.

`pthread_attr_setstacksize(3T)`   Sets a stack size attribute value.

```
#include <pthread.h>

int pthread_attr_setstacksize(pthread_attr_t *attr, size_t
stacksize);
```

If the symbol `_POSIX_THREAD_ATTR_STACKSIZE` is defined, then the implementation supports a stacksize attribute for threads that defines the minimum stack size (in bytes). The function `pthread_attr_setstacksize()` sets the thread creation stacksize attribute in the *attr* object. The default stacksize is `NULL`.

`pthread_create()` uses the stack starting at the address specified by stackaddr (see `pthread_attr_setstackaddr()`) and continuing for *stacksize* bytes. *stacksize* must be greater than the value `PTHREAD_STACK_MIN`. If stackaddr is `NULL`, then `pthread_create()` allocates a stack for the new thread with at least *stacksize* bytes. If *stacksize* is zero, then a default size is used. If *stacksize* is non-zero, then it must be greater than the value returned by `PTHREAD_STACK_MIN`. A stack of minimum size might not accommodate the stack frame for new thread functions. If a stack size is specified, it must take into account the requirements of new thread functions and the functions that it might call in turn, in addition to the minimum requirement.

Upon successful completion, `pthread_attr_setstacksize()` returns zero; otherwise, an error number is returned to indicate the error.

If any of the following conditions occur, `pthread_attr_setstacksize()` returns the corresponding error number.

EINVAL	The value of *stacksize* is less than PTHREAD_STACK_MIN or exceeds a system-imposed limit.
EINVAL	The value of *attr* is not valid.

Semaphore Functions

sem_destroy(3R)   Destroys a semaphore variable.

```
/* NOTE - This call is defined in POSIX.1b, not Pthreads */
#include <semaphore.h>

int sem_destroy(sem_t *sem);
```

sem_destroy() destroys the semaphore, *sem*, which was initialized by
sem_init().

If successful, sem_destroy() returns zero; otherwise it returns -1 and sets
errno to indicate the error condition.

If any of the following conditions are detected, sem_destroy() fails and returns
the corresponding value.

>   EINVAL   *sem* is not a valid semaphore.
>
>   ENOTSUP   sem_destroy() is not supported by this implementation.
>
>   EBUSY   Other processes (or LWPs or threads) are currently blocked on
>   the semaphore.

In Solaris 2.4, these functions always return - 1 and set errno to ENOTSUP,
because this release does not support the Semaphores option. These interfaces
will be supported in future releases. However, you can use the sema_destroy()
call in the Solaris threads API.

sem_init(3R)   Initializes a semaphore variable.

```
/* NOTE - This call is defined in POSIX.1b, not Pthreads */
#include <semaphore.h>

int sem_init(sem_t *sem, int pshared, unsigned int value);
```

sem_init() initializes the semaphore, referred to by *sem*, to *value*. This
semaphore may be used in subsequent calls to sem_wait(), sem_trywait(),

`sem_post()`, and `sem_destroy()`. This semaphore remains usable until the semaphore is destroyed.

If *pshared* is non-zero, then the semaphore is sharable among processes. If the semaphore is not being shared among processes, the application should set *pshared* to zero.

If successful, `sem_init()` returns zero and initializes the semaphore in *sem*; otherwise it returns -1 and sets `errno` to indicate the error condition.

If any of the following conditions are detected, `sem_init()` fails and returns the corresponding value.

EINVAL	*value* exceeds `SEM_VALUE_MAX`.
ENOSPC	A resource required to initialize the semaphore has been exhausted. The resources have reached the limit on semaphores, `SEM_NSEMS_MAX`.
ENOTSUP	`sem_init()` is not supported by this implementation.
EPERM	The calling process lacks the appropriate privileges to initialize the semaphore.

In Solaris 2.4, the semaphore functions always return - 1 and set `errno` to ENOTSUP, because this release does not support the Semaphores option. However, you can use the `sema_init()` call in the Solaris threads API.

`sem_post(3R)`   Increments the count of a semaphore variable.

```
/* NOTE - This call is defined in POSIX.1b, not Pthreads */
#include <pthread.h>

int sem_post(sem_t *sem);
```

If, prior to the call to `sem_post()`, the value of *sem* was zero and other processes (or LWPs or threads) were blocked, waiting for the semaphore, then one of them will be allowed to return successfully from its call to `sem_wait()`. The process to be unblocked will be chosen in a manner appropriate to the scheduling policies and parameters in effect for the blocked processes. In the case of the policies SCHED_FIFO and SCHED_RR, the highest-priority waiting process is unblocked; if there is more than one highest-priority process blocked, waiting for the semaphore, then the highest-priority process that has been waiting the longest is unblocked.

If, prior to the call to `sem_post()`, no other processes (or LWPs or thread) were blocked for the semaphore, then its value is incremented by one.

`sem_post()` is reentrant with respect to signals (it's async safe) and may be invoked from a signal handler.

If successful, `sem_post()` returns zero, otherwise it returns - 1, and sets `errno` to indicate the error condition.

If any of the following conditions are detected, `sem_post()` fails and returns the corresponding value.

EINVAL   *sem* does not refer to a valid semaphore.

ENOTSUP   `sem_post()` is not supported by this implementation.

In Solaris 2.4, these functions always return - 1 and set `errno` to ENOTSUP, because this release does not support the Semaphores option. These interfaces will be supported in future releases. However, you can use the `sema_post()` call in the Solaris threads API.

sem_trywait(3R)   Tries to decrement a semaphore variable.

```
/* NOTE - This call is defined in POSIX.1b, not Pthreads */
#include <semaphore.h>

int sem_trywait(sem_t *sem);
```

`sem_trywait()` is the function by which a calling thread waits or proceeds, depending on the state of a semaphore. A synchronizing process can proceed only if the value of the semaphore it accesses is currently greater than zero.

If at the time of a call to `sem_trywait()`, the value of *sem* is positive, the function decrements the value of the semaphore, returns immediately, and allows the calling process to continue.

If the semaphore's value is zero, `sem_trywait()` fails, returning immediately.

If successful, `sem_trywait()` returns zero; otherwise, it returns -1 and sets `errno` to indicate the error condition, leaving the state of the semaphore unchanged.

If any of the following conditions are detected, `sem_trywait()` fails and returns the corresponding value.

EAGAIN   The value of *sem* was zero when `sem_trywait()` was called.

EINVAL   *sem* does not refer to a valid semaphore.

ENOTSUP   `sem_trywait()` is not supported by this implementation.

EDEADLK   A deadlock condition was detected; that is, two separate processes are waiting for an available resource to be released via a semaphore "held" by the other process.

In Solaris 2.4, these functions always return - 1 and set `errno` to ENOTSUP, because this release does not support the Semaphores option. These interfaces will be supported in future releases. However, you can use the `sema_trywait()` call in the Solaris threads API.

sem_wait(3R)   Decrements a semaphore variable.

```
/* NOTE - This call is defined in POSIX.1b, not Pthreads */
#include <semaphore.h>

int sem_wait(sem_t *sem);
```

`sem_wait()` is the function by which a calling thread waits or proceeds, depending on the state of a semaphore. A synchronizing process can proceed only if the value of the semaphore it accesses is currently greater than zero.

If at the time of a call to `sem_wait()`, the value of *sem* is positive, the function decrements the value of the semaphore, returns immediately, and allows the calling process to continue.

If the semaphore's value is zero, `sem_wait()` blocks, waiting for the semaphore to be released by another process (or LWP or thread).

`sem_wait()` can be interrupted by a signal, which may result in its premature return.

≡ H

If successful, `sem_wait()` returns zero, otherwise it returns -1 and sets `errno` to indicate the error condition, leaving the state of the semaphore unchanged.

If any of the following conditions are detected, `sem_wait()` fails and returns the corresponding value.

EINVAL   *sem* does not refer to a valid semaphore.

EINTR   Interrupted by a signal.

ENOTSUP   `sem_wait()` is not supported by this implementation.

EDEADLK   A deadlock condition was detected.

In Solaris 2.4, these functions always return - 1 and set `errno` to `ENOTSUP`, because this release does not support the Semaphores option. These interfaces will be supported in future releases. However, you can use the `sema_wait()` call in the Solaris threads API.

Glossary ≡

active thread

A thread that is currently on an LWP. The LWP may actually be on a CPU, or it may not.

adaptive lock

A variation of a spin lock, which is used in the Solaris kernel but is not available to the user-level programmer.

API

The set of function calls in a library, along with their arguments, and their semantics. APIs are published so programmers can always know which interface a vendor supports. Programmers have been known to go looking through the source code for library calls to use, ignoring the API. These programmers get burned when that unsupported interface changes.

application programmer's interface

See *API*.

asynchronous signal

A signal that is sent to a process independently of what the process happens to be doing. An asynchronous signal can arrive at any time whatsoever, with no relation to what the program happens to be doing (cf: synchronous signal).

async I/O

An abbreviation for *Asynchronous Input/Output* — Normally, I/O calls block in the kernel while waiting for data to come off of a disk, a tape, or some other "slow" device. But async I/O calls are designed not to block. Such calls return immediately, so the user can continue to work. Whenever the data comes off the disk, the process will be sent a signal to let it know the call has completed.

atomic operation

An operation that is guaranteed to take place "at a single time." No other operation can do anything in the middle of an atomic operation that would change the result.

barrier

A synchronization variable that allows numerous threads to wait until they have all completed some task.

BLAS

An abbreviation for *Basic Linear Algebra Subroutines* — A package of routines commonly used in numerical programs. Many companies implement the same set of routines but add value by making the routines faster or by giving better support.

blocking system call

A system call that blocks in the kernel while it waits for something to happen. Disk reads and reading from a terminal are typically blocking calls.

bound thread

A thread that is bound permanently to an LWP.

cache memory

A section of very fast (and expensive) memory that is located very close to the CPU. It is an extra layer in the storage hierarchy and helps "well-behaved" programs run much faster.

CAD

An abbreviation for *Computer Aided Design* — Heavily numeric applications that always want more CPU.

CDE

An abbreviation for *Common Desktop Environment* — The specification for the look and feel that the major UNIX vendors have adopted. CDE includes a set of desktop tools.

CDE is the major result of the Cose agreement. It is a set of tools and window toolkits (Motif 1.2.3), along with supporting cross-process communications software (ToolTalk®), which will form the basis of the window offerings of all major UNIX vendors. HP, IBM, and Sun have cooperated in the creation of CDE and have released a joint CD containing all the software. They will each productize CDE in their own fashion, and ultimately maintain separate source bases, doing their own value-add and their own bug fixing.

co-routining

An older, more primitive (but simpler!) version of multithreading in which the programmer specifically stated when context switching was to occur.

coarse-grained locking

See *fine-grained locking*.

condition variable

A synchronization variable that allows the users to specify arbitrary conditions on which to block.

context switch

The process of moving one process (or LWP or thread) off a CPU and another one on.

Cose

The agreement by the major UNIX vendors to complete the unification of UNIX by implementing CDE and SPEC 1170.

critical section

A section of code that must not be interrupted. If it doesn't complete atomically, then some data or resource may be left in an inconsistent state.

daemon

A process or a thread that works in the background. The pager is a daemon process in UNIX.

DBMS

An abbreviation for *Database Management System* — Very demanding programs that are obvious candidates for threading (most of them are already threaded).

DCE

An abbreviation for *Distributed Computing Environment* — A set of functions that were deemed sufficient to write network programs. It was settled upon and implemented by the original OSF (Open Software Foundation). DCE is the environment of choice of a number of vendors including DEC and HP, while Sun has stayed with ONC+™. As part of the Cose agreement, all of the vendors will support both DCE and ONC+.

deadlock

A situation where two things are stuck waiting for the other to do something first. More things could be stuck in a ring, waiting for each other, and even one thing could be stuck, waiting for itself.

device driver

A program that controls a physical device. The driver is always run as part of the kernel, with full kernel permissions. Device drivers may be threaded, but they would use the kernel threads library, not the library discussed in this book.

distributed objects

Objects (as in object-oriented programming) that are not all located on a single machine but that can be spread out over the network. Distributed objects are thought to be the future of computing.

dynamically loadable module

Any program module (such as a library) that is dynamically loadable. This term typically refers to kernel modules such as device drivers and scheduling classes.

dynamic library

A library of routines that a user program can load into core "dynamically." That is, the library is not linked in as part of the user's executable image but is loaded in only when the user program is run.

errno

An integer variable that is defined for all ANSI C programs (PCs running DOS as well as workstations running UNIX). It is the place where the operating system puts the return status for system calls when they return error codes. Because a system call often returns an integer (such as the number of bytes read during a file read operation), there's no way to put the error code there. So system calls are defined to return -1 when there's an error; the programmer must then look at the value of errno to determine exactly what the error was.

external cache

Cache memory that is not physically located on the same chip as the CPU. External cache (aka "E$") is slower than internal cache (typically around five cycles versus one) but faster than main memory (upwards of 100 cycles, depending upon architecture).

FIFO

An abbreviation for *first in, first out* — A kind of a queue. Contrast to *last in, first out*, which is a stack.

file descriptor

An element in the process structure that describes the state of a file in use by that process. The actual file descriptor is in kernel space, but the user program also has a file descriptor that refers to this kernel structure.

file position pointer

A part of the file descriptor that is a pointer into a file the process is using.

fine-grained locking

The concept of putting lots of locks around tiny fragments of code. It's good because it means that there's less contention for the individual locks. It's bad because it means that the program must spend a lot of time obtaining locks. Coarse-grained locking is the opposite concept and has exactly the opposite qualities.

GID

An abbreviation for *Group ID* — UNIX users are assigned to groups that share permissions for accessing files.

GUI

An abbreviation for *Graphical User Interface* — Everything the user sees on the screen, along with the protocol for how the various objects work.

internal cache

Cache memory (aka I$) that is located on the same chip as the CPU, hence is very fast.

interprocess communication

See *IPC*.

interrupt

An external signal that interrupts the CPU. Typically, when an external device wants to get the CPU's attention, it asserts a voltage level on one of the CPU pins. This causes the CPU to stop what it's doing and run an interrupt handler.

interrupt handler

A section of code in the kernel that is called when an interrupt comes in. Different interrupts will run different handlers.

IPC

An abbreviation for *Interprocess Communication* — The idea that different processes can communicate via different means. Typically, this refers to a specific API.

kernel mode

A mode of operation for a CPU where all instructions are allowed (cf: user mode).

kernel module

A module of code that is used in the kernel.

kernel space

The portion of memory that the kernel uses for itself. User programs cannot access it (cf: user space).

kernel stack

A stack in kernel space that the kernel uses when running system calls on behalf of a user program. All LWPs must have a kernel stack.

kernel threads

Threads that are used in the kernel. The Solaris kernel threads library is similar to the user threads library, but it does have some different calls.

LADDIS

A standardized set of calls used to benchmark NFS performance. It was created by and is monitored by SPEC.

library

A collection of routines that many different programs may wish to use. Similar routines are grouped together into a single file and called a library.

library call
> One of the routines in a library.

LWP
> An abbreviation for *LightWeight Process* — A kernel schedulable entity.

MAP_NORESERVE
> A keyword that can be used when asking the operating system for more memory. Memory mapped in as "no reserve" does not have to exist in any form until it is actually used.

memory management unit
> See *MMU*.

memory-mapped file
> A file that has been "mapped" into core. This is just like loading the file into core, save that any changes will be written back to the file itself. Because of this, that area of memory does not need any "backing store" for paging. It is also much faster than doing reads and writes.

MMU
> An abbreviation for *Memory Management Unit* — The part of the computer that figures out which physical page of memory corresponds to which virtual page and takes care of keeping everything straight.

Motif
> A description of what windows should look like, how mouse buttons work, etc. Motif is the GUI that is the basis for CDE. The word Motif is also used as the name of the libraries that implement the Motif look and feel.

MP
> An abbreviation for *multiprocessor* — A computer with more than one processor.

MT
> An abbreviation for *multithreading* — A paradigm for programming in which a single process can have more than one line of execution.

multiprocessor

> See *MP*.

multitasking OS

> An operating system that can run one process for a while, then switch to another one, return to the first, etc. UNIX, VMS, MVS, TOPS, etc., are all multitasking systems. DOS and Microsoft® Windows™ are single-tasking operating systems. (Although MS-Windows™ can have more than one program active on the desktop, it does not do any kind of preemptive context-switching between them.)

multithreading

> See *MT*.

mutex

> See *mutual exclusion lock*.

mutual exclusion lock

> A synchronization variable used to protect a section of code.

NFS

> An abbreviation for *Network File System* — A kernel program that makes it possible to access files across the network without the user ever knowing that the network was involved.

NIS

> An abbreviation for *Network Information System* — A kernel program that supplies information about such things as users, printers, host names and addresses, etc.

page fault

> The process of bringing in a page from disk when it is not memory-resident. When a program accesses a word in virtual memory, the MMU must translate that virtual address into a physical one. If that block of memory is currently out on disk, the MMU must load that page in.

page table

> A table used by the MMU to show which virtual pages map to which physical pages.

POS

An abbreviation for *Portable Operating System* — A definition for UNIX that is intended to eliminate the incompatibilities between different vendors' implementations. It is now a group under IEEE.

POSIX

An acronym for Portable Operating System Interface. This refers to a set of committees in the IEEE that are concerned with creating an API that can be common to all UNIX systems. There is a committee in POSIX that is concerned with creating a standard for writing multithreaded programs.

PowerPC

An architecture for a RISC CPU designed by IBM, Apple, and Motorola. It was created as the logical follow-on for the x86 CPU family.

preemption

The act of forcing a thread to stop running.

preemptive scheduling

Scheduling that uses preemption. Time-slicing is preemptive, but preemption does not imply time-slicing.

process

A running program and all the state associated with it.

process structure

A kernel structure that describes all of the relevant aspects of a process.

program counter

A register in the CPU that defines which instruction will be executed next.

race condition

A situation in which the outcome of a program depends upon the luck of the draw—which thread happens to run first.

reader/writer lock

A kind of a lock that allows any number of threads to read the protected data, but only one at a time to write it.

real time

Anything that is timed by a wall clock. Typically this is used by external devices that require servicing within some period of time, such raster printers and aircraft autopilots. Real time does not mean any particular amount of time, but is almost always used to refer to sub-100-millisecond (and often sub-1-millisecond) response time.

semaphore

A kind of a synchronization variable that contains a count.

shadowed call

A function that has had some code inserted at the front of it that first performs some other function. That other function may eventually call the original function. It may not.

shared memory

Memory that is shared by more than one process. Any process may write into this memory, and the others will see the change.

SIGLWP

A signal that is implemented in Solaris and used to preempt a thread.

signal

A mechanism that UNIX systems use to allow a process to be notified of some event, typically asynchronous and external. It is a software analog to hardware interrupts.

signal dispatch table

A table kept in the process structure that the kernel uses to decide what to do when sending a signal to a process.

signal mask

A mask that tells the kernel (or threads library) which signals will be accepted and which must be put onto a "pending" queue.

SIGSEGV

A signal that is generated by UNIX systems when a user program attempts to access an address that it has not mapped into its address space.

Threads Primer

SIGWAITING

A signal that is implemented in Solaris and used to tell a threaded process that it should consider creating a new LWP.

Single UNIX Specification

See SPEC 1170.

sleep queue

A queue of threads that have been put to sleep.

SMP

An abbreviation for *Symmetric Multiprocessor.*

SPARC

A specific RISC CPU architecture that was invented by Sun Microsystems and used in their machines.

SPARCstation

A workstation based on a SPARC RISC chip.

SPEC

An organization that creates benchmark programs and monitors their use.

SPEC 1170

The specification for an API for all UNIX systems. It is the result of several of the major vendors agreeing on a set of interfaces that is sufficient for programming just about anything and that will be supported by the majority of the vendors. It was arrived at by going through a large number of programs and noting the system calls that were actually used. After the first pass, the committee had found 1170 calls. A few were added later on. This is part of the Cose agreement.

The new, official name for SPEC 1170 is *Single UNIX Specification.*

SPILT

The Solaris POSIX Interface Layer for Threads — A library that defines those functions that are in the Solaris threads library but not in POSIX.

spin lock

A specialization of a mutex lock, which can give better performance in a limited number of situations.

stack

An area of memory used to store intermediate results and return addresses for functions while they are calling other functions.

stack pointer

A register in the CPU that tells the CPU where the next unused location in the stack is.

store buffer

A buffer in a CPU that caches writes to main memory, allowing the CPU to run without waiting for main memory. It is a special case of cache memory.

SunOS 4.x

A set of operating systems (4.0, 4.1, 4.1.1, etc.) from Sun, based on the work at UC Berkeley. First shipped in the late 80s, now superseded by Solaris 2.

SVR4

An abbreviation for *System Five, Release 4* — The merger of several different flavors of UNIX that was done by Sun and AT&T. SVR4 has become the basis for SPEC 1170 and (presumably) all future UNIX implementations.

synchronization variable

Any of a number of variables that can be used to synchronize different threads.

synchronous signal

A signal that is sent to a process "synchronously." This means that it is the direct result of something that process did, such as dividing by zero. Should a program do a divide-by-zero, the CPU will immediately trap into a kernel routine, which in turn will send a signal to the process (cf: asynchronous signal).

system call

A function that sets up its arguments, then traps into the kernel in order to have the kernel do something for it. This is the only means a user program has for communication with the kernel.

thread local storage

See TLS.

threads library
> A library that implements threads.

thread-specific data
> See *TSD*.

time-sliced scheduling
> An algorithm that allocates a set amount of time for a process (or LWP or thread) to run before it is preempted from the CPU and another one is given time to run.

TLS
> An abbreviation for *Thread Local Storage* — A different method of effecting TSD, but which requires changes to the compiler. TLS is not part of POSIX, Solaris, OS/2, Windows NT, or any other common threads library.

trap
> An instruction that causes the CPU to stop what it is doing and jump to a special routine in the kernel (cf: system call).

TSD
> An abbreviation for *Thread-Specific Data* —Variables that are global to all functions being run by a single thread, but independent of those same variables for other threads (cf: TLS).

UID
> An abbreviation for *User ID* — A number that is associated with a user. When a user account is created on a UNIX system, it is assigned a number.

user ID
> *See UID.*

user mode
> An operating mode for a CPU in which certain instructions are not allowed. A user program runs in user mode (cf: kernel mode).

user space
> That area of memory devoted to user programs. The kernel sets up this space but generally never looks inside (cf: kernel space).

virtual memory

> The memory space that a program thinks it is using. It is mapped into physical memory by the MMU. Virtual memory allows a program to behave as if it had 100 Mbytes, even though the system only has 32 Mbytes.

VMS

> An abbreviation for *Virtual Memory System* — The name of the operating system DEC designed for the VAX.

XView

> A library of routines that draws and operates GUI components on a screen. It is based on the SunView™ library of the mid-80s and has been superseded by CDE Motif.

x86

> The set of CPUs based on the CISC architecture designed by Intel back in the 70s. The 8086, 80186, 286, 386, 486, and Pentium™ are all members, along with numerous clones from other companies.

Index

▇ *Index*

API description 220
in matrix multiplication example 165
POSIX equivalent 242

cond_signal
API description 220
in matrix multiplication example 167
in producer/consumer example 157, 158
POSIX equivalent 243
use 67

cond_timedwait
API description 221
limiting sleep time 68
POSIX equivalent 244

cond_wait
API description 221
in matrix multiplication example 166
in producer/consumer example 156, 158
POSIX equivalent 245
use 154

condition variable
attribute object, pthreads 111
code example 68
definition 293
how it works 67
limiting sleep time 68

context switch
and critical sections 63
causing 45
definition 293
how it works 49–52
unbound threads 31

co-routining, definition 41, 293

Cose 293

counting semaphore 69

CPU-intensive problems 161

critical section 63, 71, 293

cross-process synchronization variable 72

D

-D_REENTRANT 95, 144, 210

daemon threads 57, 106, 117, 151, 159

daemon, definition 293

Dakota Scientific Software, Inc. 24

data
encapsulation 140
locking 141
race 119, 125

Database Management System 293

DBMS, definition 293

dbx
and SPARCworks Debugger 131
options 215
use 215

DCE 42, 102, 293

deadlock
avoiding 75, 141
bugs in multithreaded programs 214
cancellation 112
caused by random termination 182
definition 294
demonstration 186
detection 119
LockLint example 125
occurrence 74
recovering from 77
recovery features 28
recursive 75, 142
self- 142

debugger
See also SPARCworks Debugger
adb 215
dbx 215
interface for Solaris threads 102
multithreaded 119

debugging 214–215

DEC 102

DEC UNIX 43

detach state, for thread attribute object 108

detached thread 58, 173

device driver, definition 294

Dijkstra, E.W. 69

dispatch latencies 93

Distributed Computing Environment,
definition 293

distributed objects 13, 294

Distributed Objects Everywhere (DOE) 101

≣ *Index*

≡ Index

≣ Index

threads library specification 85
threads library type 28
World Wide Web 205
`write`, MT safe 94

X

X11 168, 169
X11R6 169
`XCreateEvent` 94
XView 94, 304

Y

yielding, context switching 46

Z

zombie 47